Introductory

MICROECONOMICS

(For CBSE and other State Boards, Class XI & XII)

Dr. Harjeet Singh

[B.Com, M.A. (Economics), M.Phil, Ph.D, (O level, PGDCA)]

Assistant Professor,

Govt. Rajindra College,

Bathinda.

Contents

CHAPTER 1

BASIC CONCEPTS OF ECONOMICS

Introduction:

There are two basic facts i.e. human wants and resources that are required for the existence of an economy. Human wants are unlimited and mostly are repetitive in nature. On the other side resources used to fulfill them are limited and have alternative uses. These features of resources compel individuals to make choice among countless wants which are to be satisfied or which are to be sacrificed. It is clear that economic behaviour of the individuals is essentially the choice making behavior with aim of maximizing their gains. Scarcity of resources having alternative uses forces us to make choice. In this context, J.R. Hicks described economics as "the logic of choice". This is what which forms the central theme of economics, which we are going to discuss in the chapter.

Economy is a system spread over a particular area that reveals the nature and level of economic activities in that area. It shows how people of the concerned area earn their living.

Economic System: Economic System refers to those norms and rules or institutions which direct an economy.

According to Nicholson, *"An economic system is a social framework of rules, goals and incentives that govern economic relationships among people in a society and provide a framework for answering the basic economic questions".*

Types of Economic Systems

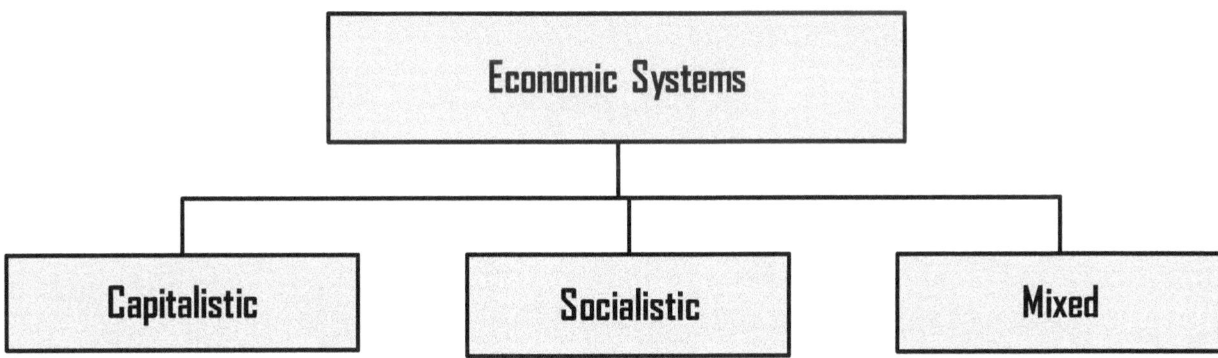

1. **Capitalistic System** is that system of economic organization in which free enterprise, competition and the private ownership of property generally prevail.

Economy with capitalistic system is known as free/ market/capitalistic economy.

Main Features
1. *Private ownership of means of production*
2. *Price mechanism guides the producers and consumers*
3. *Freedom of enterprise (laissez faire policy)*
4. *Cut throat competition*
5. *Profit motive (Self interest is the prime consideration)*
6. *Labour as commodity*
7. *Sovereignty of consumer*

2. **Socialistic System** is a kind of system under which the economic system of a country is controlled by the government so as to ensure welfare and equality of opportunity to the people in a society. Economy with socialistic system is known as command/ planned/socialistic economy.

Main Features
1. *Social/Private ownership of means of production*
2. *There are set objectives*
3. *Economic planning (The central planning authority will decide about the goods to be produced in accordance with national priorities)*
4. *Government control over use of resources*
5. *Lack of competition*
6. *Motive of Social welfare (Collective welfare is the prime consideration)*

3. **Mixed System** is the system in which both government and private individuals exercise control over economic activities.

Main Features
1. *Co-existence of private property and public sector*
2. *Profit motive and Social welfare*

Economic Problem or Problem of Choice

It is well known fact that human wants are unlimited and resources to fulfill them are limited and have alternative uses. It is not possible to satisfy all the needs with limited resources, because with limited resources we can produce limited goods. Thus, society has to make choice among the vast array of wants that are to be satisfied. Scarcity of resources compels us to choose among various channels of production to which resources to be used. In this way, scarcity of resources arise the problem of allocating limited resources so to achieve the greatest possible satisfaction of wants, which in economics is termed as economic problem.

"The economic problem is essentially a problem arising from the necessity of choice: Choice of the manner in which the limited resources with alternative uses are disposed of. It is the problem of husbandry of resources."-**Erich Roll**

"Economic problem is concerned with the use of scarce resources among alternative human wants and in using these resources towards the end of satisfying wants as fully as possible." –**Leftwitch**

Causes of Economic Problem or Why the Economic Problem Arises?

Economic problem or problem of choice arises of because of the following three reasons

1. Human wants are unlimited
2. Resources (Natural, Human, Man-made, Technological etc.) are limited.
3. Resources have alternative uses. Suppose, we have coal which can be used for cooking, generating electricity, in steel plants etc. In this way coal have alternative uses but due to its limited availability, we cannot fulfill all our requirements, we have to sacrifice some amount of coal used in cooking if we want to generate more electricity, because more of electricity and more availability of coal for cooking cannot be possible.

What is Scarcity?

Scarcity – *A core parameter in economics*

Scarcity is a situation where requirement of goods exceeds their availability. It is the scarcity of resources which is mother of all economic problems. That's why this is considered as core parameter in economics. If there was no scarcity or resources were unlimited or abundant in relation to human wants, there would be no economic problem or no need to make choice and perhaps, no existence of economics. Because, economics as such nothing but a study of scarcity and choice. It can be said that economics is a study of mechanism that an economy uses to make choices and to allocate the scarce resources to the fields with maximum possible and optimum gains.

Scarcity and Choice go hand in hand or are inseparable

Scarcity of resources having alternative uses forces us to make choice. If there was no scarcity or resources were unlimited in relation to human wants, there would be no need to make choice. The need for choice arises because of scarcity. If we have to make choice it means we are confronting scarcity and if we are confronting scarcity then we have to make choice. In this way scarcity and choice are inseparable and they go hand in hand.

What is Economics?

Economics *deals with the rational management of scarce resources in such a way so that consumers get maximum satisfaction, producers get maximum profit and society can maximize its social welfare.*

"Economics is a science which studies human behaviour as a relationship between ends and scarce means which have alternative uses." – **Robbins**

Prof. Ragnar Frisch who coined the terms Micro and Macro economics in 1933, said that proper allocation of resources and their optimum use are two main objectives of economic activities. The study of Microeconomics is related with the proper allocation of resources and Macro economics is related with the efficient use of resources.

Micro Economics studies economic relationships or economic problems at the level of an individual firm, an individual household etc.

Macro Economics is concerned with economy as whole or large segments of it. In macroeconomics, attention is focused on such problems as level of unemployment, the rate of inflation, the nation's total output and other matters of economy wide significance.

Prof. Adam Smith (1723-1790)	**Prof. Ragnar Frisch (1895-1973)**
Known as Father of Modern Economics	Coined the Term Micro & Macro Economics
Book: An Inquiry into the Nature and Causes	(1933) and also Econometrics (1926)
of the Wealth of Nations (1776)	Won I[st] Noble Prize with Jan Tinbergen (1969)

Difference between Micro and Macro Economics

Basis of Difference	Micro Economics (Price/Value Theory)	Macro Economics (Theory of Income)
Meaning	Microeconomics studies economic relationships or economic problems at the level of an individual firm, an individual household etc.	Macroeconomics studies economic problems from the point of view of entire economy. E.g. Aggregate Consumption, Aggregate Saving etc.
Objective	Main aim of micro economics is to study the principles and policies relating to optimum allocation of resources.	Aim of macro economics is to study the principles, problems and policies concerning full employment and growth of the resources of economy.
Degree of Aggregation	There is limited degree of aggregation in microeconomic study.	There is significant degree of aggregation in macroeconomic study.
Methods of Study	Micro economics is based upon partial equilibrium analysis.	Macro economics is based upon quasi general equilibrium analysis.
Importance to Variables	The main determinant of problems of the microeconomics is 'Price'.	The main determinant of problems of the macroeconomics is 'Income'.
Analytical Difference	Micro economics deals with the study of the behaviour of economic variables in equilibrium position.	Macro economics deals with the study of the behaviour of economic variables in disequilibrium position.

Positive and Normative Economics/Statements

Positive Economics/Statements is concerned with accurate and true description of phenomenon or economic situations, it explains what is, how it works, and what are its effects. It describes theories and laws to explain observed economic phenomena. (Economists like Robbins, Friedman, Senior are of the view that economics is only positive science)

1. These statements can be tested, proven or disproven. (If someone says that fiscal deficit of India is 4% of GDP and other says that it is 4.4%, then we can verify whether 4% is correct or 4.4% is correct)

2. These statements do not involve any suggestion/opinion or personal judgment. Example: 1. The higher interest rate causes people to save more. 2. Determination of price and wages 3. Minimum wage law causes unemployment.

Normative Economics/Statements is concerned with explaining what should be or what ought to be the things. In this sense, economics offers suggestions and opinions. These suggestions and opinions of economists can be regarded as solution to the various economic problems. (Economists like Marshall, Pigou are of the view that economics is a normative science)

1. These statements cannot be tested and verified.

2. These statements involve personal value judgments.

Example: 1. People should save more. 2. Government should tax the rich to help the poor. 3. Saving is a vice or virtue

*** Economics is both a positive and a normative economics**

Difference between Positive and Normative Economics/Statements

Positive Economics	Normative Economics
1. *Positive economics* is concerned with accurate and true description of events as they happen.	1. *Normative Economics* is concerned with explaining what ought to be the things.
2. These statements are descriptive.	2. These statements are prescriptive.
3. It does not involve any personal value judgment or suggestions.	3. It involves the personal value judgment or suggestions.
4. These statements can be tested, proven or disproven	4. These statements cannot be tested and verified.
Example- The rate of inflation at present is 9%. Minimum wage cause unemployment.	Example- Inflation rate should be below 4%. Minimum wage should be increased.

Basic or Central Problems of an Economy

1. **What to produce and in what quantities? (Problem of allocation of resources):** Every economy has limited resources to satisfy unlimited wants of the people. Due to scarcity of resources in relation to wants, we cannot satisfy all needs of a nation. To fulfill the need of food we may have to sacrifice weapons or other goods that may have been produced with resources allocated to produce food. That is why, the problem of what goods should be produced and in what quantities arises. Will we use scarce resources to produce more consumption goods or more capital goods? The production of consumer goods

is essential to raise standard of living while capital goods are required to raise production capacity for growth. An economy has to make choice of the wants according to national priorities. We have to allocate limited resource to produce those goods which are considered as urgent or important. The decision of allocation of resources is central theme of micro economics.

2. **How are goods produced? (Problem of choice of production method):** After deciding the goods to be produced and their quantity, the next problem confronted by the nation is to determine who will do production, with what resources and with what production techniques. Who bakes and who treats? Is electricity generated from water, or from coal or from sun or from the nuclear? Will factories be run by people or machines? As far as techniques of production is concerned there are two types of techniques i.e. labour intensive and capital intensive. In labour intensive technique, more of labour and less capital in the form of machines etc. is used. Hence it is employment oriented. While in capital intensive technique, more capital and less labour is used and it is considered as more efficient and contributes more to growth. Every nation tries to use such a technique of production which ensures the optimum use of resources and maintain right balance between employment and efficiency.

3. **For whom to produce (The problem of distribution of national product)**: This is the problem of distribution of national product. It is related with who gets more or who gets less and how should the national product be distributed among the individuals in the economy? Will the composition of output benefit the .whole society or only a small section of rich people? The answer of this will be determined by the size of income obtained by these individuals or households from various sources. More equal is the distribution of income, more equal or justified will be the distribution of national product.

> **Functional Distribution (Source of National Income):** The size of income in first instance will depends upon the ownership of means of production by individuals and further it depends upon the reward that each factor gets by rendering their services.
>
> **Personal Distribution:** The distribution of national income among various individuals is known as personal distribution. This concept is related to the size of the income of an individual. The distribution may be equal or unequal.

Production Possibility (Frontier, Boundary) Curve/ Transformation Curve
It is an important tool of modern economics that is widely used in economics like explaining the, basic economic problems, theories of international trade etc.

*Production possibility curve is graphic representation of alternative production possibilities of two commodities that a country can produce by making the best use or optimal use of its given (available at point of time) resources and technological knowledge. **(See Table 1 & Diagram 1)***

Or

PPC shows the maximum possible production that a country can produce with available resources using existing level of technology, on the condition of fuller utilization of resources.

It is called *transformation curve* because in moving from one point to another on it, one good is transformed into another, not physically but by transferring resources from one use to other.

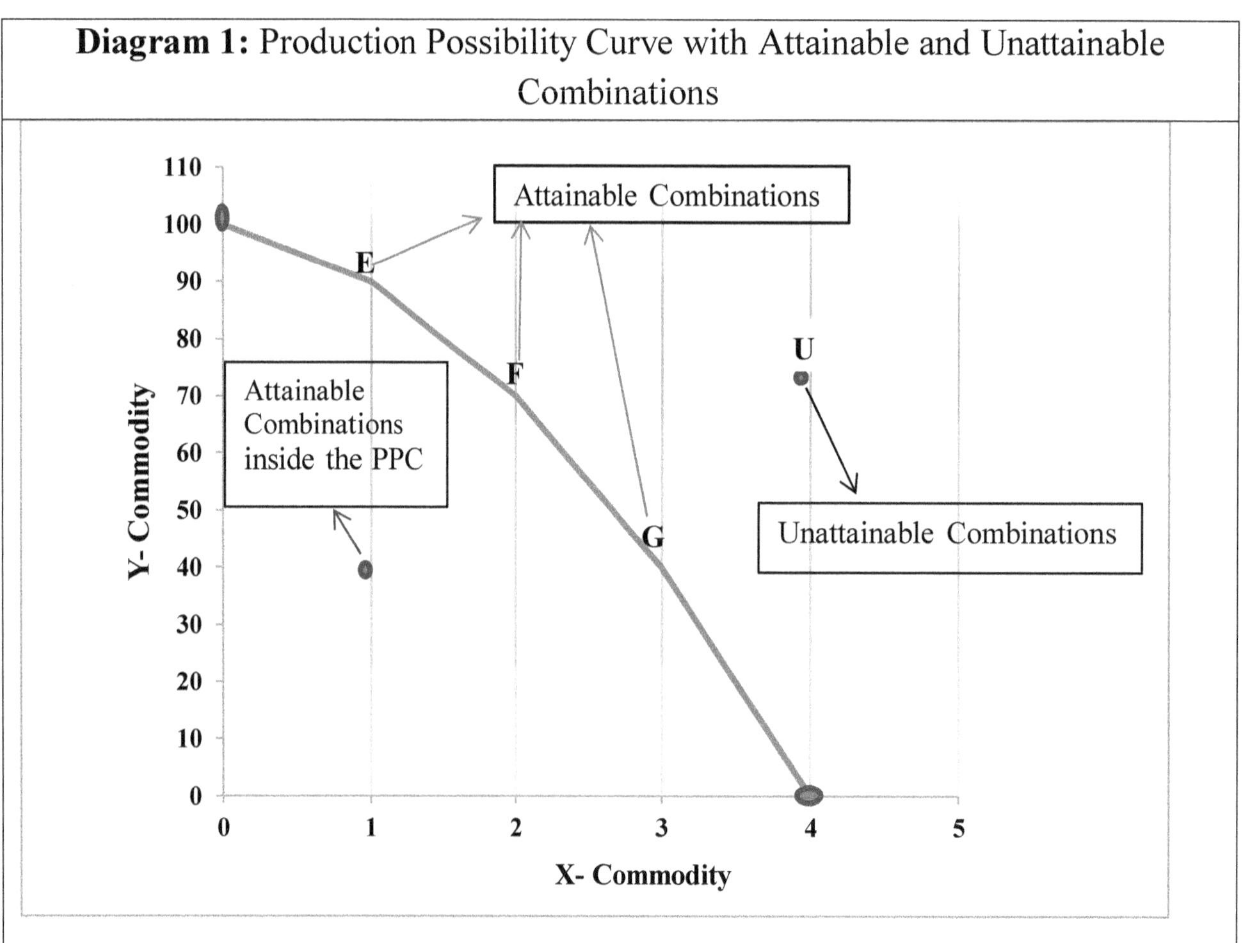

Diagram 1: Production Possibility Curve with Attainable and Unattainable Combinations

All points inside or on the PPC are attainable points while points outside the PPC are unattainable under given conditions. A country producing inside its PPC, say at point U, using its resources inefficiently (Under utilization of resources or Actual Output < Potential Output) and producing on the PPC, say at points E, F and G, means country is fully utilizing its resources (Actual Output = Potential Output). Points outside the PPC are unattainable under given circumstances.

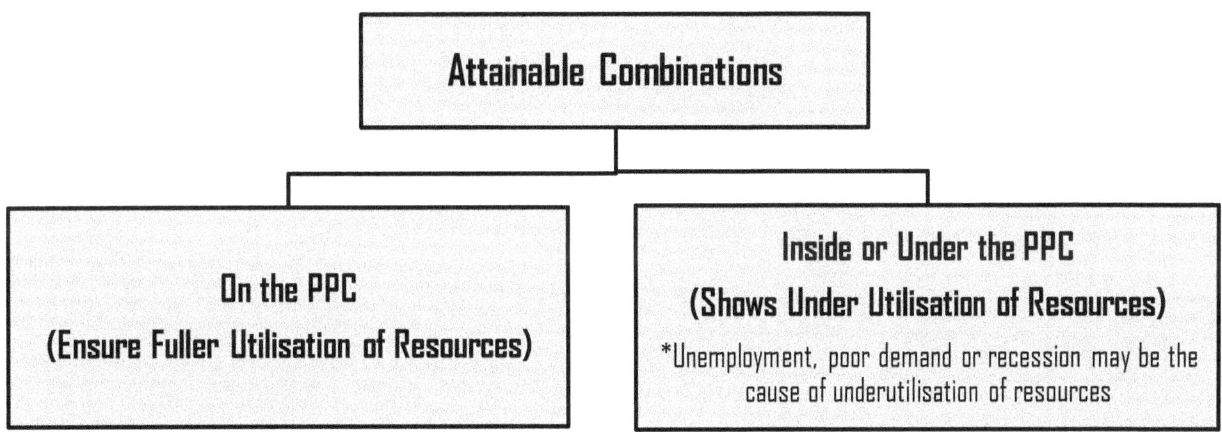

Table: 1				Diagram: 2
Production Possibilities	Good X	Good Y	MOC = $\frac{\Delta Y}{\Delta X}$	
A	0	100	-	
B	1	90	10	
C	2	70	20	
D	3	40	30	
F	4	0	40	

Characteristics/ Features/ Properties of PPC

1. **PPC slopes downward (Negative Slope).** It slopes downward from left to right. Because in case of given resources, more of one good say X can be produced only with less of other good say Y.
2. **PPC is concave to the point of origin**. It is concave due to increase in marginal opportunity cost. **(See Table 1 and Diagram 2)**

PPC will be convex to the point of origin, if MOC is falling and it will be straight line if MOC is constant.

Opportunity Cost

It is the cost of next best alternative foregone.

"The opportunity cost of producing one unit of commodity X is the amount of commodity Y that must be sacrificed in order to use resources to produce X rather than Y".

Marginal Opportunity Cost (MOC) is described as a rate at which output of commodity Y is to be sacrificed for producing one additional unit of commodity X.

$$MOC = \frac{\Delta Y}{\Delta X} \ \ or \ \ \frac{\text{Loss of output of commodity Y}}{\text{Gain of output of commodity X}}$$

Marginal Rate of Transformation (MRT) *is the rate at which resources from one product are transferred to produce one extra unit of the other product.*

*****Marginal opportunity cost is also known as slope of PPC.***

An example of concave PPC is given in figure 1. Suppose the country is producing at point E, on the PPC. It can increase its output of cloth only by switching factors of production from the wine sector to cloth sector. The opportunity cost of increasing its cloth is the reduction in wine production, and we would measure this by **ΔWine/ΔCloth**. This PPC is concave because opportunity cost of cloth increases as we increase the production of cloth.

Why PPC is concave to the point of origin?
Because of the application of, diminishing returns or law of increasing opportunity costs. This law operates when economic resources are not equally suited or adaptable to alternative uses. This is known as specificity of resources.

Shifting of PPC
Production possibility curve shifts either outward or inward due to change in resources and technological knowledge. The outward shifting of PPC implies increase in potential or production capacity of the country to produce more goods. PPC shifts to the right due to growth of resources, discovery of new resources, improvement in technology, innovations, scientific inventions, various policies and programmes by government to increase potential the country etc. This is shown by diagram 3. On the other side, the inward shifting of PPC implies decrease in potential of the country. PPC shifts to the left due to decrease in resources, depletion of natural resources, etc. This is shown by diagram 4.

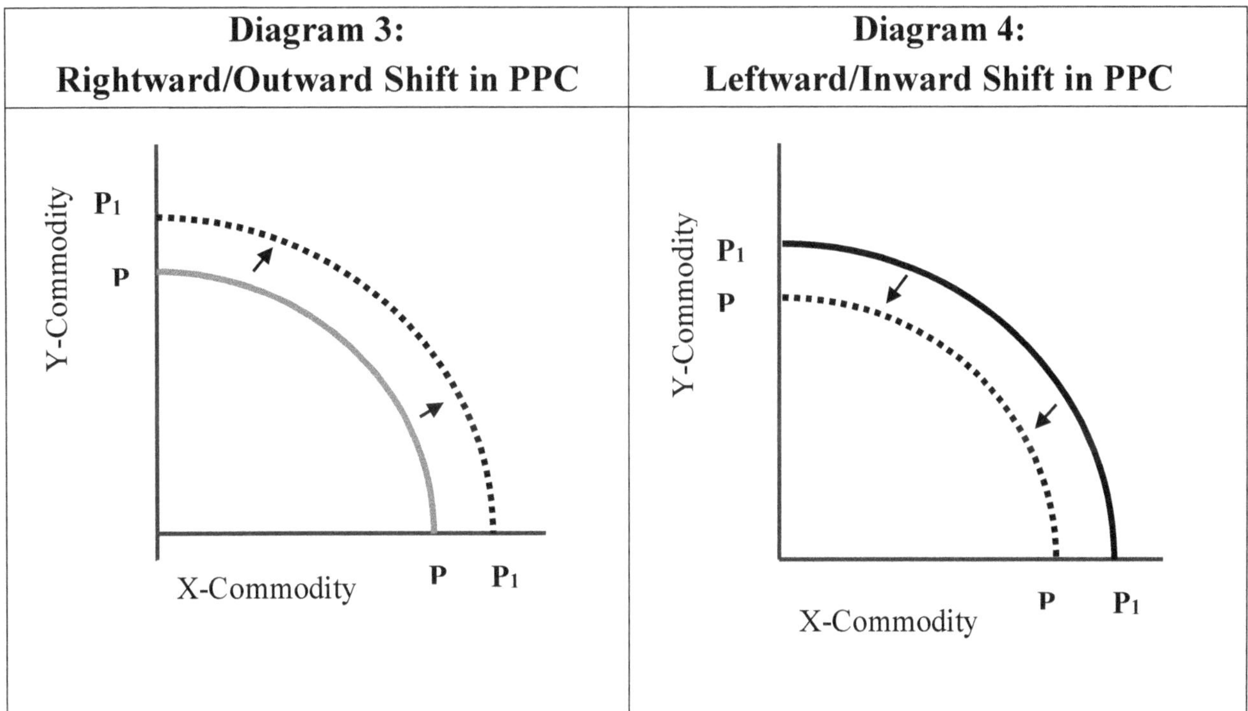

Rotation of PPC

Production possibility curve rotate either towards X-axis or **towards** Y-axis due to change in technology. If technological changes have neutral effect on Y commodity and have favourable impact on X commodity then PPC will shift to the right on X-axis only as shown in diagram 5 and If technological changes have neutral effect on X commodity and have favourable impact on Y commodity then PPC will move upwards on Y-axis only as shown in diagram 6.

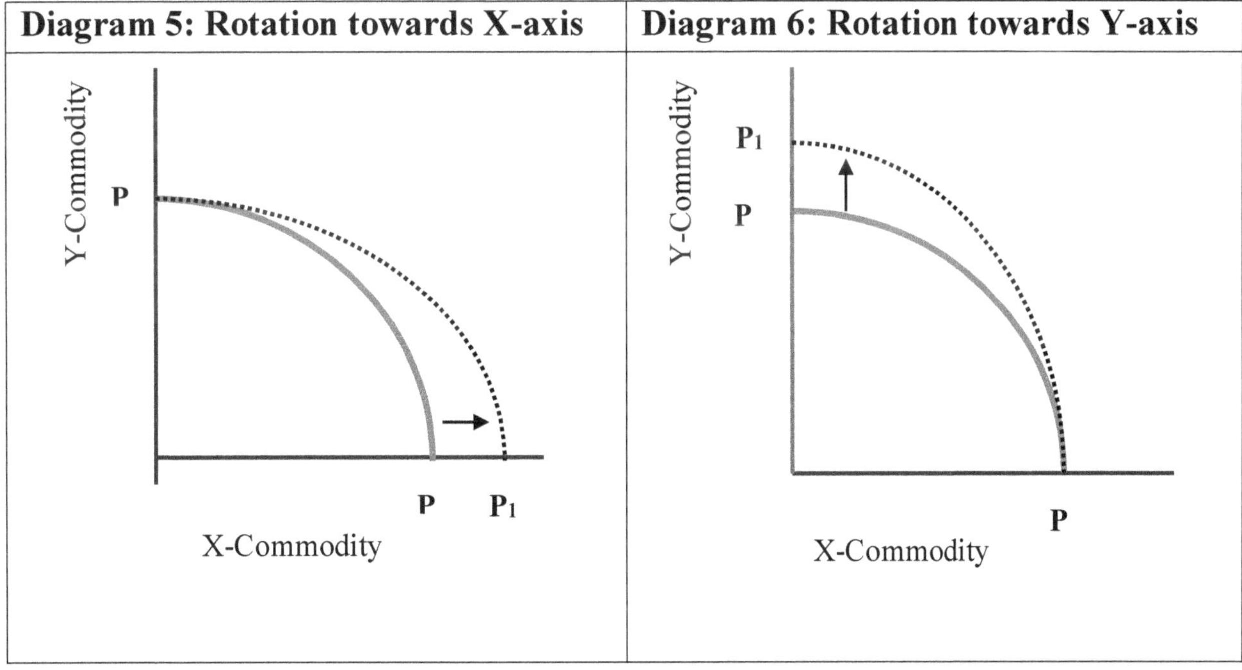

***

Exercise

1. Which one is not the feature of free market economy? 1. Public ownership 2. Consumer preference 3. Freedom of enterprise 4. Keen competition
2. Which studies belong to micro economics? 1. Study of General Price level 2. National Income 3. Study of a Rubber industry 4. Study of personal distribution of Income
3. _______________Statements can't be verified. 1. Positive 2. Negative 3. Normative 4. All of the above
4. Price mechanism belongs to _____________ economy. 1. Capitalistic 2. Mixed 3. Socialistic 4. All of the above
5. Under _______________ system more focus is on consumer's preferences. 1. Capitalistic 2. Mixed 3. Socialistic 4. All of the above
6. Which of the following does not belong to basic economic problem? 1. Problem of choice of technique 2. Problem of distribution of national output 3. Problem of allocation of resources 4. Problem of inflation
7. Choice is the outcome of__________.
8. Under___________ system, a decision regarding what to produce is taken by planning authority. 1. Capitalistic 2. Mixed 3. Socialistic 4. All of the above
9. Under ___________ economics there is limited degree of aggregation. 1. Micro 2. Macro 3. Both 1 & 2 4. None of the above
10. Economic problem arises due to the fact that: 1. Resources are scarce 2. Human wants are unlimited 3. Resources have alternative uses 4. All of these
11. Shape of production possibility curve is 1. Straight line 2. Convex to the point of origin 3. Concave to the point of origin 4. None of these
12. Which of the following is related to the problem 'how to produce'? 1. Distribution of income 2. Choice of technique 3. Choice of product 4.None of these
13. Growth of resources implies that production possibility curve: 1. Shifts to the right 2. Shifts to the left 3. Rotates to the right 4. None of these
14. Concavity of PPC implies: 1. Increasing MOC 2. Decreasing MOC 3. Constant MOC 4. None of these
15. A country producing under the PPC implies that 1. Actual output = Potential output 2. Actual output > Potential output 3. Actual output < Potential output 4. None of the above
16. Economising the use of resources means________ 1. Resources are easily available 2. Resources should be reserved for future 3. Optimum use of resources 4. All of the above

17. "Subsidies will make the people unproductive and parasites." This is the __________ statement given by the eminent economist. 1. Positive 2. Normative 3. Both 1 & 2 4. None of the above

18. "Opportunity cost is avoidable cost." True or False

19. Which of the following will shift the PPC to right? 1. Make in India 2. Skill India Campaign 3. Growth of Resources 4. All of the above

20. How will PPC react to increase in workforce given the labour force? 1. Shifts to the right 2. Shifts to the left 3. Rotates to the right 4. No change

Answers:

1. 1	2. 3	3. 3	4. 1	5. 1
6. 4	7. Scarcity	8. 3	9. 1	10.4
11.3	12.2	13.1	14.1	15.3
16.3	17.2	18.F	19.4	20.4

Schedules:

1. An economy produces two goods Watch and LED Bulb. The following table summarizes its production possibilities. Calculate the marginal opportunity cost of Watches at various combinations and draw PPC. Also comment on the behavior of MOC and the shape of PPC.

Watch	0	1	2	3	4
LED Bulb	50	45	35	20	0

Ans: MOC is increasing and shape of PPC will be concave.

Watch	0	1	2	3	4
LED Bulb	50	45	35	20	0
MOC	-	5/1	10/1	15/1	20/1

2. An economy produces two goods Clothes and LED TV's. The following table summarizes its production possibilities. Calculate production possibility of LED TV's from the given marginal opportunity cost of Watches at various combinations.

Clothes	0	1	2	3	4
LED TV's	100	-	-	-	-
MOC	-	5/1	10/1	15/1	20/1

Ans:

Clothes	0	1	2	3	4
LED TV's	100	95	85	70	50
MOC	-	5/1	10/1	15/1	20/1

3. A country produces rice and wheat. Their production possibilities are shown in the following table. Plot the PPC in a graph paper and identify its appearance.

Possibility	A	B	C	D	E
Rice	0	10	20	30	40
Cotton	100	90	70	40	0

Ans: PPC will be concave

Possibility	A	B	C	D	E
Rice	0	10	20	30	40
Cotton	100	90	70	40	0
MOC	-	10/1	20/1	30/1	40/1

4. The following is a production possibility table for war goods and civilian goods. Plot the PPC in a graph paper and identify its appearance by calculating marginal opportunity cost.

Combinations	A	B	C	D	E	F
War goods	0	1	2	3	4	5
Civilian goods	10	8	6	4	2	0

Ans: MOC is constant and PPC will be straight line.

Combinations	A	B	C	D	E	F
War goods	0	1	2	3	4	5
Civilian goods	10	8	6	4	2	0
MOC	-	2/1	2/1	2/1	2/1	2/1

5. The following is a production possibility table for war goods and civilian goods. Plot the PPC in a graph paper and identify its appearance by calculating marginal opportunity cost.

Combinations	A	B	C	D	E	F
War goods	0	1	2	3	4	5
Civilian goods	15	10	6	3	1	0

Ans: MOC is decreasing and PPC will be convex.

Combinations	A	B	C	D	E	F
War goods	0	1	2	3	4	5
Civilian goods	15	10	6	3	1	0
MOC	-	5/1	4/1	3/1	2/1	1/1

6. Prof. Demagi Lal is getting Rs.60000 p.m. as salary and rent free house with other facilities in university (all of worth of Rs. 360000 p.a). If he wanted to start tuition work by leaving university job. He is expected to earn Rs. 75000 p.m. What would be his opportunity cost of starting tuition work? Ans: University Job (Salary & Benefits Rs. 1080000)

7. Identify which of the following is the subject matter of microeconomics or macroeconomics:

1. General Price level
2. National income

3.   Gross Domestic Product
4.   Demand for Dora Cakes by all buyers
5.   Reliance Industry
6.   Supply by a firm
7.   Information and Technology industry
8.   Government budget
9.   Price determination of a smart phone
10. Agriculture Sector contribution to GDP

Answers: [Microeconomics: 4,5,6,7,9], [Macroeconomics: 1,2,3,8,10]

Practice Questions including NECERT Questions:

1. Define the subject matter of economics.
2. Distinguish between a centrally planned economy and a market economy.
3. Distinguish between microeconomics and macroeconomics.
4. Discuss the central problems of an economy.
5. What do you mean by the production possibilities of an economy?
6. What is production possibility frontier?
7. What is market economy?
8. Why is production possibility curve concave? Explain
9. What is planned economy?
10. Define an economy.
11. Define macroeconomics.
12. How is production possibility curve affected by unemployment in the economy? Explain
13. Define microeconomics.
14. What is opportunity cost?
15. Explain how a production possibility curve is affected when resources are inefficiently employed in an economy.
16. State reasons why an economic problem arises.
17. What is opportunity cost? Explain with the help of a numerical example.
18. What is 'marginal rate of transformation? Explain with the help of an example.
19. Explain the central problem of 'how to produce'.
20. Define production possibilities curve. Explain why it is downward sloping from left to right.
21. Explain the meaning of opportunity cost with the help of production possibility schedule.

22. With the help of suitable example explain the problem of 'for whom to produce'.

23. Why there is huge unemployment in India when scarcity of resources is a universal fact? (Hint: Due to shortage of capital or investment)

24. "Massive unemployment shifts PPC to the left." Defend or Refute.

25. "Growth of resources shifts PPC to the right." Defend or Refute.

26. Explain the problem of 'what to produce'.

27. "A country always produces on the PPC." Defend or Refute.

CHAPTER 2

CONSUMER'S EQUILIBRIUM: UTILITY ANALYSIS

The consumers demand a commodity because they derive utility from that commodity. It is a utility that is considered as basis of demand for commodity. In this chapter we will go through the meaning, concepts of utility and various laws associated with utility.

Utility: Utility is the want satisfying power of a commodity.

"Utility is the quality of a good to satisfy a want." **Hibbdon**

Features of Utility:
1. Utility is subjective in nature.
2. Utility is relative as it varies with time and place.
3. Utility is not essential useful.
4. Utility is independent of morality.

Measurement of Utility

Cardinal Concept of Utility: *According to cardinal concept of utility, it can be measured in cardinal numbers. This analysis was developed by Dupit, Gossen, Walras, Menger and Jevons etc. in cardinal utility function a person is able to describe by how much one good is preferred to other good. Prof. Alfred Marshall, devised a method of measuring utility. He measured utility with amount of money that a consumer is willing to pay for a unit of the commodity. Prof. Fisher has used the term* **'Util'** *as a measure of utility. Thus in terms of cardinal utility analysis it can be said that one gets 10 utils from a cup of tea.*

Ordinal Concept of Utility: This approach is given by J.R. Hicks and R.G.D. Allen and is also called Hicks and Allen approach. *According to ordinal concept of utility, it cannot be measured in terms of cardinal numbers. The consumer is able to rank the various 'basket of goods' according to the satisfaction that each bundle gives him. He is able to determine his order of preference among different bundles of goods. He can express only whether one good is more or less preferable to another good.*

Concepts of Utility

Total Utility (TU): Total utility refers to the entire amount of satisfaction obtained from consuming various quantities of a commodity.

$$TU = f(Q) \text{ or } TU_n = U^{Ist} + U^{2nd} + \ldots + U^{nth}$$

Marginal Utility (MU): Marginal utility is the addition made to total utility by consuming one more unit of a commodity. $MU = \frac{\Delta TU}{\Delta Q}$, $MU_{nth} = TU_n - TU_{n-1}$

$$TU_n = U^{Ist} + U^{2nd} + \ldots\ldots + U^{nth} \text{ and } MU = \frac{\Delta TU}{\Delta Q}, MU_{nth} = TU_n - TU_{n-1}$$

Relationship between TU and MU

1. Both TU and MU can be obtained from each other if value of one of them is given. TU can be obtained from MU using $TU = \Sigma MU$ and MU can be obtained from TU like $MU = TU_n - TU_{n-1}$ as shown in table 1 and diagram 1.
2. As long as MU falls, TU increases at diminishing rate.
3. TU is at highest point when MU is zero and it is known as point of saturation.
4. TU starts falling when MU becomes negative.
5. MU is considered as slope of TU.

Table 1			Diagram 1
Q	**MU**	**TU**	
0	**-**	**0**	
1	**10**	**10**	
2	**8**	**18**	
3	**6**	**24**	
4	**4**	**28**	
5	**2**	**30**	
6	**0**	**30**	
7	**-2**	**28**	

Difference between Total Utility and Marginal Utility

Total Utility	Marginal Utility
Total utility refers to the entire amount of satisfaction obtained from consuming various quantities of a commodity.	Marginal utility is the addition made to total utility by consuming one more unit of a commodity. (MU is a slope of TU)

TU can be calculated using formula. $$TU = \Sigma MU$$	MU can be calculated using formula. $$MU = \frac{\Delta TU}{\Delta Q}, \quad MU_{nth} = TU_n - TU_{n-1}$$
TU cannot be negative.	MU can be negative.
TU refers to utility obtained from aggregate units.	MU refers to utility obtained from an additional unit.
TU increases with increase in quantity consumed of a commodity.	MU falls with increase in quantity consumed of a commodity due to application of law of diminishing MU.
Point of saturation occurs when TU is maximum.	Point of saturation occurs when MU is zero.

Law of Diminishing Marginal Utility or Gossen's First Law

This law is the fundamental law of utility analysis. It is universal in nature and we all experience this law in our daily life. This law states that it is psychological fact that when a consumer gets more and more units of a commodity, during a particular time, the utility from the successive units will diminish.

"As the amount consumed of a good increases, the marginal utility of the good tend to decrease." - **Samuelson**

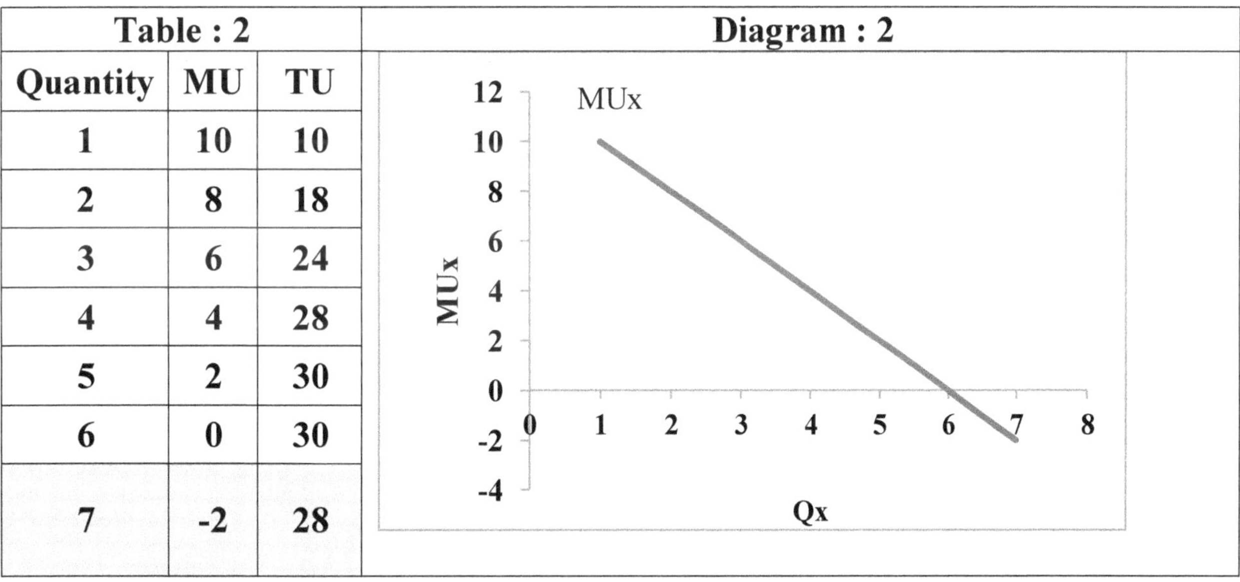

Quantity	MU	TU
1	10	10
2	8	18
3	6	24
4	4	28
5	2	30
6	0	30
7	-2	28

Table 2 and diagram 2 explain the law of diminishing marginal utility. The table and the diagram show that MU tends to diminish as consumption increases. TU will increase only at the diminishing rate, because MU is diminishing.

Consumer's Equilibrium

Consumer's equilibrium refers to a situation where in a consumer gets maximum satisfaction out of his limited income and he has no tendency to make any change in his existing expenditure as long as circumstances remain unchanged.

Consumers' equilibrium based on the following assumptions:

1. Utility can be measured in cardinal numbers.
2. Consumer is rational, he always tries to get maximum satisfaction and use his resources in rational manner.
3. Consumer has perfect knowledge.
4. Marginal utility of money remain constant.
5. There is no change in Habit, Fashion, Income and Price of commodities.
6. Utility obtained from one commodity is independent of another commodity.

Consumer Equilibrium in Case of One Commodity

To achieve equilibrium position in case of one commodity, the consumer should purchase that much quantity of the commodity at its given price so that he/she can maximise total consumer surplus (Total utility) from his/her purchase.

Conditions of Consumer's Equilibrium in Case of One Commodity

$\dfrac{MUx}{Px} = MUm$ (See Table 2) or $\dfrac{MUx}{MUm} = P_x$ (See Table 3)

(Where MUx means MU derive from consumption of X Commodity, Px means actual price of a X commodity, MU_m means worth of one unit of money in terms of utils)

Table 3:

Units of X	MUx	Px	$\dfrac{MUx}{MUm}$ Assuming MUm = Rs. 1 = 2 utils (Utility gained in terms of money or Price willing to pay to get one unit)	Consumer Surplus = (Price willing to pay – Actual price)	
				Per unit	Total
1	10	2	5	3	3
2	8	2	4	2	(3+2 = 5)
3	6	2	3	1	(3+2+1 = 6)
4	*4*	*2*	*2*	*0*	(3+2+1+0 = 6) Max
5	2	2	1	-1	(3+2+1+0+(-1)) = 5

Table 4:

Units of X	MUx	Px	$\dfrac{\text{MUx}}{\text{Px}}$ (Utility gained by spending one rupee)	MUm (in Utils) (Utility sacrificed by spending one rupee)
1	10	2	5	2
2	8	2	4	2
3	6	2	3	2
4	*4*	*2*	*2*	*2*
5	2	2	1	2

Explanation: Consumer's equilibrium in one commodity case is explained with the help of table 3 & 4 and diagram 3. Suppose the consumer wants to purchase X-commodity whose actual price is Rs. 2 and MUm = 2 utils as declared by consumer. Utility gained in terms of money ($\frac{\text{MUx}}{\text{MUm}}$) from different units of X is shown in table 3. MUx goes on diminishing with purchase of additional units due to operation of law of diminishing marginal utility. Consumer attains equilibrium position when he/she purchases 4 units of X commodity where $\frac{\text{MUx}}{\text{MUm}}$ = **Px**. In diagram 3, the downward sloping $\frac{\text{MUx}}{\text{MUm}}$ curve and horizontal line **Px** showing price of the commodity X intersect at point 'E' corresponding to 4 units of X commodity. This point shows the consumer's equilibrium position where consumer surplus (Shown by area ABEC) is maximised. As long as $\frac{\text{MUx}}{\text{MUm}}$ > **Px**, consumer continuous to buy commodity X because every additional unit positively contributes to consumer surplus and total value of consumer surplus is increasing. In other words, utility gained by spending one rupee on X commodity is more than the utility sacrificed as shown in table 4. He/she will stop where $\frac{\text{MUx}}{\text{MUm}}$ = Px corresponding to 4 units of X commodity, where consumer surplus is maximised. At any point right side to 'E', consumer will not like purchase because utility gained by spending one rupee on X commodity is less than the utility sacrificed, that means consumer surplus will be negative. Thus, point 'E' is the point of equilibrium where consumer gets maximum satisfaction.

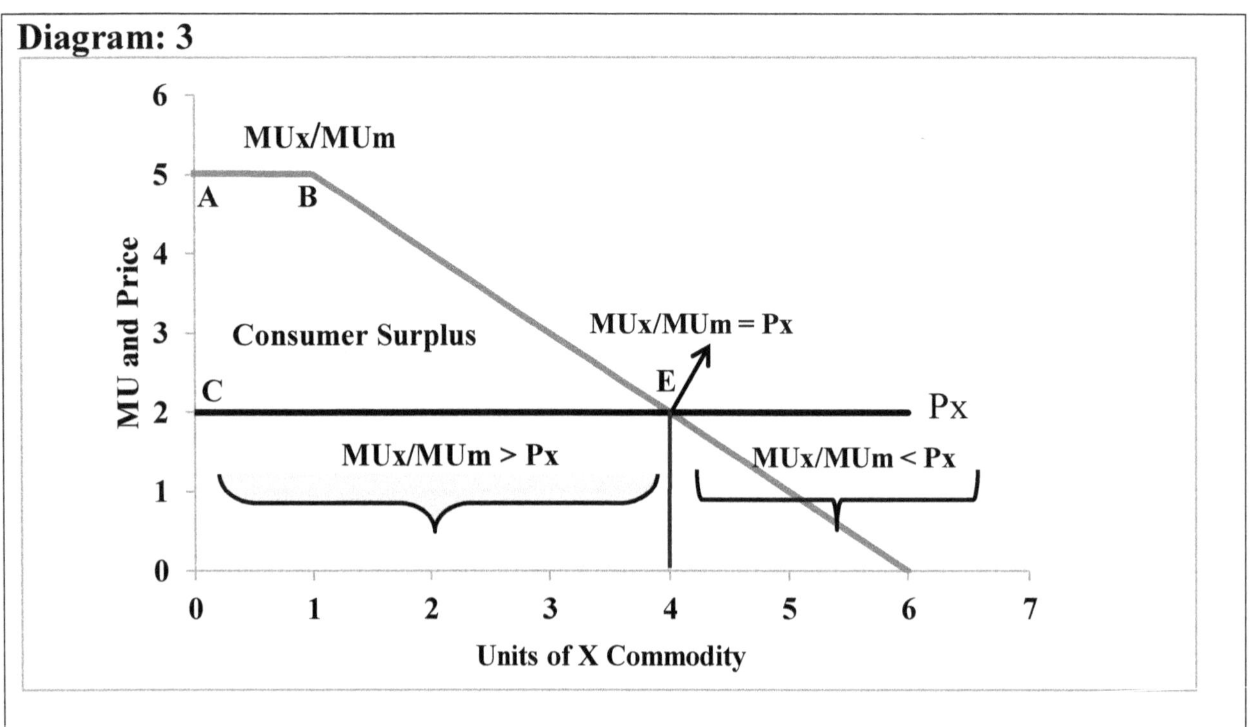

Consumer's Equilibrium in Case of Several Commodities (Two Commodities)
Consumer's equilibrium in case of two or more commodities can be explained with the help of **"Law of equi- marginal utility"**. This law states that a consumer gets maximum satisfaction from his limited resources when he spends his limited resources on different commodities in such a way that last rupee spent on different commodities yields equal marginal utility.

Conditions of Consumer's Equilibrium in case of Two Commodities

1. $\dfrac{\text{MUx}}{\text{Px}} = \dfrac{\text{MUy}}{\text{Py}} = \textbf{MUm}$

2. $\textbf{P}_x\textbf{Q}_x + \textbf{P}_y\textbf{Q}_y = \textbf{M}$ (P_x is price of X-Commodity, P_y is price of Y-Commodity, Q_x is quantity consumed of X-Commodity, Q_y is quantity consumed of Y-Commodity and M is Money income of the consumer)

Table 5

Rupee	Units of X	MU_x	$\dfrac{MUx}{Px}$	Units of Y	MU_y	$\dfrac{MUy}{Py}$
1st	1st	10	10	1st	12	12
2nd	2nd	8	8	2nd	10	10
3rd	3rd	6	6	3rd	8	8
4th	4th	4	4	4th	6	6
5th	5th	2	2	5th	4	4

Explanation: Consumer's equilibrium in case of two commodities is explained with the help of table 5 and diagram 4. Suppose consumer has five rupees to spend and price of X and Y commodity is Rs. 1 each. Table 5 shows MU of Good X and Good Y. From table 5 it is clear that the proportionality rule $\frac{MUx}{Px} = \frac{MUy}{Py}$ or $[\frac{8}{1} = \frac{8}{1}]$ along with second order condition $P_xQ_x + P_yQ_y = M$ or $[(1\times2) + (1\times3) = Rs. 5]$ is fulfilled when consumer is buying 2 units of X and 3 units of Y. TU from X commodity will be 10+8= 18 utils and TU from Y commodity will be 12+10+8= 30 utils corresponding to 2 units of X commodity and 3 units of Y commodity. Total utility from both the commodities will be 30+18= 48 utils which is maximum possible utility under given conditions. This is the situation of consumer's equilibrium shown by point 'E' on diagram 5. If $\frac{MUx}{Px} > \frac{MUy}{Py}$, it means consumer is getting more utility per rupee in case of X commodity than Y commodity. The utility maximizing consumer will increase quantity of X commodity and will decrease quantity of Y commodity as long as $\frac{MUx}{Px} > \frac{MUy}{Py}$. He/she will continue to switch his/her expenditure from Y to X commodity till $\frac{MUx}{Px} = \frac{MUy}{Py}$. On the other side, if $\frac{MUx}{Px} < \frac{MUy}{Py}$, it means consumer is getting more utility per rupee in case of Y commodity than X commodity. The utility maximizing consumer will increase quantity of Y commodity and will decrease quantity of X commodity as long as $\frac{MUx}{Px} < \frac{MUy}{Py}$. He/she will continue to switch his/her expenditure from X to Y commodity till $\frac{MUx}{Px} = \frac{MUy}{Py}$.

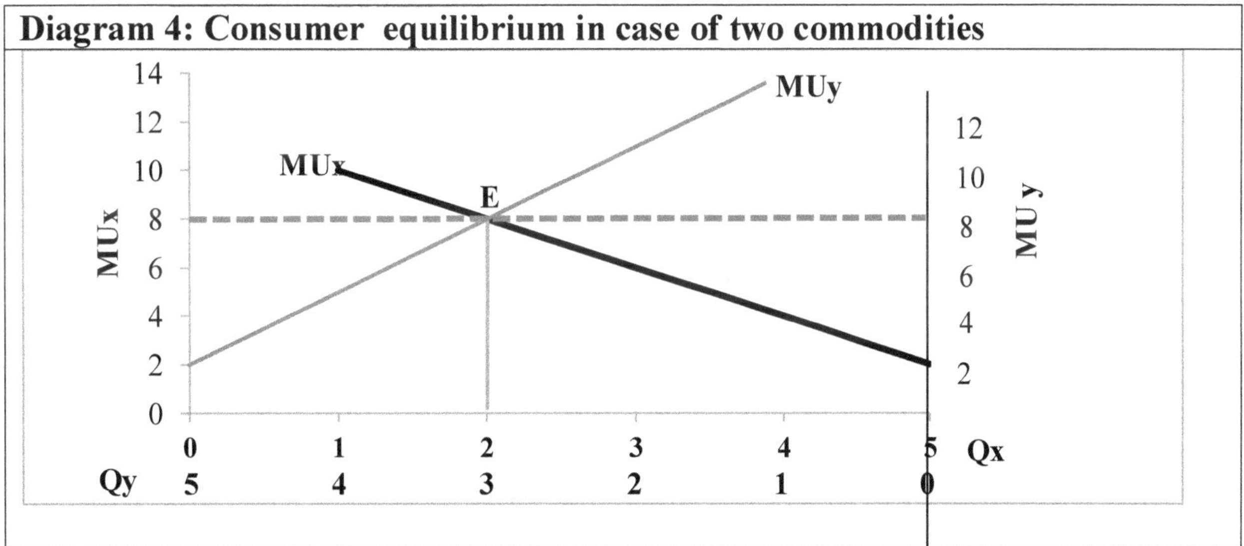

Diagram 4: Consumer equilibrium in case of two commodities

In case of N commodities condition of consumer equilibrium would be

$$\frac{MU1}{P1} = \frac{MU2}{P2} = \ldots\ldots = \frac{MUn}{Pn} = MUm, \quad P_1Q_1 + P_2Q_2 + \ldots\ldots\ldots + P_nQ_n = M$$

(P$_1$ is price of 1-Commodity, P$_2$ is price of 2-Commodity, Q$_1$ is quantity consumed of 1-Commodity, Q$_2$ is quantity consumed of 2-Commodity, P$_n$ is price of n-Commodity, Q$_n$ is quantity consumed of n-Commodity and M is Money income of the consumer, where P$_1$Q$_1$ shows expenditure on commodity 1, where P$_n$Q$_n$ shows expenditure on commodity 'n')

Consumer's Equilibrium:

One Commodity: $\dfrac{MUx}{Px} = MUm$

Two Commodities: $\dfrac{MUx}{Px} = \dfrac{MUy}{Py} = MUm$, $P_xQ_x + P_yQ_y = $ **Money Income**

'N' Commodities: $\dfrac{MUx}{Px} = \dfrac{MUy}{Py} = \ldots = \dfrac{MUn}{Pn} = MUm$, $P_xQ_x + P_yQ_y + \ldots + P_nQ_n = M$

****

Exercise

1. Utility can be measured in cardinal numbers according to 1. Cardinal concept 2. Ordinal concept 3. Both 1&2 4. Statement is wrong

2. Which of the following equations is correct? 1. $MU = TU_{n+2} - TU_{n+1}$ 2. TU = ΣMU 3. $MU = TU_n - TU_{n-1}$ 4. All of the above

3. When there is point of saturation, then total utility will be 1. Zero 2. Diminishing 3. Maximum 4. Minimum

4. When TU is increasing, then MU must be: 1. Increasing 2. Decreasing 3. Both 1&2 4. Negative

5. Initially $\dfrac{MU_X}{P_X} = \dfrac{MU_Y}{P_Y}$. With a fall in the price of Y, the consumption of the commodity-Y: 1. Diminishes 2. Increases 3. Remains constant 4. Becomes zero

6. Utility is a _________ concept. 1. Subjective 2.Objective 3. Both 1&2 4. None of the above

7. Consumer surplus is ___________, when consumer is in equilibrium. 1. Maximum 2. Minimum 3. Zero 4. Equal to price

8. Consumer surplus is difference between 1. Actual price and Price willing to pay 2. Price willing to pay and Actual price 3. TU and MU 4. None of the above

9. Which of the following is true about consumer's equilibrium in case of 'n' commodities? 1. MU$_1$/P$_1$ = MU$_2$/P$_2$ and P$_1$Q$_1$+ P$_2$Q$_2$ = M, 2. MU$_1$/P$_1$ + MU$_2$/P$_2$ and P$_1$Q$_1$+ P$_2$Q$_2$ = M, 3. MU$_1$/P$_1$ = MU$_2$/P$_2$ =…= MUn/Pn and P$_1$Q$_1$+ P$_2$Q$_2$+……+PnQn = M, 4. MU$_1$/P$_1$+MU$_2$/P$_2$ +…+ MUn/Pn and P$_1$Q$_1$+ P$_2$Q$_2$+……+PnQn = M

---

10. Other things being constant, if price of commodity falls then consumer surplus will 1. Decrease 2. Increase 3. No change 4. Nothing can be said.

11. Area under the MU curve represents the _______ 1. TU 2. MU 3. Consumer Surplus 4. None of the above

12. Which of the following is true when TU is positive? 1. MU=0 2. MU is falling 3. MU is negative 4. All of the above

Answers:

1. 1	2. 4	3. 3	4. 3	5. 2	6. 1
7. 1	8. 2	9. 3	10.2	11.1	12.4

NCERT Questions:

1. State the condition of consumer's equilibrium.

2. Starting from the initial situation of consumer's equilibrium, suppose that the marginal utility of a rupee increases. Will it increases or decreases the quantity demanded of a product?

3. Ice-cream sell for Rs.30. Lakshmi who loves ice cream, has already eaten 3. Her MU from eating 3 ice creams is 90. Suppose further that, for her, the MU of one rupee is 3. Should she eat more ice cream or should the stop? (Ans: She is at point of equilibrium, she should stop consuming more ice cream. Use $\frac{MUx}{Px} = MUm, \frac{90}{30} = 3$)

Schedules

1. A person's total utility schedule is given below. Derive the marginal utility schedule.

Q	0	1	2	3	4	5
TU	0	10	25	38	48	55

Ans:

Q	0	1	2	3	4	5
MU	-	10	15	13	10	7

2. A person's total utility schedule is given below. Derive the marginal utility schedule.

Q	0	1	2	3	5	8
TU	0	10	25	38	48	60

Ans:

Q	0	1	2	3	5	8
MU	-	10	15	13	10/2	12/3

3. A person's schedule is given below. Calculate TU from this schedule.

Q	1	2	3	4	5	6

| MU | 8 | 10 | 8 | 6 | 3 | 0 |

Ans:

Q	1	2	3	4	5	6
TU	8	18	26	32	35	35

4. Complete the following table,:

Q	1	2	3	4	5
TU	-	19	-	29	-
MU	10	-	7	-	-3

Ans:

Q	1	2	3	4	5
TU	10	19	26	29	26
MU	10	9	7	3	-3

5. Complete the following table, assuming point of saturation attained when consumer consumed 4 units:

Q	1	2	3	4	5
TU	50	-	120	-	110
MU	-	-	30	-	-

Ans:

Q	1	2	3	4	5
TU	50	90	120	120	110
MU	50	40	30	0	-10

6. The price of the good is Rs. 3. How many units of the commodity the person will purchase to reach equilibrium position? Schedule is given below. (Assuming MUm= 1util = 1Rs.) Ans: 3 units

Q	1	2	3	4	5
MU	5	4	3	2	1

7. The following schedule gives the number of **Toffees** consumed and the total utility derived of each level of consumption by a consumer. Given that the price of **Toffees** is fixed at Rs.2. determine the optimal level of consumption: Ans: 7 units

No. of Toffees	1	2	3	4	5	6	7	8
TU	5	9.5	13.5	17	20	22.5	24.5	26

8. What are the conditions of consumer equilibrium given that consumer consumes two goods X and Y. The ratio of price of good X that of Y is 2:1. Total money income available with consumer is Rs.52 and price of Y is Rs.2.

Units	1	2	3	4	5	6	7	8	9	10
MU (X)	112	96	84	80	64	52	36	20	12	4
TU (Y)	64	122	176	222	262	298	332	364	386	396

Ans: 8 Units of X and 10 units of Y

Units	1	2	3	4	5	6	7	8	9	10
MU (X)	112	96	84	80	64	52	36	20	12	4
MU (X)/Px	28	24	21	20	16	13	9	5	3	1
MU (Y)	64	58	54	46	40	36	34	32	22	10
MU (Y)/Py	32	29	27	23	20	18	17	16	11	5

9. Gulabjamun sells for Rs. 10 per piece. Ladoo who is very fond of gulabjamun, has already consumed 2 pieces and marginal utility from 2nd unit is 15 utils. His marginal utility of one rupee is 2. What will be the behavior of Ladoo in this situation? Should he consume more or stop the consumption? (Ans: $\frac{MUx}{Px} =$ **MUm, Given MUx =15, Px = Rs. 10, MUm = 2,** $\frac{15}{10} < 2$, Consumer is not in equilibrium position, he should decrease the consumption of Gulabjamun)

10. How consumer will attain equilibrium position under cardinal concept of utility in case of two commodities. From the following schedule find out how much quantity of X commodity and Y commodity he will buy to get maximum satisfaction if he has Rs. 24 to spend and price of X commodity and Y commodity is Rs. 2 and Rs. 3 respectively?

Units	1	2	3	4	5	6
MUx	20	18	16	14	12	10
MUy	24	21	18	15	12	9

Ans: 6 units of X and 4 units of Y

Units	1	2	3	4	5	6
MUx	20	18	16	14	12	10
MUx/Px	10	9	8	7	6	5
MUy	24	21	18	15	12	9
MUy/Py	8	7	6	5	4	3

11. How consumer will attain equilibrium position under cardinal concept of utility in case of two commodities. From the following schedule find out how much quantity of X commodity and Y commodity he will buy to get maximum satisfaction if he has Rs. 24 to spend and price of Y commodity is one and half times the price of X commodity.?

Units	1	2	3	4	5	6
MUx	20	18	16	14	12	10
MUx/Px	10	9	8	7	6	5
TUy	24	45	63	78	90	99

Ans: Px = Rs. 2 and Py = Rs. 3, 6 units of X and 4 units of Y

Units	1	2	3	4	5	6
MUx	20	18	16	14	12	10
MUx/Px	10	9	8	7	6	5
MUy	24	21	18	15	12	9
MUy/Py	8	7	6	5	4	3

Practice Questions

1. Define utility.
2. What is law of diminishing marginal utility?
3. State and explain the conditions of consumer's equilibrium with the help of utility analysis if consumer consumes only two goods.
4. Explain the conditions determining how many units of a good the consumer will buy at a given price.
5. A consumer consumes only two goods X and Y. At a consumption level of these two goods, he finds that the ratio of marginal utility to price in case of X is higher than in case of Y. Explain the reaction of the consumer.
6. A consumer consumes only two goods X and Y. At a consumption level of these two goods, he finds that the ratio of marginal utility to price in case of X is lower than in case of Y. Explain the reaction of the consumer.
7. Explain the law of diminishing marginal utility with the help of a total utility schedule.
8. Explain the relation between total utility and marginal utility.
9. A consumer consumes only two goods X and Y and is in equilibrium. Price of X falls. Explain the reaction of the consumer through the utility analysis.
10. A consumer consumes only two goods X and Y and is in equilibrium. Price of X rises. Explain the reaction of the consumer through the utility analysis.
11. What is meant by consumer's equilibrium?
12. Explain the conditions of consumer's equilibrium with the help of utility analysis.
13. By spending his entire income only on two goods X and Y a consumer finds that $\frac{MU\ of\ X}{Price\ of\ X} > \frac{MU\ of\ Y}{Price\ of\ Y}$. Explain how consumer will react.
14. By spending his entire income only on two goods X and Y a consumer finds that $\frac{MU\ of\ X}{Price\ of\ X} < \frac{MU\ of\ Y}{Price\ of\ Y}$. Explain how consumer will react.
15. A consumer consumes only two goods. Explain consumer's equilibrium with the help of utility analysis.

CHAPTER 3

CONSUMER EQUILBRIUM: INDIFFERENCE CURVE ANALYSIS

We had discussion on the consumer equilibrium with cardinal concept of utility in the previous chapter. In this chapter we will discuss the ordinal approach of consumer's equilibrium using indifference curve technique and its related concepts. This approach is developed by Prof. Hicks and Prof. Allen.

Indifference Curve or Equal/Iso Utility Curve: Indifference curve shows all those combinations of market baskets that provide a consumer with same level of satisfaction. That means consumer is indifferent among these market baskets. Market basket or bundle represents the list with specific quantities of one or more goods (See diagram 1).

"A single indifference curve shows the different combinations of X and Y that yields equal satisfaction to the consumer".- **Leftwitch**

Indifference Curve Schedule: An indifference curve schedule refers to a schedule that indicates different combinations of two commodities which yield equal satisfaction. Table 1 shows that consumer gets equal satisfaction from all the four combinations.

Table 1: Indifference Curve Schedule			Diagram 1: Indifference Curve
Combinations	**Good X**	**Good Y**	
A	1	10	
B	2	7	
C	3	5	
D	4	4	

Indifference Map: An indifference map displays consumer's scale of preference. It is a collection of various indifference curves showing various levels of satisfaction.

"An indifference map is a collection of indifference curves corresponding to different levels of satisfaction, each curve on the right hand side represents a higher level of satisfaction as compared to the indifference curves on the left hand side as it represents greater quantities of both commodities. A lower indifference curve on the other hand, represents lesser quantities of both the commodities and hence it represents lesser level of satisfaction". –**Handerson & Quant**

Indifference Set: It is a set of those combinations of two goods which offers same level of satisfaction and is displayed by single IC as shown in diagram 1.

Monotonic Preferences: Consumer's preferences are said to be monotonic if and only if between any two bundles the consumer prefers the bundle which has more of at least one of the goods and no less of the other good as compared to the other bundle. E.g. suppose consumer has two bundles B1 = (10 units of Coke, 15 units of Samosa) and B2 = (12 units of Coke, 15 units of Samosa). According to monotonic preferences consumer will prefer B2 bundle.

Difference between Indifference Set and Indifference Map

Indifference Set	Indifference Map
Indifference set is a set of those combinations of two goods which offers same level of satisfaction and is displayed by single IC as shown in diagram.	Indifference map is a set of various IC's that displays various levels of satisfaction.
All combinations of Indifference set are equally preferable.	Combinations on higher IC are preferable to combinations placed on lower IC, as these offer more satisfaction.

Marginal Rate of Substitution of X for Y (MRSxy): Marginal rate of substitution of X for Y is the maximum amount of Y commodity that a person is willing to give up to obtain one additional unit of X commodity by keeping his level of satisfaction at same level.

"The marginal rate of substitution of X for Y (MRSxy) is defined as the amount of Y, the consumer is willing to give up, to get one more unit of X and maintain the same level of satisfaction." **– Bilas**

MRXxy $= \frac{\Delta Y}{\Delta X}$ (where ΔY measures the change in Y commodity, ΔX measures the change in X commodity)

Diminishing Marginal Rate of Substitution (DMRS): In general MRSxy falls as we moved down along the indifference curve. This behavior of MRS is termed as DMRS. This happens because as the consumer has more and more of a commodity the intensity for his want for that commodity goes on declining as result of which the sacrifice made in terms of another commodity declines also as shown in table 2 and diagram II. In this way, DMRS reflects important features of consumer preferences. This is the reason behind the convex or bowed inward IC's.

Table 2: Marginal Rate of Substitution of X for Y

Combination	X-Commodity	Y-Commodity	MRXxy $= \frac{\Delta Y}{\Delta X}$
A	1	15	-
B	2	10	5/1
C	3	6	4/1
D	4	3	3/1
E	5	1	2/1

Properties/Features/Characteristics of IC

1. **IC has Negative Slope:** This property implies that IC slopes downward from left to right. To keep the level of satisfaction same, if a consumer consumes more of one commodity then he must consume less quantity of other commodity. If consumer will not reduce the quantity of other commodity for gain of quantity of one commodity, then as per monotonic preference his level of satisfaction will increase. This requires that an IC must be negatively sloped and all other possibilities viz. horizontal IC, vertical IC and positively sloped IC are ruled out.

IC with negative slope	Horizontal IC
Vertical IC	**IC with positive slope**

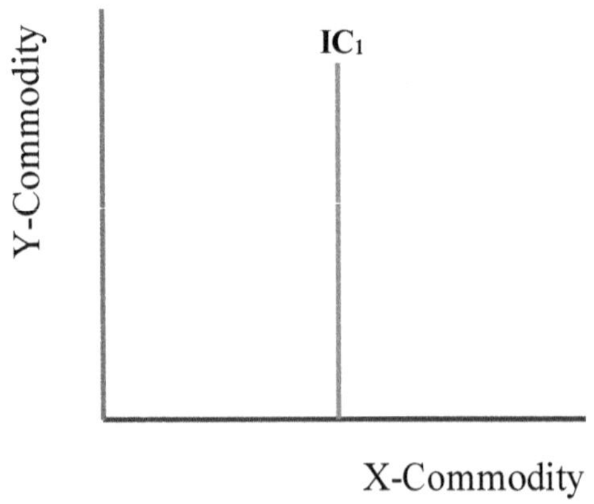

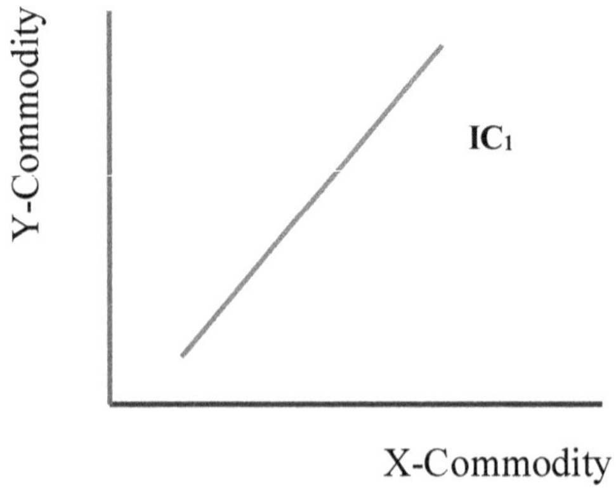

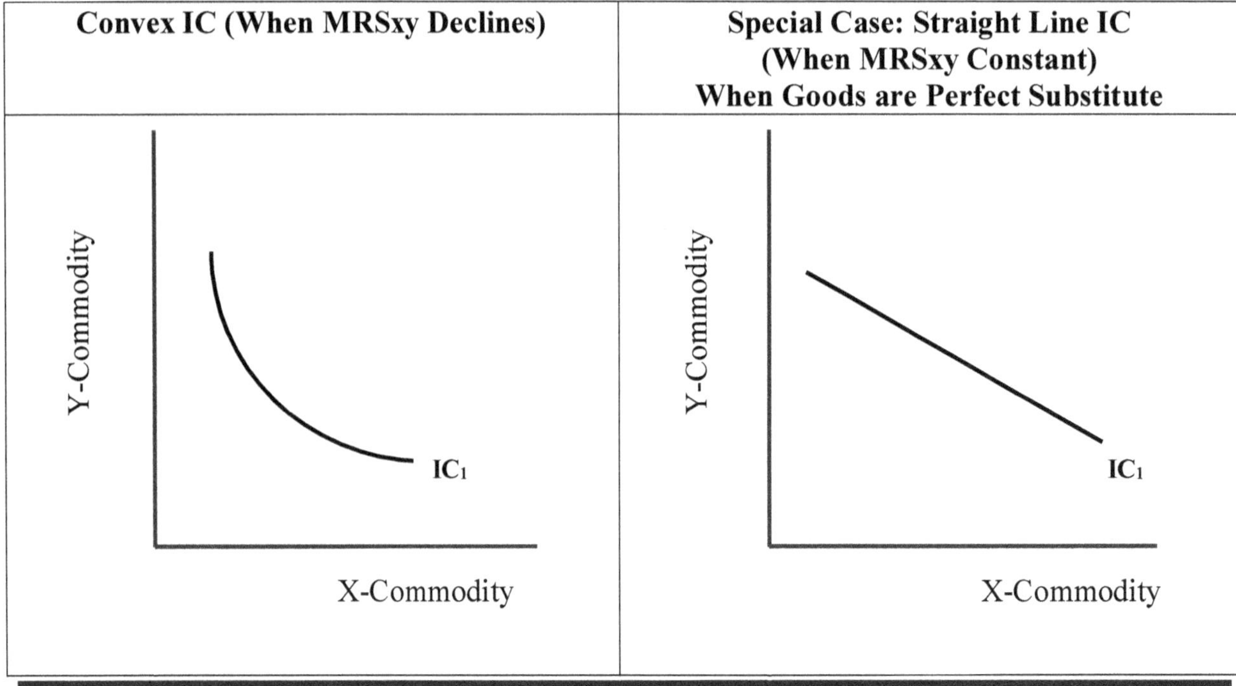

2. **IC is Convex to the Point of Origin:** In general IC is convex to the origin due to diminishing marginal rate of substitution. Convexity of IC implies that as we move down the indifference curve marginal rate of substitution of X for Y falls.

Convex IC (When MRSxy Declines)	Special Case: Straight Line IC (When MRSxy Constant) When Goods are Perfect Substitute

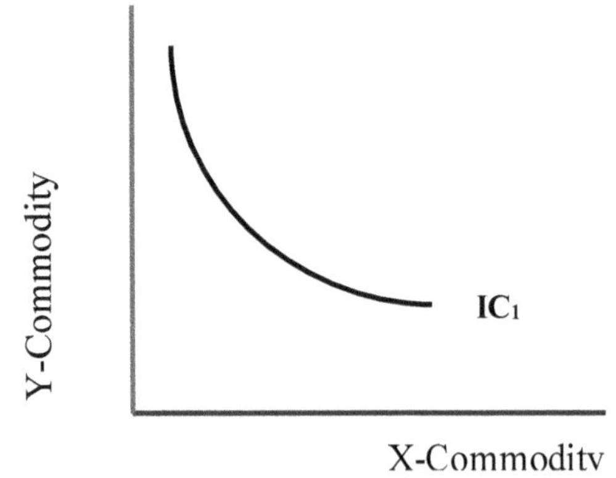

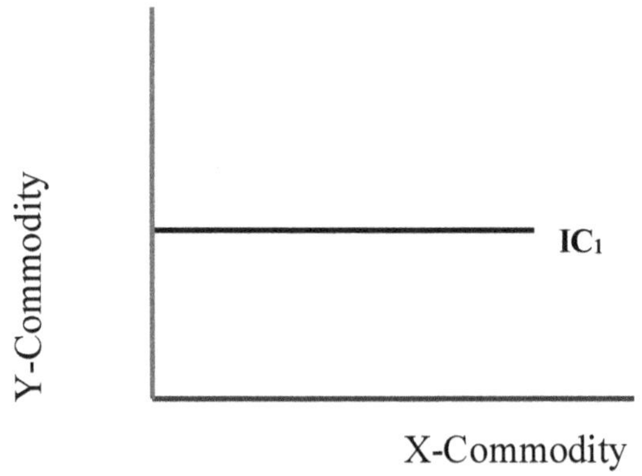

This happens because as the consumer has more and more of a commodity the intensity for his want for that commodity goes on declining as result of which the sacrifice made in terms of another commodity declines.

Special Case: Concave IC (When MRSxy Increases)	Special Case: Right Angled IC (When MRSxy =0) In case of Complementary Goods
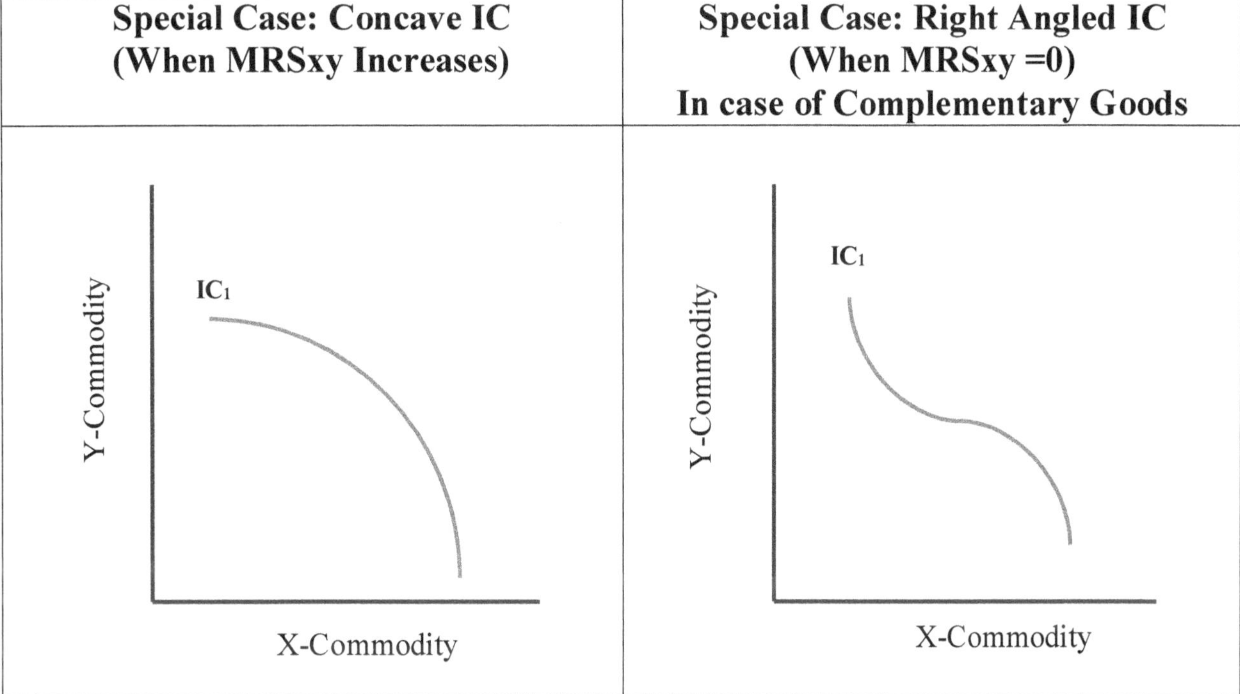	

3. **ICs Can Neither Tangent or Intersect Each Other:** This property means that two ICs can never cut each other. If two ICs intersect each other or tangent with one another, it produces

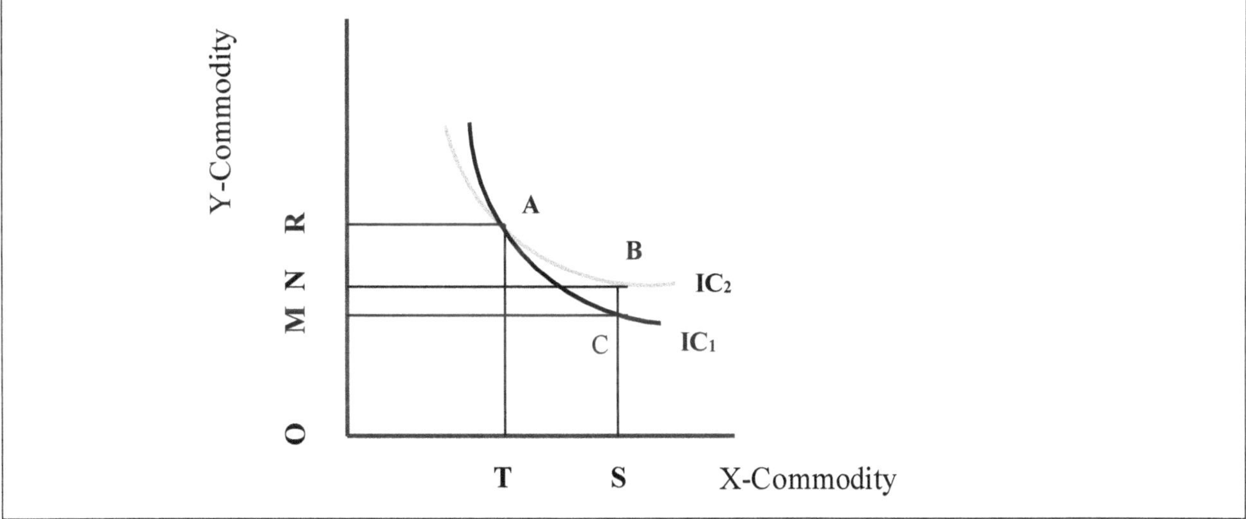

contradictory results or impossible conclusions. As shown in the given diagram, two Indifference curves IC₁ and IC₂ are intersecting at point A. To show that two ICs never cut each other, take two combinations B and C one on IC₁ and on IC₂ respectively. Now, there are two combinations on IC₁ i.e. A and B, being on same IC they will offer same satisfaction. Similarly, on IC2 there are two combinations A and C offering same level of satisfaction. Intersection of two ICs implies that A=B, A=C, B=C. But satisfaction derived from 'Combination B (OT of X commodity and OM of Y commodity) is not equal to satisfaction derived from 'Combination C (OT of X commodity and ON of Y commodity) as per monotonic preferences. Hence, intersection of two ICs leads to inconsistence results.

4. **Higher ICs Represents Higher Levels of Satisfaction:** Every IC to the right represents higher level of satisfaction. Higher IC includes combinations of two commodities that contain either more quantity of one commodity with same quantity of another or represents more quantity of both the commodities. According to monotonic preferences consumers will prefer those combinations which either contains larger quantity of one commodity or both the commodities. In this way higher IC shows more satisfaction as compared to the lower ones as shown in figure B. There are three ICs, IC_1, IC_2 and IC_3; IC3 showing the higher level of satisfaction and IC_2 shows higher satisfaction as compared to IC_1.

5. **ICs Need Not to be Parallel to Each Other:** ICs may or may not be parallel to each other. It depends upon the marginal rate of substitution of the various ICs in the indifference map. If all ICs have same MRS_{xy} then they will be parallel to each other otherwise they may not be parallel.

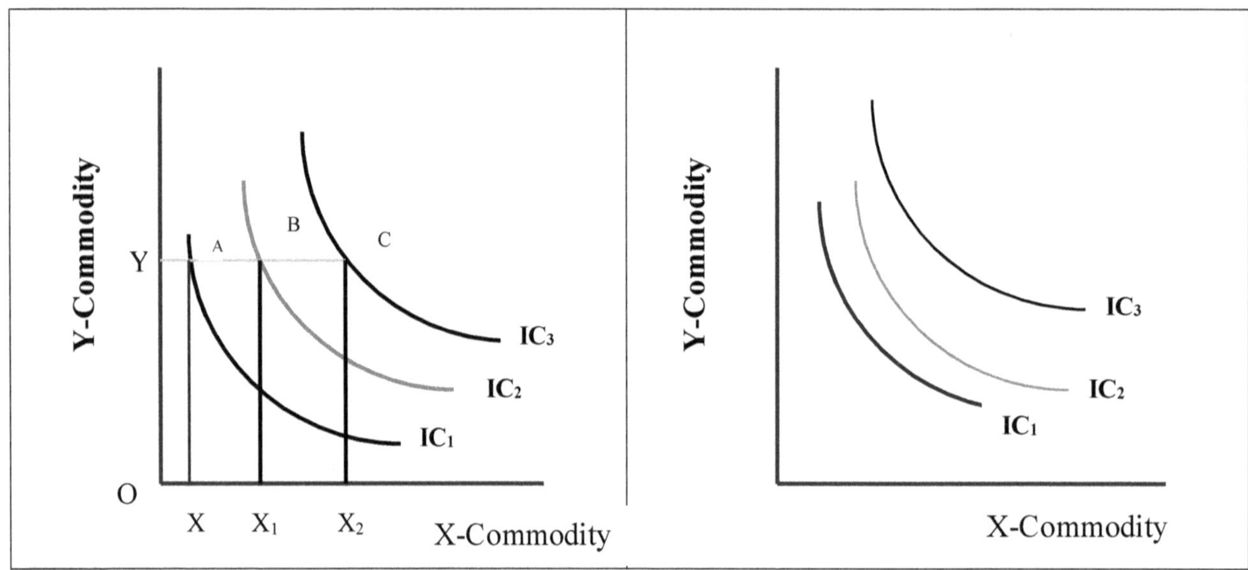

Price Line/Budget Line/Line of Attainable Combinations/Consumption Possibility Line

"The budget line shows all the different combinations of two commodities that a consumer can purchase given his money income and the price of two commodities." – **Hibbdon**

Suppose consumer has an income of Rs. 100 to spend on X and Y commodity. Price of X commodity is Rs. 20 and price of Y commodity is Rs. 10.with his given income and given prices of X commodity and Y commodity, the different combinations that the consumer can buy of these two goods are displayed in Table 3. The graphical presentation of all these combinations is shown by PL line. It is called Price Line. This line has negative slope which shows that consumer can have more of one commodity only by sacrificing some of the other.

Table: 3				Diagram: 5
Possibilities	**Q_X**	**Q_Y**	**Income = $P_x.Q_x+P_y.Q_y$ (Budget Equation)**	
A	0	10	100	
B	1	8	100	
C	2	6	100	
D	3	4	100	
E	4	2	100	
F	5	0	100	

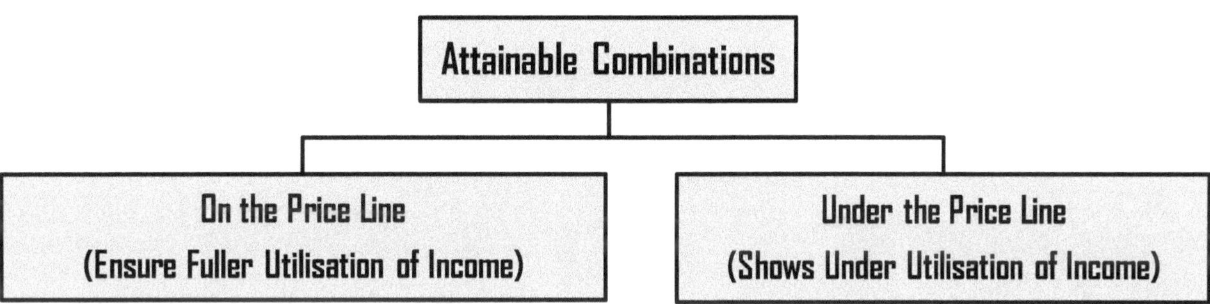

Attainable Combinations with Given Money Income at Given Prices of Commodities

Attainable Combinations

On the Price Line
(Ensure Fuller Utilisation of Income)

Under the Price Line
(Shows Under Utilisation of Income)

Slope of the Price Line can be determined by the ratio of price of X commodity to price of Y commodity i.e. **P_x/P_y.**

Budget Equation is $P_x.Q_x+P_y.Q_y$ = Income. $P_x.Q_x$ shows expenditure on X commodity and $P_y.Q_y$ shows expenditure on Y commodity.

> **Budget Equation is $P_x.Q_x+P_y.Q_y$ = Income & Slope of Price Line = P_x/P_y**

Shifting of the Price Line: Shifting of the price line occurs due to change in income at given prices of the commodities. Price line shows parallel shifting either to left side or to right side with change in income.

Diagram 6: Increase in Income

Diagram 7: Decrease in Income

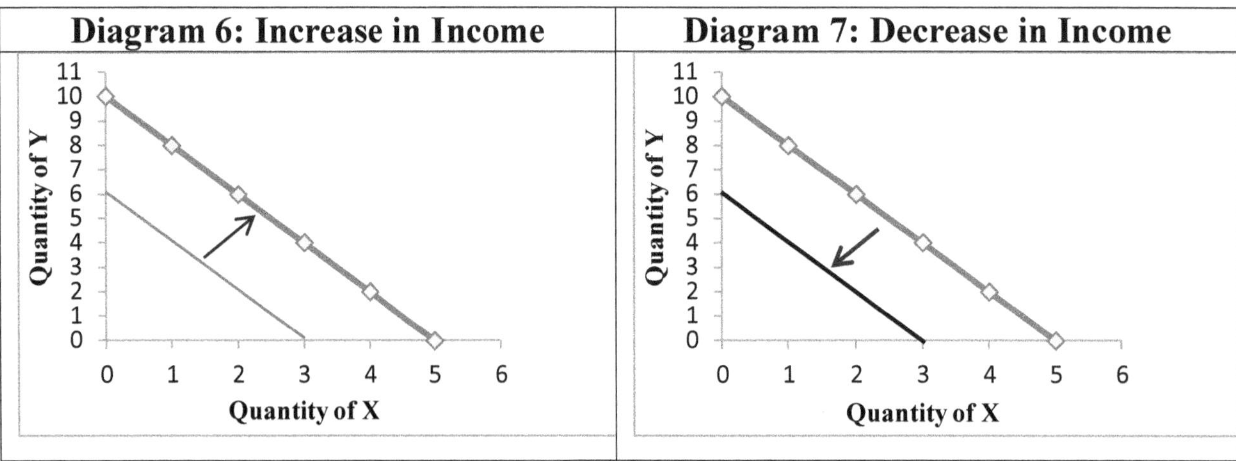

Rotation of the price line: Rotation of the price line occurs due to change in prices of one of the commodities keeping other factors constant.

Diagram 8: Increase in Price of X

Diagram 9: Decrease in Price of X

Diagram 10: Increase in Price of Y

Diagram 11: Decrease in Price of Y

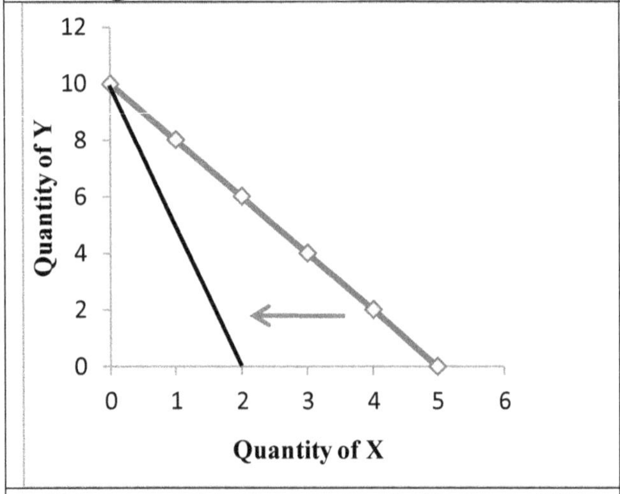

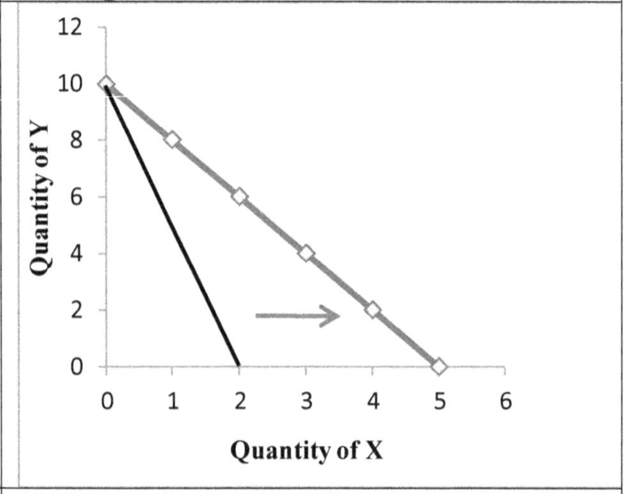

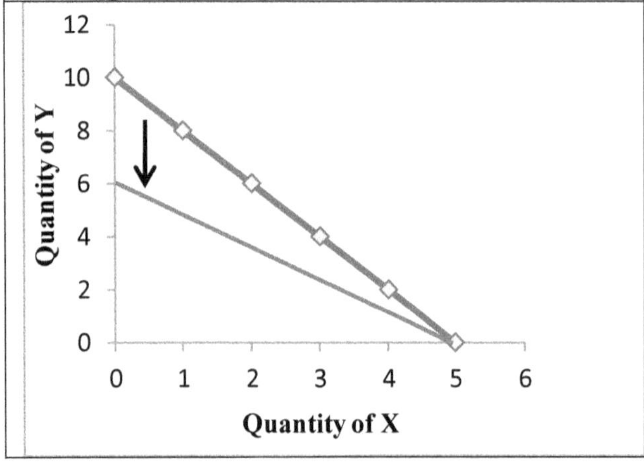

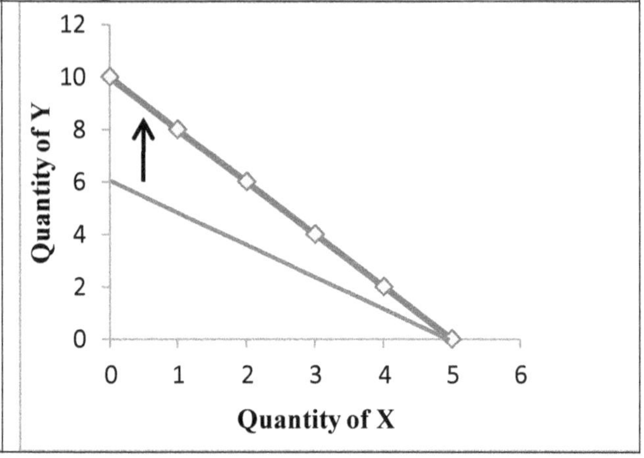

Increase in Income cause price line shifts parallel to the right. It shows that consumer can buy more quantity of the two commodities when his income increases. It is shown in diagram 6.

Decrease in Income cause price line shifts parallel to the left. It shows that consumer can buy less quantity of the two commodities when his income decreases. It is shown in diagram 7.

Consumer's Equilibrium with the help of Indifference Curve Technique Or Using Ordinal Concept Approach: Consumer's equilibrium refers to a situation in which a consumer with given income and given prices purchases such a combination of goods and services which gives him maximum satisfaction and he is not willing to make any change in it.

"A consumer is in equilibrium, when he regards his actual behavior as the best possible under the circumstances and he feels no urge to change in his behavior as long as circumstances remain unchanged." – **Tiber Scitovsky**

Assumptions: Consumer equilibrium is based upon the following assumptions
1. Consumer is rational and has perfect knowledge.
2. He is aware of the indifference map.
3. Analysis is based upon ordinal concept of utility.
4. Income of the consumer and prices of commodities are given and assumed to be constant.
5. Goods are finely divisible.
6. Consumer's choices are assumed to be transitive and consistent.
7. It is also assumed that consumer has not reached the point of saturation. This means consumer is not over supplied with goods in question.

Conditions of Consumer's Equilibrium
1. **Necessary Condition:** *Price line should be tangent to indifference curve. It means that at point of equilibrium slope of IC (MRS_{xy}) and of the Price line (P_x/P_y) should be the same. or*

$$MRS_{xy} = \frac{Px}{Py}$$

2. **Sufficient Condition:** *IC should be convex to the point of origin.*

Consumer's equilibrium is explained in diagram 12. Various IC's i.e. IC_1, IC_2 and IC_3 show the scale of the preferences of the consumer. Line PL, shows the Budget line of the consumer, that shows various combinations of two commodities that a consumer can buy with its given money income at given prices of commodities. It is clear from the diagram that consumer can buy A, B and E combinations with his given income. But he will never choose combinations A & B as they are on lower IC i.e. on IC_1, but he will choose combination E which is on higher IC i.e. IC_2 and where both the conditions of consumer's equilibrium are fulfilled, or where MRS_{xy} = P_x/P_y. It is also clear from the diagram that due to budget constraint consumer cannot move to higher IC i.e. IC_3. In diagram 13, at equilibrium point 'E', IC is concave to the point of origin, instead of convex IC. This equilibrium position will not be considered as stable, because at this point MRS is increasing and there is violation of sufficient condition.

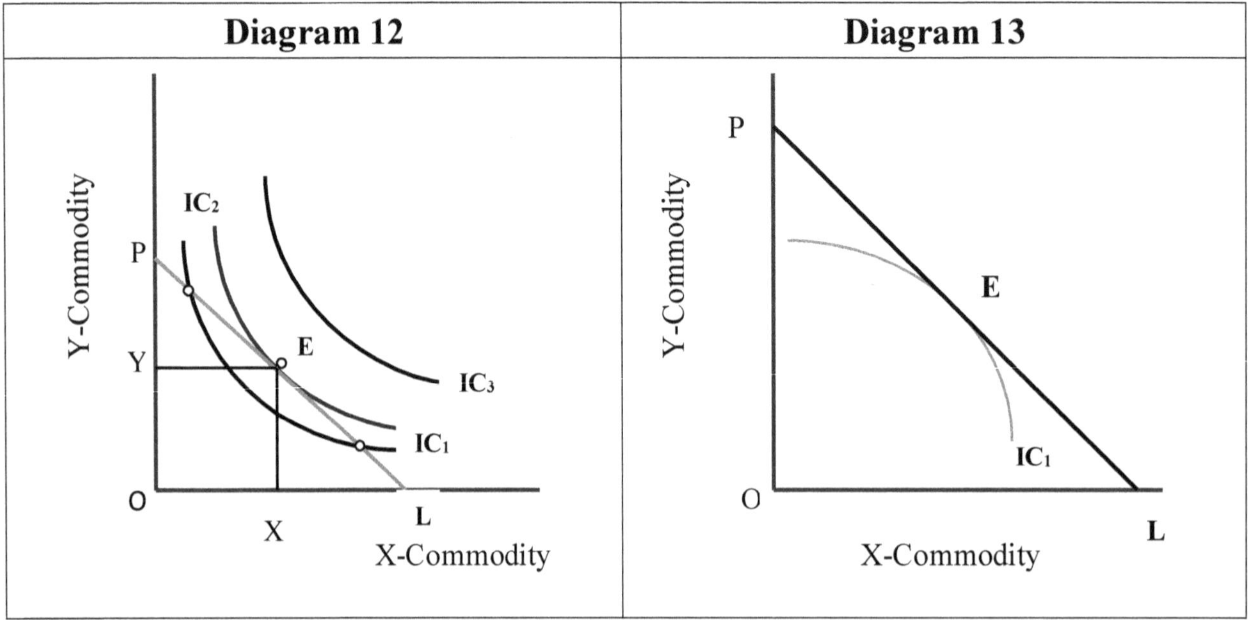

Reaction of consumer when $MRS_{xy} > P_x/P_y$: In this situation consumer will buy more of X commodity and less of Y commodity.

Reaction of consumer when $MRS_{xy} < P_x/P_y$: In this situation consumer will buy less of X commodity and more of Y commodity.

****

Exercise:

1. IC analysis of consumer's equilibrium is based on the concept of ______ measurement of utility. 1. Cardinal 2. Ordinal 3. Both 1&2 4. None of the above
2. Which is/are the property/properties of IC? 1. IC is positively sloped 2. IC is concave to the point of origin 3. Lower IC shows lower level of satisfaction. 4. None of the above
3. Which of the following is/are true to achieve consumer's equilibrium under IC analysis? 1. MRS_{xy}=Px/Py 2. Slope of IC = Slope of Price line 3. Both 1&2 4. MUx/MUm = Px
4. Slope of price line is determined by 1. Px/Py 2. Income of the consumer 3. Preferences of the consumer 4. MRS

5. In budget equation $P_xQ_x+P_yQ_y = M$, P_xQ_x shows 1. Expenditure on X commodity 2. Expenditure on Y commodity 3. Total expenditure 4. TU from X commodity

6. IC slopes downward due to 1.Constant money income 2.DMRS$_{xy}$ 3.Monotonic preferences 4. Perfect knowledge of the consumer

7. What will be the shape of IC if MRS$_{xy}$ decreases with use of every additional unit of X commodity? 1. Concave 2. Convex 3. Right Angled 4. Straight Line

8. Diagrammatic presentation of consumer's indifference set is called: 1. Indifference curve 2. PP curve 3. Budget line 4. None of the above

9. Marginal rate of substitution indicates: 1. Slope of production possibility curve 2. Slope of indifference curve 3. Slope of budget line 4. None of the above

10. In a situation where, $MRS_{XY} > \dfrac{P_X}{P_Y}$, the consumer would react by: 1. Diminishing the consumption of commodity – X 2. Increasing the consumption of commodity-Y 3. Increasing the consumption of commodity-X 4. None of these

11. What will be the impact on price line if money income is halved and prices of both the commodities remain same? 1. Outward parallel shift 2. No change 3. Inward parallel shift 4. Nothing can be said

12. All points on indifference curve represents: 1. Same expenditure on goods 2. Same price of goods 3. Bundles which are considered indifferent by the consumer 4. Bundles which are considered same by the consumer

13. When MRS is constant, then IC will be straight line. Statement is true or false.

14. Calculate MRS$_{xy}$ from the given schedule. Also Comment on the shape of IC.

Qx	1	2	3	4
Qy	15	10	6	3
MRS$_{xy}$				

15. Complete the Indifference Schedule given below. Also Comment on the shape of IC.

Qx	1	2	3	4
Qy	20			
MRS$_{xy}$	-	6	5	4

16. Complete the Indifference Schedule given below. Also Comment on the shape of IC.

Qx	10	20	30	40
Qy	200	160	110	50
MRS$_{xy}$				

---

17. If a consumer has monotonic preferences, can she be indifferent between the bundles (10, 8) and (10, 6)?

18. If Px = 50, Py = 100, and Money income is Rs. 500, then slope of price line will be?

19. Draw price line when P_x = 20, P_y =10 and Money Income is Rs. 100. What will happen to price line if (a) P_x falls to Rs. 10, (b) Money income doubles, (c) Money income halved and P_x and P_y also decrease by 50%.

20. A consumer has total money of Rs. 250 to be spent on two goods X and Y with prices of Rs.25 and 10 per unit respectively. On the basis of the information given, answer the following questions:

 (a) Give the equation of the budget line and its slope.

 (b) How many units can the consumer buy if he is to spend all his money income on good Y?

 (c) How does the budget line change if there is a fall in price of good Y by Rs 5?

Answers

1. 2	2. 3	3. 3	4. 1	5. 1	6. 3
7. 2	8. 1	9. 2	10. 3	11. 3	12. 3
13. T	14.Convex (MRS = - ,5/1,4/1,3/1)	15.Convex (Qy = 20,14,9,5)			
16.Concave (-, 40/1, 50/1, 60/1)			17.No		18.1/2
19. (a) Outward Rotation on X axis (b) Price line parallel shifts to right (c) No change					
20.(a) 25Qx+10Qy = 250, slope = 2.5 (b) 25 units (c) Outward Rotation on Y axis					

NCERT QUESTIONS:

1. What do you mean by budget set of a consumer?

2. What is budget line?

3. Explain why the budget line is downward sloping.

4. A consumer wants to consumer two goods. The prices of the goods X and Y are Rs. 4 and Rs. 5 respectively. The consumer's income is Rs.20.

 a) Write down the equation of budget line. (Ans: 4Qx+5Qy = Rs. 20)

 b) How much of Good-1 can the consumer consume if she spends her entire income on that good?

 c) How much of Good-2 can she consume if she spends her entire income on that good?

 d) What is the slope of the budget line? (Ans: 4/5)

e) How does the budget line change if the consumer's income increases to Rs.40 but the prices remain unchanged?

5. Suppose a consumer can afford to buy 6 units of Good-1 and 8 units of Good-2, if she spends her entire income. The prices of the two goods are Rs.6 and Rs.8 respectively. How much is the consumer's income?

6. What do you mean by 'monotonic preferences'?

7. If a consumer has monotonic preferences, can she be indifferent between the bundles (10,8) and (8,6)?

8. Suppose a consumer's preferences are monotonic. What can you say about her preferences ranking over the bundles (10, 10), (10, 9), (9, 9)?

9. Suppose your friend is indifferent to the bundles (5,6) and (6,6). Are the preferences of your friend monotonic?

Practice Questions

1. Define budget set and budget space.
2. What is MRS?
3. What is indifference set and indifference map?
4. What are monotonic preferences?
5. What is a budget line? Why is it downward sloping?
6. Explain the distinction between budget set an budget line.
7. What is budget equation? Explain with the help of numerical example.
8. Explain consumer's equilibrium with the help of indifference curve analysis.
9. Explain the three properties of indifference curves.
10. Explain the concept of marginal rate of substitution (MRS) by giving an example. What happens to MRS when consumer moves downwards along the indifference curve? Give reasons for your answer.
11. Explain the conditions of consumer's equilibrium with the help of the indifference curve analysis.
12. Explain the concept of marginal rate of substitution. Explain the reaction of the consumer when marginal rate of substitution is higher than the ratio of prices.
13. Define an indifference curve. Explain why an indifference curve is downward sloping from left to right.
14. Define marginal rate of substitution. Explain why an indifference curve is convex.
15. Define an indifference map. Explain why an indifference curve to the right shows higher utility level.

16. Explain with suitable example, the difference between cardinal utility and ordinal utility.

17. Define a budget line. When can it shift to right?

18. What is budget set? Explain what can lead to change in budget set.

19. Explain why an indifference curve is downward sloping from left to right. State the conditions of consumer's equilibrium in indifference curve analysis.

20. Explain the concept of marginal rate of substitution with the help of numerical example.

21. What are monotonic preferences? Explain why an indifference curve to the right shows higher utility.

CHAPTER 4

THEORY OF DEMAND

Theory of demand is an important and integral part of the price theory. It studies the consumer's behaviour in the market when he buys goods from the market. As we know price is determined by both, the demand and supply of the product. In present chapter, we shall have discussion on concept of demand.

In common parlance the word desire, want and demand are used in the same sense. In economics all these words have different meanings.

Desire is a wishful thing that a person desire to possess but he doesn't afford to have it. For example, a poor person desires to have a Royal Royce car. Then this will be termed as desire of the poor person, because he doesn't have resources to afford it.

Want: Desire of the person will become a want when a person has enough money to buy it. **Demand:** *"Demand refers to the quantities of a commodity that the consumers are able and willing to buy at each possible price during a given period of time, other things being equal."*-**Ferguson**

Three core elements of demand are as follows:
1. Demand is always backed up by enough money to pay for the good demanded.
2. Demand is always related to price and makes no sense if it is not related to price.
3. Demand is always expressed with reference to a particular time period.

Quantity Demanded: Quantity demanded refers to specific amount of a commodity to be purchased against a specific price of the commodity.

Demand Schedule: A demand schedule is a table displaying the relation between different quantities of a commodity that a consumer is willing and able to buy at various possible prices at given time, assuming other factors as constant. Demand schedule is of two types:
1. Individual Demand Schedule, 2. Market Demand Schedule

Individual Demand Schedule: An individual demand schedule is defined as the table which shows various quantities of a commodity that a single buyer in the market is willing and able to buy at various possible prices at given time, assuming other factors as constant. Table 1 shows such a demand schedule. It is clear from the table that a consumer is willing to buy 30 kg of X- commodity corresponding to Rs. 10 per Kg, 20 kg of X-commodity corresponding to Rs. 20 per kg, and 10 kg of X-commodity corresponding to Rs. 30 per kg.

Table 1: Individual Demand Schedule for X-Commodity

Price of X- Commodity (Per Kg)	Quantity Demanded of X-Commodity
10	50Kgs
20	40Kgs
30	30Kgs

Market Demand Schedule: A market demand schedule is defined as the table which shows various quantities of a commodity that all the buyers in the market are willing and able to buy at various possible prices at given time, assuming other factors as constant. Table 2 shows such a demand schedule, assuming there are three buyers of X commodity in the market. It is clear from the table that all the buyers are willing to buy 90 kg of X- commodity corresponding to Rs. 10 per kg, 60 quintal of X-commodity corresponding to Rs. 20 per kg, and 30 kg of X-commodity corresponding to Rs. 30 per kg.

Table 2: Market Demand Schedule for X- Commodity

Price of X-Commodity (Rs. Per Kg)	Quantities demanded of X-Commodity (Kg)			
	Buyer Mr. Lal **(D1)**	Buyer Mr. Bal **(D2)**	Buyer Mr. Pal **(D3)**	Market Demand **(MD)**
10	10	25	50	10+25+50=85
20	8	20	40	8+20+40=68
30	6	15	30	6+15+30=51
40	4	10	20	4+10+20=34
50	2	5	10	2+5+10=17

Demand Curve: Demand curve is diagrammatic presentation of the demand schedule. It shows the relationship between price and quantity demanded of a commodity graphically. According to relationship demand curve is negatively sloped. Like demand schedule, demand curve is also of two types: **1. Individual Demand Curve 2. Market Demand Curve**

Individual Demand Curve: It is defined as the curve which displays various quantities of a given commodity which an individual buyer is ready to buy at various prices at given time, ceteris paribus. In diagram 2, demand curve of single buyer (Mr. Pal) is shown by D3 curve.

Market Demand Curve: It is defined as the curve which displays various quantities of a given commodity which all buyers are willing to buy at different prices at given time, other things being constant. It is obtained by horizontal summation of demand curves of individual buyers in the market. In diagram 1, negatively sloped market demand curve is shown by curve MD.

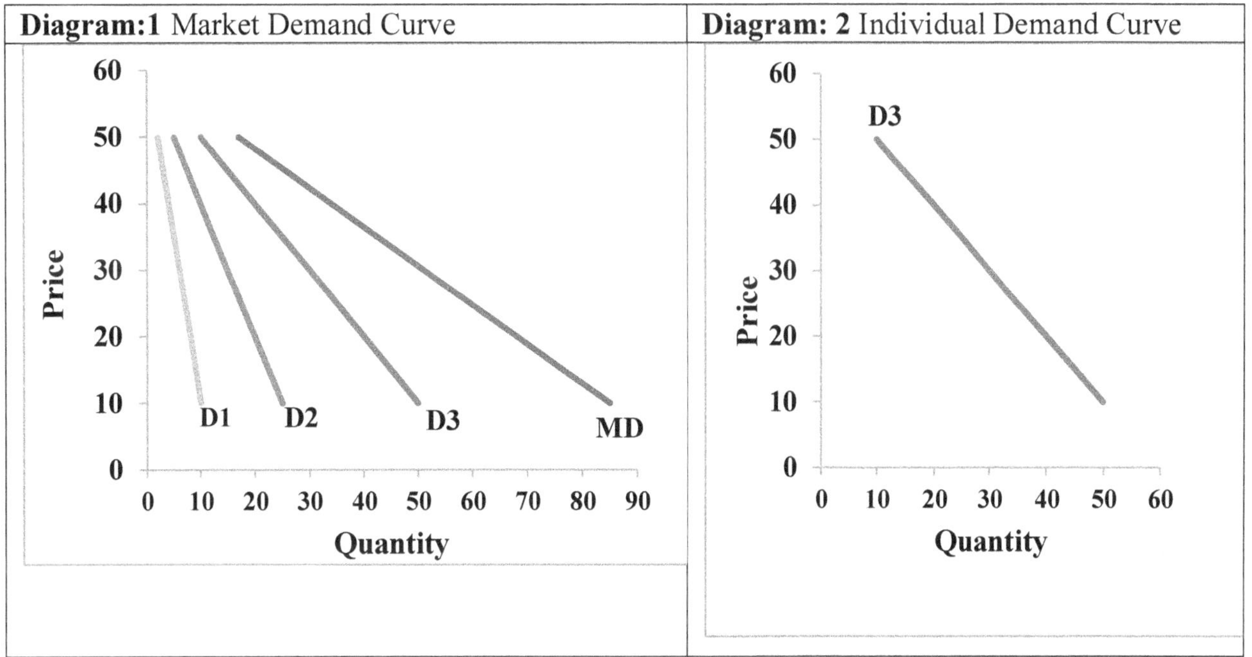

Demand Function (Factors Affecting Demand or Determinants of Demand)

Demand function studies the functional relationship between demand for a commodity and its various determinants. Demand is a function of several factors expressed as $Q_x = f(P_x, P_r, Y, T, E, P_o, Y_d, C_F....)$.

It is very difficult to analyse the effect of simultaneous change in all factors on demand, that's why we study the effect of one factor at one time by assuming other factors as constant. The important factors which determine the demand of commodity are as follows:

1. **Price of the Commodity (Px):** The most important determinant of the demand of commodity is its own price. Assuming other factors constant (Ceteris Paribus), quantity demanded falls with increase in price of the commodity and vice versa. This relationship, which shows inverse relation between demand of a commodity and the price of it, also known as Law of demand.

2. **Price of Related Goods (Pr):** The demand for a commodity is also affected by changes in price of its related goods. The influence of change in price of related goods on the demand of a commodity depends upon whether the related good is either substitute or complementary. In case of *substitute goods* there is positive relationship between demand for commodity and price of its substitute goods, keeping other factors as constant. For example, demand for coke is influenced

by the change in price of its substitute good like pepsi. This relationship can be shown in the table 3.

Table 3: Relationship between QD of a commodity and price of its substitute good

Price (Pepsi)	Quantity Demanded (Coke)
Rise	Rise
Fall	Fall

In case of ***complementary goods*** there is negative relationship between demand for commodity and price of its complementary goods, keeping other factors as constant. For example, demand for ink pen is influenced by the change in price of its complementary good like ink. This relationship can be shown in table 4.

Table 4: Relationship between QD of a commodity and price of its complementary good

Price (Ink)	Quantity Demanded (Ink Pen)
Rise	Fall
Fall	Rise

3. **Income of the Consumer (Y):** It is very important determinant of the quantity demanded of a commodity. In case of normal goods, there is direct relationship between income of the consumer and his demand for the commodity. Demand for commodity increases with increase in income and vice versa. On the other hand, demand for the inferior goods decreases with increase in income and vice versa.

Normal Goods (Positive Income Effect)		Inferior Goods (Negative Income Effect)	
Income	Quantity Demanded	Income	Quantity Demanded
Fall	Fall	Fall	Rise
Rise	Rise	Rise	Fall

4. **Tastes and Preferences (T):** Taste and preference of the consumers significantly influenced the demand of a commodity. They depend upon habits, social customs, geographic regions, fashion, general life style of the people, etc. Demand for those goods will increase for which consumers develops taste. In general, goods which are in fashion or in trends have more demand and goods which are old fashioned have less demand. For example, the craze for off-roading among people leads to an increase in demand for SUV's. The craze for toned body among the youngsters has increased the demand for food having low fat and carbohydrates.

Quantity Demanded (X-commodity)	Change in Tastes and Preferences (X-commodity)
Rise	Favourable
Fall	Unfavourable

5. **Expectations (E):** It is another important determinant of demand function which affects the demand for a commodity. As we know that man is always forward looking. His expectations with regard to future price of the commodity, income, availability of a commodity affects the demand for a commodity in current period. If consumers have expectations that price of the commodity will increase in the future, he will increase the demand for commodity in current period. On the contrary, if consumers have expectations that price of the commodity will decrease in the future then he will decrease the demand for commodity in current period.

6. **Size and Composition of Population (P_o):** The market demand for a commodity is directly related to the size of population. Increase in population will lead to increase in the demand for goods and services and decrease in population will cause decrease in market demand of a commodity. Composition of the population also is very important determinant of demand for a commodity. This refers to the description of population according to its characteristics like age, sex etc. Composition of population according to sex will show the proportion of male population and female population in total population. The demand for ladies apparels and accessories will be high in a country with dominating share of female population in his total population. Composition of population according to age will show the total population according to different age groups. A country with more proportion of teenagers in total population will have more demand for videogames, story books, skateboard etc. In this way, composition of the population is very important factor that affects the demand because the types of goods demanded by the different people are different.

7. **Distribution of Income (Y_d):** This factor also affects the demand for goods. In general, there will be more demand if distribution of income is equal. If there is greater degree of inequality in distribution of income there will be more demand for luxury goods in the market. In case of fair distribution of income demand for necessities will be more.

8. **Availability of Consumer Credit Facilities (C_F):** In the modern times with the expansion of banking system demand for goods increased by manifold. This is due to availability of credit to the consumers at reasonable interest rates at all

times. Consumer didn't have to wait till money gets accumulated to buy the goods. They can now buy the goods if they don't have enough money through credit facilities offered by banks.

Law of Demand

Law of demand studies the relationship between price and demand of a commodity.

"Law of demand states that people will buy more at lower prices and buy less at higher prices ceteris paribus or other things remaining the same." – Samuelson
 In other words, there is inverse relationship between quantity demanded and price of commodity (see table 5 and diagram 3).

Table 5		Diagram 3
Price of X	**QD of X (Kg)**	
10	50	
20	40	
30	30	
40	20	
50	10	

Law of demand is based on the following assumptions.
1. There is no change in price of related goods, income and tastes of the consumer.
2. There is no expectation of change in price of the commodity in near future.
3. There is no change in distribution of income and size and composition of population.

Why does the demand curve slopes downward from left to right? Why more quantity is demanded at a lower price or vice versa?
Negatively sloping demand curve shows the inverse relationship between price and the quantity demanded. Following factors are responsible for the existence of this inverse relationship.
1. **Law of Diminishing Marginal Utility:** The law of diminishing marginal utility states that marginal utility of the commodity falls as consumer consumes more and more units of a commodity. To get maximum satisfaction the price which every consumer is willing to pay for a commodity is equal its marginal utility obtained i.e. $MU_x = P_x$. From this relationship, a consumer would purchase a

larger quantity only at lower price because as stock of commodity increases the marginal utility decreases.

2. **Income Effect:** Consumer is able to buy more quantity of a commodity at lower price because as price falls the real income of the consumer will increase. With increase in real income a person can buy more units of a commodity. On the contrary, rise in price of the commodity cause fall in real income of the consumer and he will be forced to buy small amount of the commodity. This is what known as income effect and the way it affects the demand.

Price	Real Income (Purchasing Power of Money)	Quantity demanded
Fall	Increase	Increase
Rise	Decrease	Decrease

3. **Substitution Effect:** It is an important factor that cause demand curve to slope downward. The fall in price of a commodity attract more consumers because now this commodity becomes cheaper in relation to its substitute goods. With fall in price of coke demand more coke will increase because it will be substituted for its substitute goods like pepsi etc.

4. **Addition of New Consumers:** Fall in price results in more quantity demanded of a commodity because new buyers will be added who were not be able to buy that commodity at higher price. For example, when the price of LED TV is Rs. 70000, then only few consumers can buy it and quantity demanded will be small. As the price falls to Rs. 35000, quantity demanded will increase manifold as more buyers will buy who could not afford LED TV at higher price.

5. **Alternative Uses of a Commodity:** Some goods can be put to alternative uses, some of which are more important while some are less important. When price of the commodity falls the quantity demanded of a commodity will increase as consumer will start using it in less important uses. On the contrary when price of the commodity increases quantity demanded for it falls as its use will be restricted to the important uses.

Exceptions to the Law of Demand

There are certain cases where law of demand doesn't apply. In such cases, consumers buy more when price of commodity rises and vice versa and demand curve have positive slope.

1. **Prestigious Goods or Articles of Distinction or Veblen Goods:** The law of demand doesn't apply to the commodities which are bought by consumer to display his richness, wealth or as status symbol. This term is firstly given by Thorstein Veblen. He called these goods as goods of conspicuous consumption.

Higher the price of these goods makes its possessor to feel more proud. Precious stones, diamonds, jewellery, rare paintings etc. are some examples of the prestigious goods.

2. **Ignorance:** Law of demand also fails when consumer take price as an index to measure quality. In other words, when thinks that high priced goods are always superior in quality and low piece goods are of low quality. In such cases he will prefer to buy more at higher price and vice versa.

Price	Quality	Q.D
High	High	More
Low	Low	Less

3. **Expectations Regarding Future Prices:** If consumers anticipate or speculate a rise in price of the commodity in future they may buy larger quantity even at rising prices today. They increase their buying at existing higher prices in order to store the enough quantity for future to avoid the impact of higher price in future. On the other hand, if consumers anticipate a fall in price of the commodity in future they may buy smaller quantity even at falling prices. Because they start postponing their purchases in anticipation of further fall in prices of the commodities. In these cases law of demand fails to operate because of speculative effect.

4. **Giffen Paradox:** This is an exception to the law of demand which was given by Sir Robert Giffen (1837-1910). He found that working class families of Britain were taking bread and meat as their food items. Bread was the main food item for these workers due to its low price and meat was consumed by these families on special occasions or less frequently due its high price. When price of bread rose, they had to spend more for a given quantity of bread, as result they compelled to curtail their consumption of meat in order to be able to spend more on bread. Bread still being comparatively cheaper was substituted for meat even at higher price and hence even at higher price of bread they buy more of bread.

5. **Fear of Shortage or Emergencies:** Law of demand will not apply in case where consumer is panicked by the shortage of goods during emergencies like war, floods or any other natural disaster. In these situations consumer tries to store goods for future even by paying higher prices in current period.

Change in Quantity Demanded or Movement along the Demand Curve: Change in quantity demanded occurs when the quantity demanded of the commodity changes due to change in its own price, keeping other things as constant. It is indicated by a movement along a particular demand curve and it is of two types:

Extension of Demand or Increase in Quantity Demanded: When quantity demanded of a commodity rises due to fall in its own price, other things being constant, it is called extension in demand.

Table 6: Extension of Demand

Price (X-commodity)	Quantity Demanded (X-commodity)
6	5
4	10

Table 6 shows that when price of X commodity falls from Rs. 6 to Rs. 4 its demand rises from 5 units to 10 units. This is called extension in demand and it is shown by downward movement along the demand curve DD from point A to point B as shown in diagram 4.

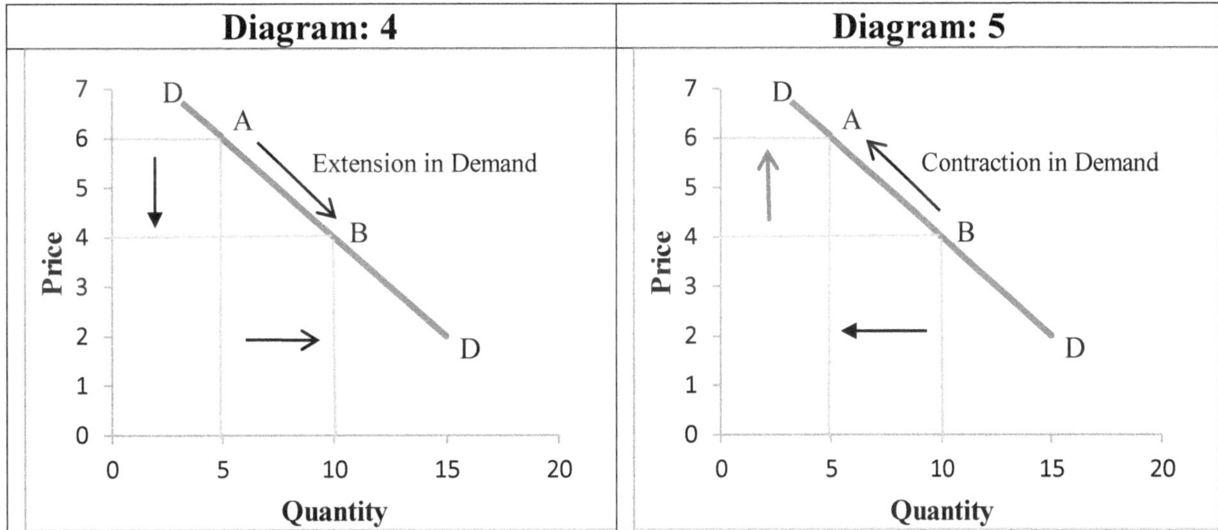

Contraction of demand or decrease in quantity demanded: When quantity demanded of a commodity falls due to increase in its own price, other things being constant, it is called contraction of demand.

Table 7: Contraction of Demand

Price (X-commodity)	Quantity Demanded (X-commodity)
4	10
6	5

Table 7 shows that when price of X commodity rises from Rs. 4 to Rs. 6 its demand falls from 10 units to 5 units. This is called contraction of demand and it is shown by upward movement along the demand curve DD from point B to point A as shown in diagram 5.

Change in Demand or Shifting of the Demand Curve: Change in Demand refers to either increase or decrease in quantity demanded of a commodity at same price due to change in determinants of demand function other than the own price of commodity. It is caused by change in other factors like change in price of related goods, income of the consumer, taste and preferences of the consumer, expectations regarding price, population, distribution of income etc. It produces shifting of the demand curve either leftward or rightward. Change in demand is classified as increase in demand and decrease in demand.

Increase in Demand: Increase in demand implies a rightward shift of the demand curve, displaying that buyers are willing to buy more quantity of a commodity at same price, due to favourable change in other determinants of demand function. For example, decrease in prices of complementary goods, increase in price of substitute goods, expectations of rise in the price of a commodity in future, increase in income of the consumer, favourable change in taste and preference etc. It is shown by right ward shift in demand curve from DD to D_1D_1 in diagram 6.

Decrease in Demand: Decrease in demand implies a leftward shift of the demand curve, displaying that buyers are willing to buy less quantity of a commodity at same price, due to unfavourable change in other determinants of demand function. For example, increase in prices of complementary goods, decrease in price of substitute goods, expectations of fall in the price of a commodity in future, decrease in income of the consumer, unfavourable change in taste and preference etc. It is shown by left ward shift in demand curve from DD to D_0D_0 in diagram 7.

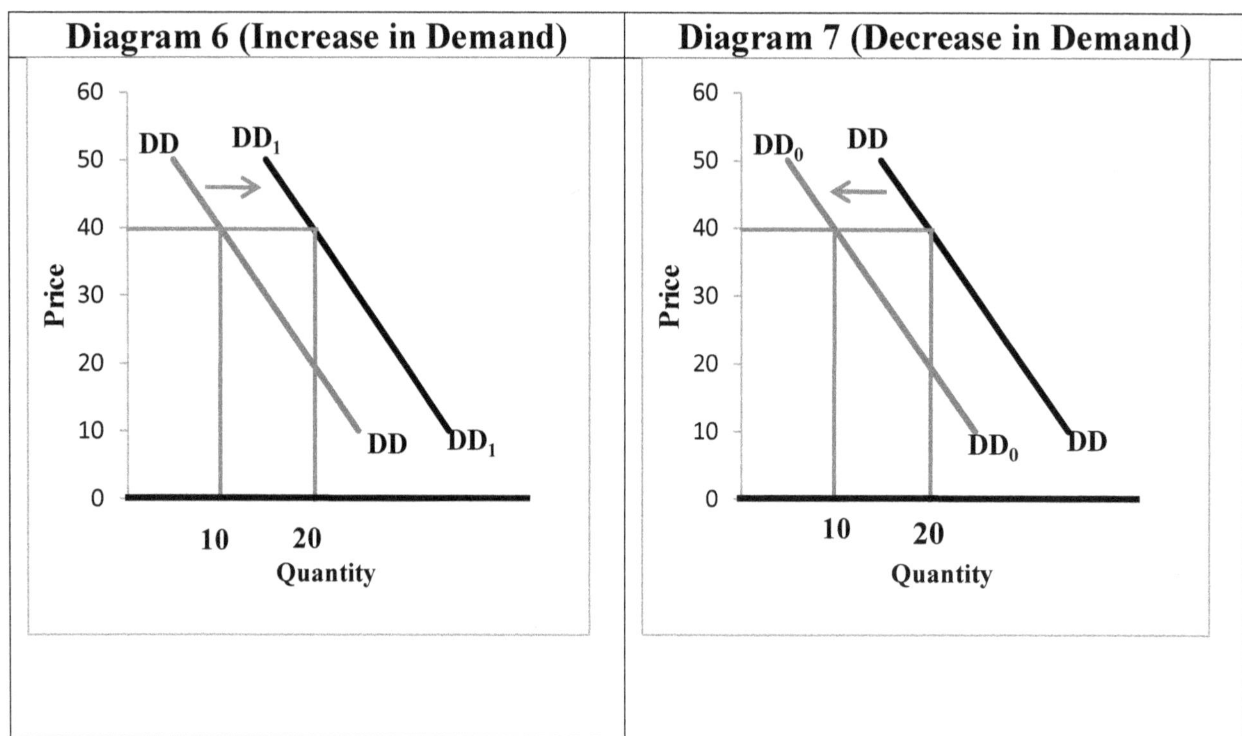

Difference between Extension in Demand and Increase in Demand

Extension in Demand	Increase in Demand
Extension in demand refers to increase in quantity demanded of a commodity due to fall in its own price, other things being constant.	Increase in demand implies a rightward shift of the demand curve, displaying that buyers are willing to buy more quantity of a commodity at same price.
It is caused by fall in price of the commodity.	It is caused by favourable change in other factors affecting the demand functions. E.g. increase in income of the consumer, favourable change in taste and preference etc.
It is shown by downward movement along the demand curve DD from point A to point B as shown in diagram.	It is shown by rightward shift in demand curve as shown in diagram.

Difference between Contraction in Demand and Decrease in Demand

Contraction in Demand	Decrease in Demand
Contraction in demand refers to decrease in quantity demanded of a commodity due to increase in its own price, other things being constant.	Decrease in demand implies a leftward shift of the demand curve, displaying that buyers are willing to buy less quantity of a commodity at same price.
It is caused by increase in price of the commodity.	It is caused by unfavourable change in other factors affecting the demand functions. E.g. decrease in income of the consumer, unfavourable change in taste and preference etc.
It is shown by upward movement along the demand curve DD from point B to point A as shown in diagram.	It is shown by leftward shift in demand curve as shown in diagram.

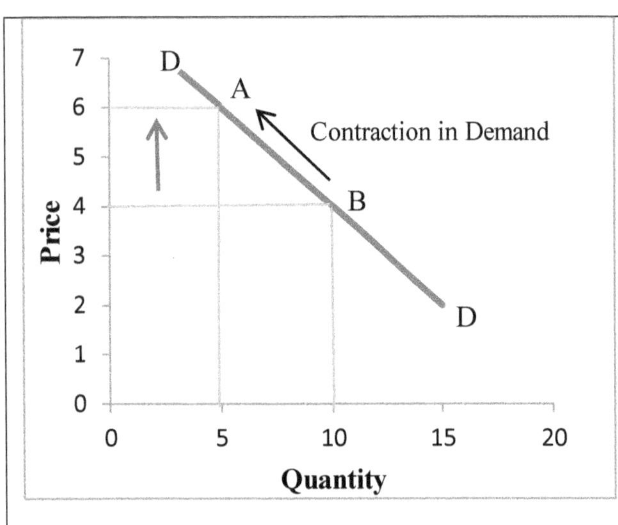

Difference between Change in Quantity Demanded and Change in Demand

Change in Quantity Demanded (Movement along the Demand Curve)	Change in Demand (Shifting of Demand Curve)
Change in quantity demanded occurs when the quantity demanded of the commodity changes due to change in its own price, keeping other things as constant.	Change in demand refers to either increase or decrease in quantity demanded of a commodity at same price due to change in determinants of demand function other than the own price of commodity.
It is caused by change in price of the commodity.	It is caused by change in other factors like change in price of related goods, income of the consumer, taste and preferences of the consumer, population, etc.
It is indicated by a movement along a particular demand curve either upward or downward. 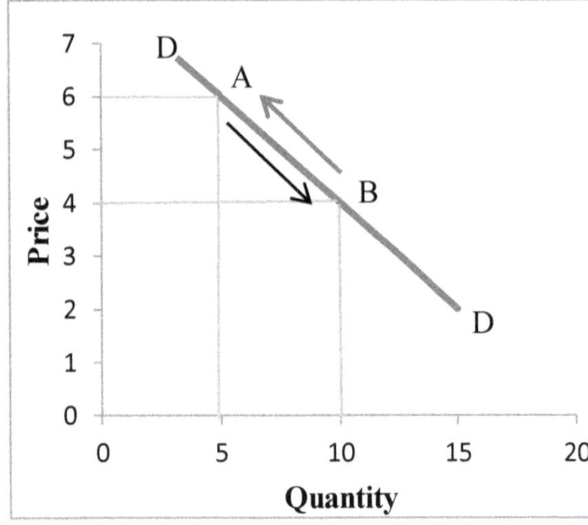	It is indicated by shifting of the demand curve either leftward or rightward. 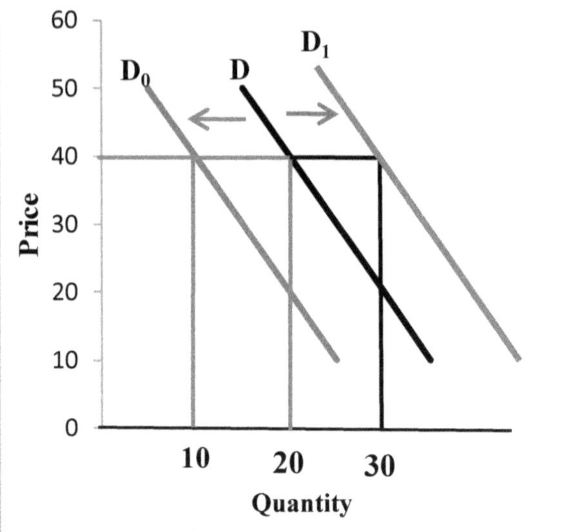
It is classified as extension in demand and contraction in demand.	It is classified as increase in demand and decrease in demand.

Extension of demand occurs when quantity demanded of a commodity rises due to fall in its own price	Increase in demand implies a rightward shift of the demand curve, displaying that buyers are willing to buy more quantity of a commodity at same price.
Contraction of demand occurs when quantity demanded of a commodity falls due to increase in its own price.	Decrease in demand implies a leftward shift of the demand curve, displaying that buyers are willing to buy less quantity of a commodity at same price.

Difference between Giffen Goods and Inferior Good

Giffen Good	**Inferior Good**
Giffen goods are those inferior goods which are consumed by poor households mostly as essential commodities. In case of Giffen goods, *income effect is negative.*	Inferior goods are those goods the demand for which is negatively related with income. In other words *income effect is negative* in case of normal goods.
Consumer is supposed to spend *larger portion* of his income on such goods.	Consumer is supposed to spend *little portion* of his income on inferior goods.
Demand curve is positively sloped in case of Giffen goods *because negative income effect is stronger than substitution effect.*	Demand curve is supposed to be negatively sloped in case of Inferior goods *because substitution effect is stronger than the negative income effect.*
All Giffen goods are inferior goods.	But, all inferior goods are not Giffen goods.

Types of Demand

Composite Demand: This refers to the demand for one commodity in order to satisfy two or more wants. For example demand for milk is composite demand as milk can be used for making butter, cheese, curd, ice cream, sweets etc.

Demand Function: Demand function shows the relationship of quantity demand of a commodity with its various determinants. Demand function is given as follows. $Q.D_x = f(P_X, P_R, Y, E, T, P, Y_D, U)$

Cross Price Effect or Cross Demand: Cross price effect refers to the effect of change in the price of commodity X, on the demand for commodity Y, when X and Y are related goods; either they are substitute goods or complementary goods.

Normal Goods: Normal goods are those goods the demand for which is positively related with income and inversely related to its own price other things being constant. In other words income effect is positive in case of normal goods and demand curve is negatively sloped.

Inferior Goods: Inferior goods are those goods the demand for which are negatively related with income and may inversely related to its own price other things being constant. In other words income effect is negative in case of inferior goods.

Substitute Goods or Competitive Goods: Substitute goods are those goods which can be used in place of one another. Demand for good decreases with decrease in price of its substitute good and vice versa. There is direct relationship between the demand for a product and the price of its substitute good. For example fall in price of Coke will decrease the demand for Pepsi. People will start substituting Pepsi with coke because Coke becomes relatively cheaper than Pepsi.

Complementary Goods: Complementary goods are those goods which are consumed together to satisfy a given want. There is inverse relationship between the demand for good and the price of its complement. For example increase in price of petrol will cause decrease in demand for petrol cars.

Joint Demand: This refers to the demand for two or more goods which are used jointly or demanded together. For example car and petrol, butter and bread, milk and sugar etc are the goods which are used together. The demand for the goods having joint demand changes simultaneously. For instance, an increase in demand for cars leads to a simultaneous increase in the demand for petrol. In case of joint demand, a rise in the price of one good leads to a fall in the demand for the other and vice versa. For example, a rise in the price of cars will lead to not only a fall in the demand for cars, but also a fall in demand for petrol.

Derived Demand: The demand for a commodity that arises because of the demand for some other commodity is called derived demand. For instance, demand for steel, bricks, cement, stones, wood etc. is a derived demand-derived from the demand for houses and other buildings. The demand for these goods arises because of the demand for houses and other buildings. Derived demand generally relates to the demand for factors of production. Demand for factors of production, such as labour, is derived from the demand for the goods produced with these factors of production. For instance, the demand for labour in a textile mill is derived from the demand for the cloth produced by the labour.

Ex-ante and Ex-post Demand: Ex ante demand refers to the amount of goods that consumers want to or willing to buy during a particular time period. It is the planned or desired amount of demand. Ex post demand, on the other hand, refers to the amount of goods that the consumer actually purchase during a specific period. It is the amount of the goods actually bought. The amount of the goods actually bought is not the same as the amount that the consumer wants to purchase. If the commodity is not available in adequate quantity, the quantity actually purchased will be less than the quantity that the consumers desire to purchase. Thus, consumers may end up buying more, or lesser quantity of goods that they planned to buy.

Snob Effect and Bandwagon Effect

Snob Effect: It refers to the desire to own unique goods and is considered as negative network externality. Market demand is less elastic in this case. E.g. rare work of art, specially designed clothes etc.

Bandwagon Effect: It is a positive network externality in which a consumer wishes to possess a good because almost everyone else has it. It refers to desire to be in style. E.g. every girl child wishes to have a Barbie doll.

****

Exercise:

1. Market demand curve is 1. Horizontal summation of individual demand curves 2. Vertical summation of individual demand curves 3. Both I and II 4. None of the above

2. What will be the reaction of market demand curve of Bricks if price of Bricks is expected to rise in future? 1. No effect on demand curve of Bricks 2. There will extension in demand of Bricks 3. There will be increase in demand of Bricks and demand will shift right side 4. There will be decrease in demand and demand will shift right side

3. What will be the effect on demand curve of 4G phones if prices of internet packs with 4G speed were declined significantly by companies? 1. There will be extension in demand of 4G phones 2. There will be contraction in demand of 4G phones 3. There will be increase in demand of 4G phones and demand will shift right side 4. There will be increase in demand of 4G phones and demand will shift left side

4. _________ goods do not obey law of demand. 1. Veblen 2. Normal 3. Both 1&2 4. None of the above

5. Which of the following is not an exception to law of demand? 1. Veblen goods 2. Goods bought with irrational judgment (Ignorance) 3. Giffen goods 4. Normal goods

6. Which of the following is true? (where PE= Price effect, SE= Substitution effect, IE= Income effect) 1. P.E. = I.E. – S.E, 2. P.E. = I.E. + S.E. 3. P.E. +I.E. – S.E. 4. P.E. +I.E. = S.E.

7. Market demand of AC refers to 1. Demand for all goods by all buyers 2. Demand for AC by single buyer 3. Demand for AC by all buyers in the market 4. All of the above

8. Find out odd one out 1. Vegetables 2. Hair Oil 3. Diamonds 4. Clothes

9. Contraction in demand of mango is caused by 1. Increase in price of Apple 2. Fall in price of apple 3. Fall in income 4. None of the above

10. Decrease in demand of AC is caused by which of the following factor 1. Increase in price of electricity 2. Decrease in income of the consumer 3. Decrease in size of population 4. All of the above

11. Statement I: Giffen goods are inferior goods. Statement II: All inferiors' goods are not Giffen goods. Answers: 1. Statement I is true but statement II is wrong 2. Both statements are true 3. Both statements are false 4. Statement II is true but statement I is wrong

12. What will be the effect on demand curve of X commodity if Price of X commodity rises? 1. Decrease in demand 2. Extension in demand 3. Contraction in demand 4. Increase in demand

13. From the following diagram, shifting of demand from D to D1 curve shows

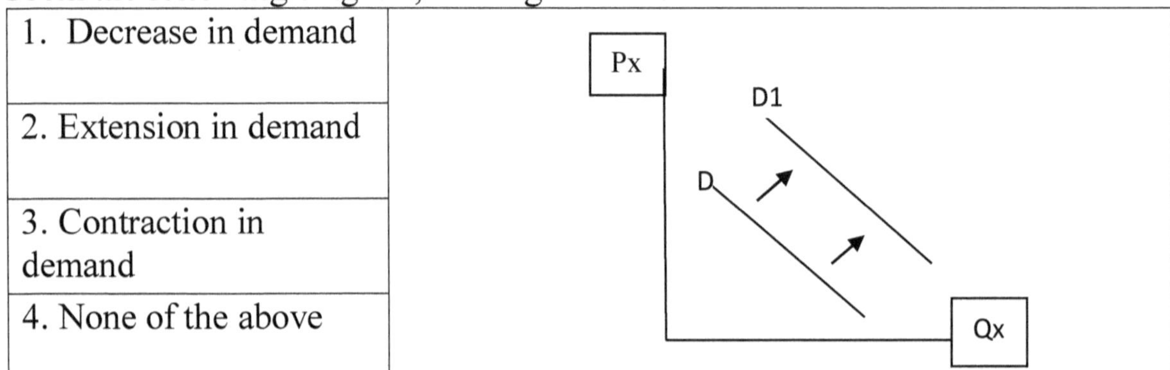

14. What will be the effect on demand curve of X commodity if income of the consumer falls (Treat X commodity as inferior) 1. Decrease in demand 2. Extension in demand 3. Contraction in demand 4. Increase in demand

15. What will be the effect on demand curve of X commodity if price of its substitute good falls 1. Decrease in demand 2. Extension in demand 3. Contraction in demand 4. Increase in demand

16. Exception to the law of demand states that there is _________ relationship between price and demand. 1. Positive 2. Negative 3. No 4. None of the above

---

17. Income effect is negative in case of ___________ goods. 1. Giffen 2. Inferior 3. Both 1&2 4. None of the above

18. Demand curve has negative slope due to 1. Law of DMU 2. Income effect 3. Substitution effect 4. All of the above

Answers:

1. 1	2. 3	3. 3	4. Veblen	5. 4	6. 2
7. 3	8. 3	9. 4	10.4	11.2	12.3
13.4	14.4	15.1	16.1	17.3	18.4

Schedules and Numerical:

1. Consider a market where there are two consumers A and B and their demands for the goods are as follows. Complete the schedule.

Price	Demand by A	Demand by B	Market Demand
5	10	3	-
10	8	-	10
15	-	1	7

2. Suppose there are three consumers in a particular market: Munna, Sona and Tona. Their demand schedules are given in the following table:

Price	Quantity demanded by Munna	Quantity demanded by Sona	Quantity demanded by Tona
10	50	50	15
20	40	40	10
30	30	25	5
40	20	10	0

   a. Derive the market demand schedule.

   b. Suppose Munna drops out of the market. Derive the new market demand schedule.

   c. Suppose Munna stays in the market and another person, Mr. Choksi, joins the market, whose quantity demanded at any given price, is twice of that of Munna. Derive the new market demand schedule.

3. Suppose that there are two consumers in the market for a good and their demand functions are as follows: $D_1 = 20-p$ for $p \leq 20$ and $d_1 = 0$ for $p > 20$, $D_2 = 30-2p$ for $p \leq 15$ and $d_2 = 0$ for $p > 15$, Find out the market demand function. (Ans: Market Demand = D1+D2 = (20-p) + (30 – 2p) = 50 – 3p, for any price greater than 15 and less than or equal to 20)

4. Suppose that there are 20 consumers for a good and they have identical demand functions: $D_1 = 10-3p$ for any price less than or equal to 10/3 and $D_1 = 0$

---

for any price greater than 10/3. What is the market demand function? (Ans: Market Demand = 20(D1) = 200-60p for any price less than equal to 10/3)

5. Given the linear demand curve: q= 12-2p. Calculate the quantity demanded at p= 5.(Ans: 2)

Practice Questions

1. What is meant by demand?
2. Define market demand.
3. What is demand function?
4. What is demand schedule?
5. What is market demand schedule?
6. What is Giffen paradox?
7. What do you mean by a normal good?
8. What do you mean by an 'inferior good'? Give some examples.
9. What do you mean by substitute goods? Give its two examples.
10. What do you mean by complementary goods? Give its two examples.
11. Explain law of demand. What are its exceptions?
12. When does demand curve is positively sloped?
13. Explain the various factors affecting the demand function.
14. What is the difference between change in quantity demanded and change in demand?
15. What is the meaning of shifting of demand curve? What are the factors responsible for this shifting?
16. Explain how the demand for a good is affected by the prices of its related goods. Give examples.
17. Explain how the following influence demand for a good. 1. Rise in income of the consumer. 2. Unfavourable change in tastes. 3. Change in price of own commodity.
18. Give one reason for a shift in demand curve.
19. Explain the difference between an inferior good and a normal good.
20. Explain the distinction between 'change in demand' and 'change in quantity demanded.
21. Explain the relationship between. 1. Prices of other goods and demand for the given good. 2. Income of the buyers and demand for a good.
22. What does a rightward shift of demand curve indicate? Explain its causes also.
23. How is the demand for a good affected by a rise in the price of other goods? Explain.

24. Give one reason for a leftward shift in demand curve.
25. What happens to the demand for a good when consumer's income changes? Explain.
26. Explain the change in demand for a good on account of change in prices of related goods.
27. What is market demand for a good? Name the factors determining market demand.
28. Give the meaning of "inferior" good and explain same with the help of an example.
29. How does change in price of a substitute good affect the demand of the given good? Explain with the help of an example.
30. How does change in price of a complementary good affect the demand of the given good? Explain with the help of an example.
31. Distinguish between an inferior good and a normal good. Is a good which is inferior for one consumer also inferior for all the consumers? Explain.
32. Distinguish between demand by an individual consumer and market demand of a good. Also state the factors leading to fall in demand by an individual consumer.
33. Derive the law of demand from the single commodity equilibrium condition "Marginal Utility=Price".

CHAPTER 5

PRICE ELASTICITY OF DEMAND

In previous chapter we had discussion on nature of relationship between demand for a commodity and its various determinants. We studied the law of demand which states that there is inverse relationship between demand for commodity and its price, keeping other factors constant. This law states that as price of commodity falls demand for that product rises and vice versa, but it fails to give answer about the magnitude of change in demand caused by change in price. In other words, the intensity with which demand response to change in price is not captured by this law. Present chapter will focus on this phenomenon. It is very essential to measure how much change is occurred in quantity demanded due to change in price, as it is very helpful in price determination, revision of tax rates, decision regarding devaluation etc.

Elasticity of demand measures the change in demand in response to change in its determinants. In the words of Dooley *"The elasticity of demand measures the responsiveness of the quantity demanded of a good, to change in its price, price of related goods and changes in consumer's income."*

To measure the sensitivity of quantity demanded to change in its various determinants of demand function are broadly classified into three concepts.

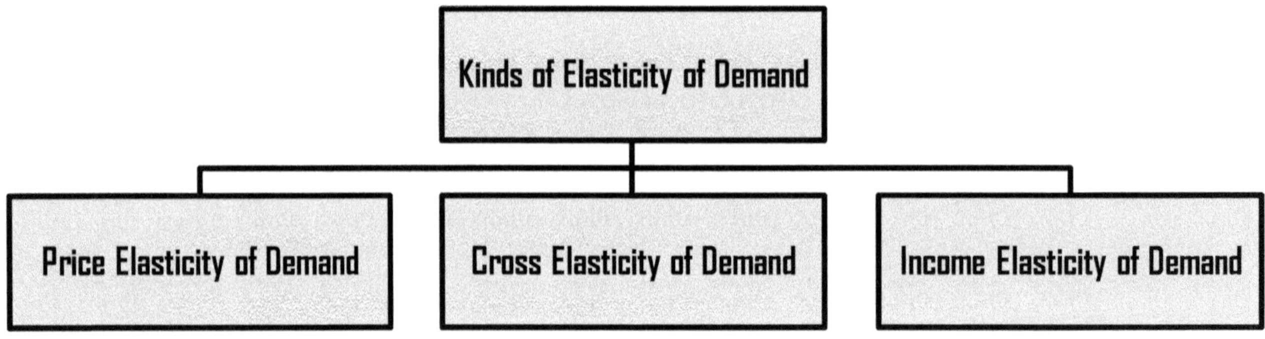

Price Elasticity of Demand: Price elasticity of demand measures the responsiveness of quantity demanded to change in its own price… Boulding

$$Ep = -\ \frac{\%\ \textbf{Change in Quantity Demanded of X– Commodity}}{\%\ \textbf{Change in Price of X–Commodity}}$$

Cross Price Elasticity of Demand: Cross price elasticity of demand measures the response of change in quantity demanded of X-commodity due to change in price of Y- commodity alone. Where, X and Y commodities are either substitute or complementary goods. In case of substitute goods cross elasticity of demand is positive and in case of complementary goods cross elasticity of demand is negative.

$$Ec = \frac{\% \text{ Change in Quantity Demanded of X} - \text{ Commodity}}{\% \text{ Change in Price of Y} - \text{Commodity}}$$

Income Elasticity of Demand: Income elasticity of demand measures the response of change in quantity demanded of commodity due to change in income alone.

$$Ey = \frac{\% \text{ Change in Quantity Demanded}}{\% \text{ Change in Income}}$$

Price Elasticity of Demand

Price elasticity of demand measures the responsiveness of quantity demanded to change in its own price… Boulding

$$Ep = -\frac{\% \text{ Change in Quantity Demanded of X} - \text{ Commodity}}{\% \text{ Change in Price of X} - \text{Commodity}}$$

Degrees of Measuring Price Elasticity of Demand

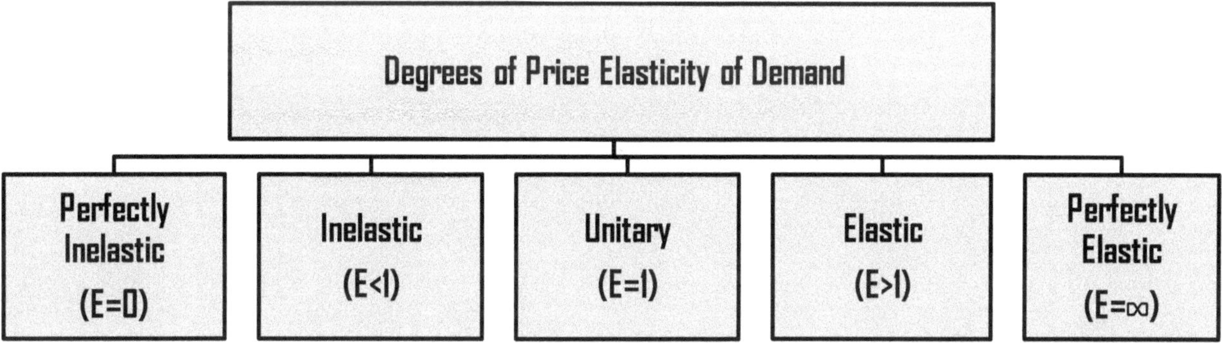

1. **Perfectly Elastic Demand (E=∞):** It is the situation where in a very small change in price (Microscopic Change) produces infinite change in quantity demanded. A very small decrease in price cause demand to extend to infinity and the small increase in price causes the demand to contracts to zero. In this case demand curve will be a horizontal line as shown in diagram 1, and will be parallel to X- axis.

2. **Perfectly Inelastic Demand (E=0):** In this case consumer will buy a fixed quantity of a good regardless of its price, that is to say whatever the change in price occurs, the demand will remain the same. In other words, there will be no change in quantity demanded due to change in price. In this case demand curve will be vertical line as shown in diagram 2.

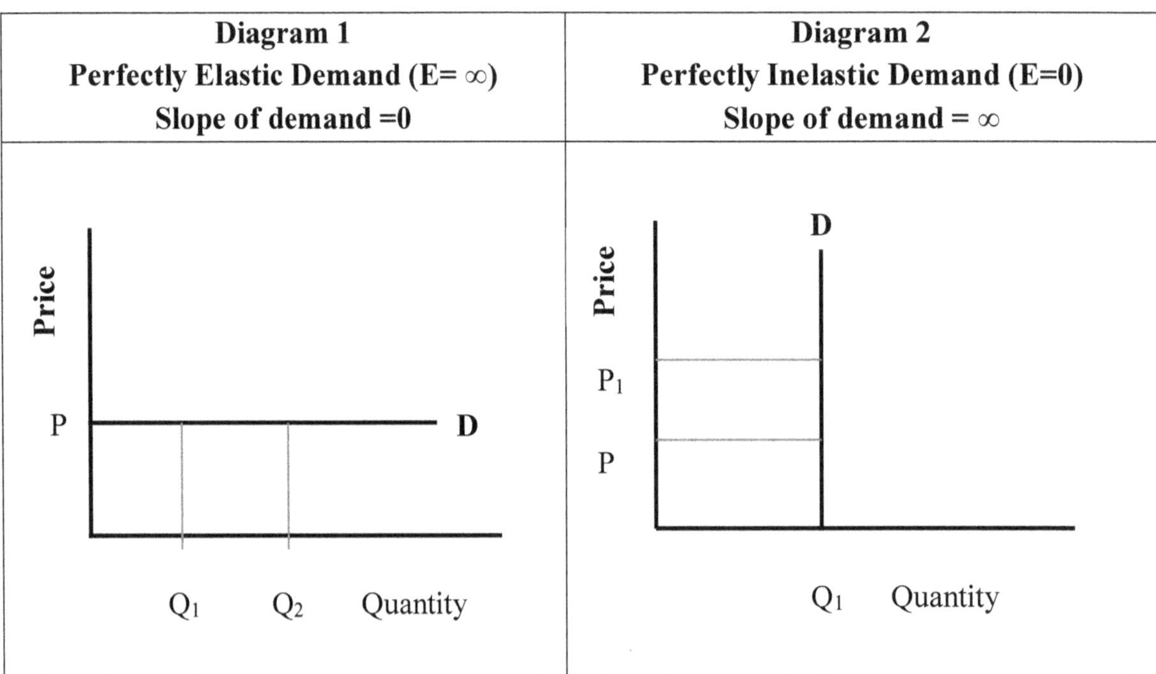

3. **Unitary Elastic Demand (E=1):** Demand is said to be unitary elastic when change in price produces equi-proportionate change in quantity demanded i.e. $(\Delta Q/Q = (\Delta P/P)$. In other words, it is case where % change in quantity demanded is exactly equal to % change in price. In this case demand curve will be rectangular hyperbola as shown in diagram 3.

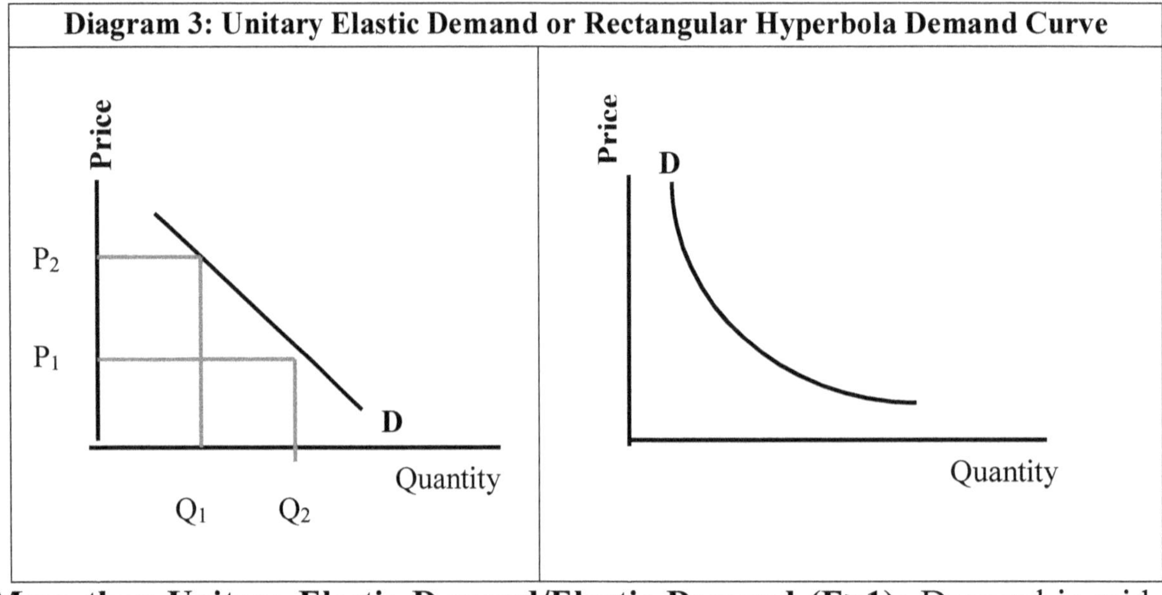

4. **More than Unitary Elastic Demand/Elastic Demand (E>1):** Demand is said to be more than unitary elastic when change in price produces more-proportionate change in quantity demanded i.e. $(\Delta Q/Q > (\Delta P/P)$. In other words, it is case where % change in quantity demanded is greater than % change in price. In this case demand curve will be flatter as shown in diagram 4.

5. **Less than Unitary Elastic Demand/Inelastic Demand (E<1):** Demand is said to be more than unitary elastic when change in price produces less-proportionate change in quantity demanded i.e. **(ΔQ/Q < (ΔP/P).** In other words, it is case where % change in quantity demanded is less than % change in price. In this case demand curve will be steeper as shown in diagram 5.

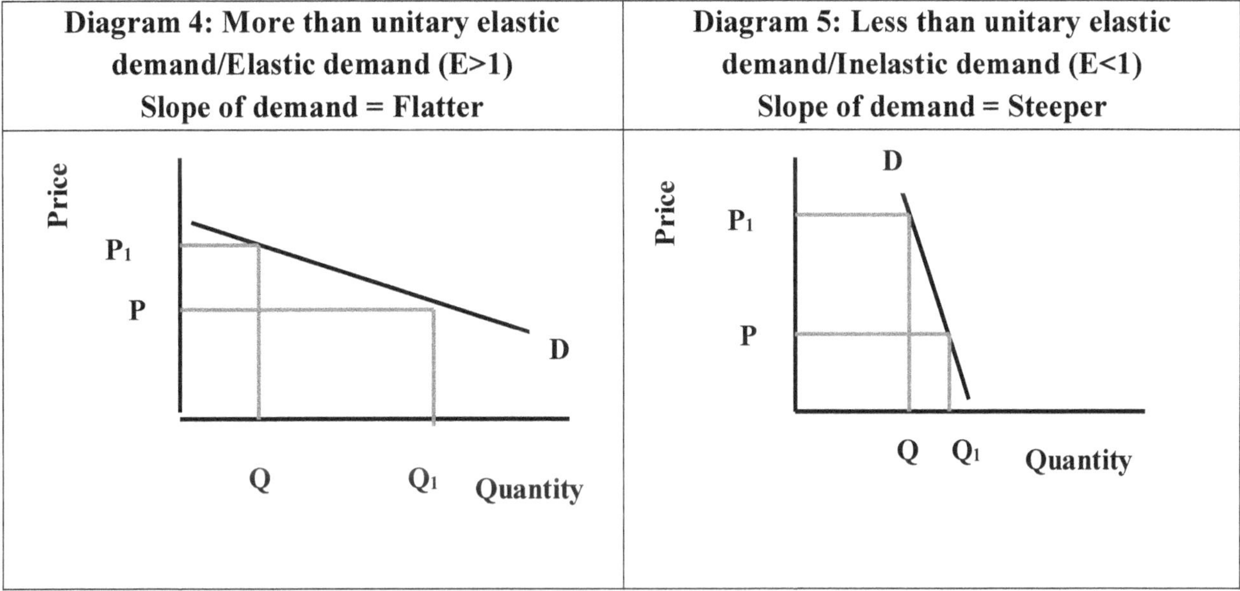

Methods of Measuring Price Elasticity of Demand

1. **Total Expenditure Method/ Total Outlay Method:** This method was evolved by Dr. Marshall. According to this method, in order to measure the elasticity of demand, it is essential to know how much and in what direction the total expenditure has changed as result of change in the price of a good. Measurement of elasticity of demand by total expenditure method is shown by the table 1 and 2.

Table 1. Total Expenditure Method

Price	Total Expenditure	Elasticity of Demand
Rise	*Fall*	*E>1*
Fall	*Rise*	*(Greater than unity)*
Price	**Total Expenditure**	**Elasticity of Demand**
Rise	*No change*	*E=1*
Fall	*No change*	*(Unitary elastic)*
Price	**Total Expenditure**	**Elasticity of Demand**
Rise	*Rise*	*E<1*
Fall	*Fall*	*(Less than unity)*

Table 2. Total Expenditure Method

Price	Quantity	Total Outlay (Price* Qty)	Elasticity of Demand
10	12	120	E>1
15 (Rise)	4	60 (Fall)	(Greater than unity)
Price	**Quantity**	**Total Outlay (Price* Qty)**	**Elasticity of Demand**
10	12	120	E=1
15 (Rise)	8	120 (Unchanged)	(Unitary elastic)
Price	**Quantity**	**Total Outlay (Price* Qty)**	**Elasticity of Demand**
10	12	120	E<1
15 (Rise)	10	150 (Rise)	(Less than unity)

2. **Point method/Geometric method:** Point method is used to measure elasticity of demand at any point on the demand curve. According to Leftwitch, *"Elasticity computed at single point on the curve for an infinitely small change in price, is point elasticity."*

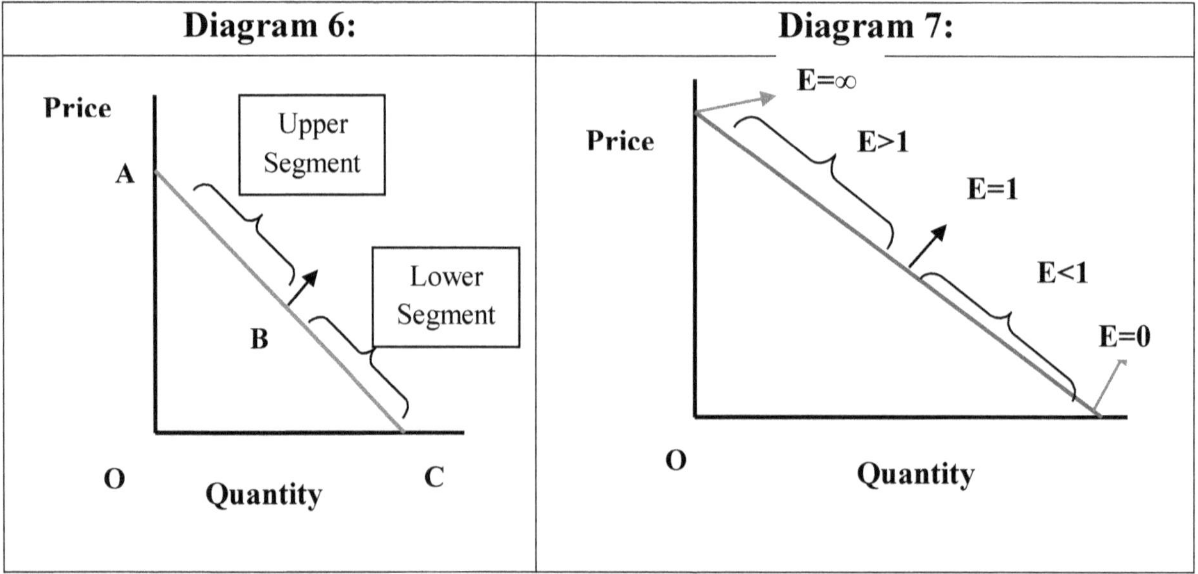

Using this method elasticity can be measured by taking ratio of **Lower Segment** of the demand curve to the **Upper Segment** of the demand curve.

$$E = \frac{\text{Lower Segment of the Demand Curve}}{\text{Upper Segment of the Demand Curve}} \quad \text{or} \quad \frac{BC}{AB} \text{ as shown in diagram 6.}$$

E>1, when lower segment of demand curve is greater than upper segment of demand curve. E<1, when lower segment of demand curve is less than upper segment of demand curve. E>1, when lower segment of demand curve is equal to upper segment of demand curve.

3. **Percentage Method or Proportionate Method or Flux Method:** This method measures the price elasticity of demand by using the following formula

$$Ep = -\frac{\%\ \textbf{Change in Quantity Demanded of X- Commodity}}{\%\ \textbf{Change in Price of X-Commodity}}$$

% Change in Quantity Demanded $= \frac{\Delta Q}{Q} \times 100$ (Where $\Delta Q = Q_1\text{-}Q$, Q_1 is the final quantity and Q is initial quantity)

% Change in Price $= \frac{\Delta P}{P} \times 100$ (where $\Delta P = P_1\text{-}P$, P_1 is the final price and P is initial price)

$$Ep = -\frac{\Delta Q}{\Delta P} \times \frac{P}{Q}$$

4. **Revenue Method:** This method measures the elasticity of demand using concepts of revenue like AR and MR. Ep= [AR/(AR-MR)]. Elasticity of demand will be equal to one when MR = 0, it will be greater than one or elastic when MR is positive, and demand will be inelastic or less than unitary elastic when MR is negative. This is depicted in diagram 8.

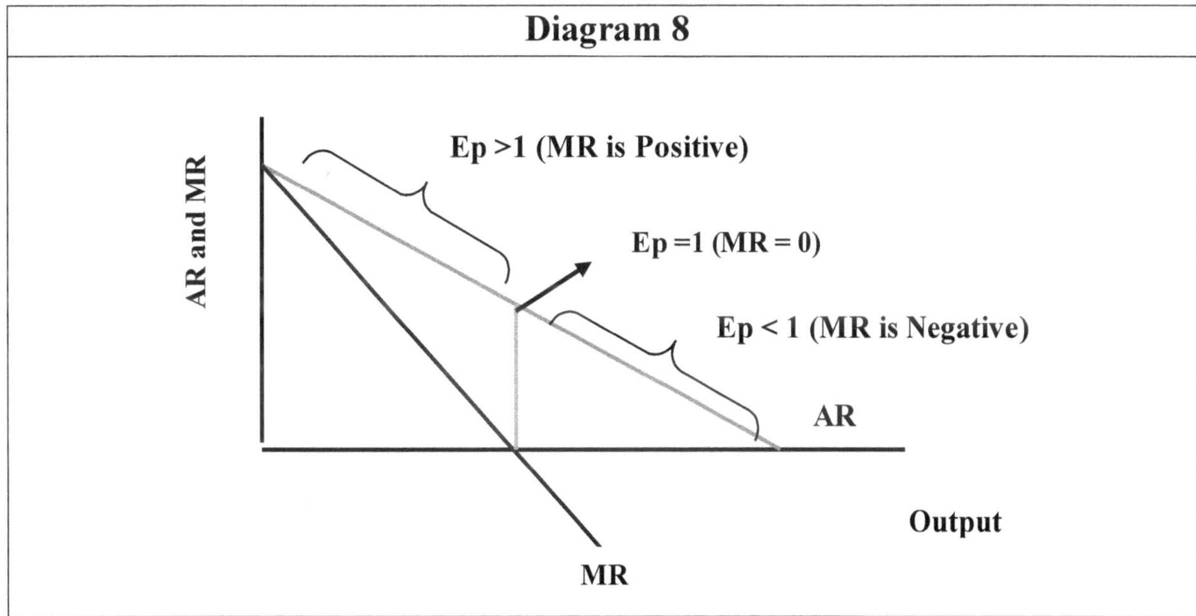

Diagram 8

Slope of Demand Curve: Slope of demand curve is determined by the ratio of change in price to change in demand $\frac{\Delta P}{\Delta Q}$.

Relationship of Slope of Demand Curve with Elasticity of Demand

There is inverse relationship between slope of demand curve and elasticity of demand curve as shown in diagram 1, 2, 4, & 5.

$$Ep = -\left[\frac{1}{\text{Slope of Demand Curve}} \times \frac{P}{Q}\right]$$

Factors Affecting Price Elasticity of Demand

The price elasticity of demand of a product ranges between 0 and ∞. There are various factors which affects the elasticity of demand.

1. **Habit or Addiction:** If consumer is habituated or addicted to use of a product, then demand for that product would be inelastic. Consumers who are addicted or habituated to the use of tobacco, alcohol etc. seldom decreases the consumption of these products in response to change in their prices.

2. **Nature of Commodity:** Commodities can be classified into necessity, comfort, prestigious or luxury according to their nature of satisfaction that they provide to consumer. Necessities like food grains, salt, clothes, sugar, medicine etc. have inelastic demand because these goods are essential for the living of the consumer. Demand for luxury goods like is relatively more elastic to necessaries, because the consumption of luxury goods can be postponed if price is too high. In case of comforts, the demand is neither inelastic like necessaries nor elastic like luxury rather it is likely to near unity.

3. **Uses of the Commodity:** Commodities with alternative uses, have more elastic demand as compared to commodity with few or limited uses.

4. **Availability of Substitutes:** Availability of substitutes of a commodity significantly affects the response of quantity demanded to change in its various determinants. Commodities with limited and poor substitutes have less elastic demand and commodities whose close substitutes are available in plenty have elastic demand, because there is opportunity for the consumer to switch over to the cheaper substitutes in case when price of one of the commodity increases.

5. **Joint Demand:** Goods which are jointly demanded like petrol and petrol vehicles, electricity and AC's, have inelastic demand. Because if we have a petrol car, then we have to buy petrol to run the car even at higher prices.

6. **Postponement of the use:** Commodities whose use or consumption can be postponed have elastic demand and which cannot be postponed have inelastic demand. E.g. hunger cannot be postponed that's why food has inelastic demand. In general, necessities have inelastic demand because consumption of these can be postponed.

7. **Weightage of Commodity in Consumer's Budget:** Elasticity of demand is also influenced by the proportion of income spent on a commodity. Commodities on which consumer spent more proportion of his income have elastic demand and commodities with low weightage in consumer's budget have inelastic demand. In other words, greater the proportion of income spent on commodity or more the weightage of commodity in consumer's budget, greater will be the elasticity of demand & vice versa.

8. **Time Factor:** It is an important factor that influences the elasticity of demand. In short period of time demand is less elastic, because consumers have not enough time to search out the substitutes or to compare the prices. In the long period demand is said to be elastic because discovery of new substitutes, changes in habits, consumer adjustments to new products, and change in production capacity are possible in the long period.

9. **Price Level:** At very low or very high range of prices demand for goods is inelastic. While in the middle range of prices demand for goods is elastic.

10. **Income level:** The level of income also influences the elasticity of demand. People with very high income or very low level of income, have inelastic demand. Because in general people with high level of income do not bothered about the change in price of the commodity. People with low level of income are buying only necessities with low income that's why due to change in price of the necessities quantity demanded of these commodities remains stable. Demand is relatively elastic in case of middle income people.

Numerical:

1. Consider the demand for a good. At price Rs. 4, the demand for the good is 25 units. Suppose price of the good increases to Rs. 5, and as a result, the demand for the good falls to 20 units. Calculate the price elasticity.

   Ans: Here, P= Rs. 4, P_1 = Rs.5, $\Delta P = P_1 - P$ = Rs. 5-Rs.4 = Rs.1

   Q= 25 units, Q_1= 20 units , $\Delta Q = Q_1 - Q$ = (20-25) units = (-) 5 units

   E_d= (-) 4/25 × -5/1 = 0.8

2. Consider the demand curve D(p) = 10-3p. What is the elasticity at price 5/3?

   Ans: Given, demand curve D(p) = 10-3p, Price $= \frac{5}{3} = 1.67$, D= $10-(3 \times \frac{5}{3})$ = 10-5 =5 units

   $$D(p) = 10-3p$$

   $$\frac{\Delta D}{\Delta P} = -3 \; or \; \frac{\Delta Q}{\Delta P} = -3$$

   $$E_d = -\frac{P}{Q} \times \frac{\Delta Q}{\Delta P} = -\frac{1.67}{5} \times -3$$

$E_d= 1$

3. Suppose the price elasticity of demand for a good is -0.2. If there is a 5 per cent increase in the price of the good, by what percentage will the demand for the good go down?

    Ans: Given, Price elasticity of demand = -0.2 and Percentage change in price = 5 per cent

    -0.2 = [Percentage change in quantity demanded/(-1)]

    Percentage change in quantity demanded = -1 per cent. It means demand for the good goes down by 1 %

4. Price of the commodity –X falls from Rs.5 per kg to Rs. 4 per kg and the demand for it rise from 4kg to 6kg. Express your opinion regarding the nature of elasticity of demand of commodity-X. If there is no change in the quantity demanded of commodity-X, what will be the nature of the price elasticity of demand?

    Ans: $(E_d) = -\dfrac{P}{Q} \times \dfrac{\Delta Q}{\Delta P}$ Here, P=5, P_1=4 & Q=4, Q_1=6, ΔP= 4-5 = -1, ΔQ=6-4 =2

    Price elasticity of demand $(E_d) = -\dfrac{5}{4} \times \dfrac{2}{-1} = \dfrac{10}{4} = 2.5$

    Price elasticity of demand will be zero. Implying a situation of perfectly inelastic demand

5. Supposing the initial demand was 100 units. With the rise in price by Rs. 5, the quantity demanded decreases by 5 units. Elasticity of demand is 1.2. Find out the price before the change in demand.

    Ans: Supposing the price (P) before change = X

    $E_d = -\dfrac{P}{Q} \times \dfrac{\Delta Q}{\Delta P}$

    ΔP=5, ΔQ = (-) 5

    P=X, Q=100 and E_d=1.2

    $E_d = -\dfrac{P}{Q} \times \dfrac{\Delta Q}{\Delta P} = 1.2$

    $-\dfrac{X}{100} \times \dfrac{-5}{5} = 1.2 \ \ or \ \ \dfrac{X}{100} = 1.2$

    X= 1.2 × 100 = 120

    Price before change in demand = Rs. 120

6. A consumer buys 100 units of Good-Y at Rs. 5 per unit. The price elasticity of demand for the good is 2. At what price will he be willing to buy 140 units of Good-Y?

    Ans: Suppose the consumer buys 140 units at price of Rs. X per unit.

$$E_d = -\frac{P}{Q} \times \frac{\Delta Q}{\Delta P}$$

$E_d=2$, $P=Rs.5$, $P_1=Rs.\ X$, $\Delta P=Rs.\ (X-5)$

$Q=100$ units, $Q_1=140$ units, $\Delta Q= Q_1-Q=140-100 = 40$ units

$$E_d = -\frac{P}{Q} \times \frac{\Delta Q}{\Delta P}$$

$$2 = (-)\frac{5}{100} \times \frac{40}{(X-5)} = (-)\frac{2}{X-5}$$

$$2 \times (X-5) = -2 \ or\ 2X-10 = -2$$

$$2X = -2 + 10 = 8$$

$$X = 4$$

The consumer will purchase 140 units of Good-Y at the price of Rs.4

7. Price of a commodity falls from Rs. 4 to Rs. 3 per unit. As a result total expenditure on it rises from Rs. 200 to Rs.300. Find out the price elasticity of demand by percentage method.

Price (Rs.)	Total Expenditure (Rs.)	Quantity Demanded (units)
4	200	$200/4 = 50$
3	300	$300/3 = 100$

Ans:

Change in Price	% Change in Price	Change in Demand	% Change in Demand
Rs. 4 to Rs. 3	$\frac{3-4}{4} \times 100$ $= 25$ per cent	50 units to 100 units	$\frac{100-50}{50} \times 100$ $=100$ per cent

$$\text{Price elasticity of demand } (E_d) = -\frac{Percentage\ change\ in\ quantity\ demanded}{percentage\ change\ in\ price} =$$

$$(-)\frac{100\%}{-25\%} = 4$$

8. The demand by a consumer for a commodity declines by 10 per cent when its price increases from Rs.5 to Rs. 6 per unit. What is the price elasticity of demand of the commodity?

Ans: $Ed= -\frac{P}{Q} \times \frac{\Delta Q}{\Delta P} = (-)\frac{Percentage\ change\ in\ quantity\ demanded}{percentage\ change\ in\ price}$

$$percentage\ change\ in\ price = \frac{\Delta P}{P} \times 100 = \frac{6-5}{5} \times 100 = \frac{1}{5} \times 100$$

$$= 20\ per\ cent$$

Percentage change in quantity demanded $= (-)\ 10$ per cent

$$E_d = -\frac{-10\%}{20\%} = 0.5$$

9. The price elasticity of demand for commodity $-X$ is known to be twice that of commodity $-Y$. Price of X falls by 5 per cent while that of commodity $-Y$ rises by 5 per cent. What is the percentage change in quantities of X and Y?

Ans. If $E_d=1$ for commodity-Y, $E_d=2$ for commodity-X

5 per cent rise in price of Y should mean 5 per cent decrease in quantity of Y and 5 per cent fall in price of X should mean 10 per cent increase in quantity of X.

10. The consumer buys 160 units of a good at a price of Rs. 8 per unit. Price falls to Rs. 6 per unit. How much quantity will the consumer buy at the new price if price elasticity of demand is (-2)?

Ans: As in the above, numerical elasticity of demand has been specified with a negative sign. Accordingly, we need not use '-'sign as a prefix to the formula of measuring elasticity of demand. Thus,

$$E_d = \frac{P}{Q} \times \frac{\Delta Q}{\Delta P}$$

Here, $E_d=$ (-) 2, P=8, $P_1=6$, $\Delta P=P_1-P=6-8=$ (-) 2

Q=160, $Q_1=X$, $\Delta Q=Q_1-Q=X-160$

$$(-)2 = \frac{8}{160} \times \frac{X-160}{-2} = \frac{X-160}{-40}$$

X-160=80

X=80+160=240

The consumer will buy 240 units at the new price.

11. There is 50 per cent fall in price of the commodity. But quantity demand remains to be 150 units. Find elasticity of demand.

Ans: Here, elasticity of demand is zero because in response to decrease price of the commodity, the quantity demanded remains the same, i.e., 150 units.

12. For a commodity, $\Delta P/P=-0.2$, and elasticity of demand = -0.5. Find quantity demanded after a fall in price when initially it was 60 units.

Ans: $\Delta P/P=-0.2$, and elasticity of demand = -0.5

Initial quantity demanded (Q)=60 units

Elasticity of demand $(E_d) = \frac{P}{Q} \times \frac{\Delta Q}{\Delta P} = \frac{\Delta Q}{Q} \times \frac{P}{\Delta P}$

$-0.5 = \frac{\Delta Q}{60} \times \frac{1}{-0.2}$

$\Delta Q=6$

$Q_1=Q+\Delta Q= 60+6=66$

New quantity =66 units.

13. If E_d=-0.2 and ΔP/P=0.6, find new expenditure if initially it was Rs. 1000.

Ans: E_d=-0.2, Percentage change in price $(\Delta P/P)*100= 60\%$

Percentage change in quantity demanded $= (-)0.2 \times 60 \ percent = -12 \ percent$

Let initial price = Rs. 100 and initial quantity = 100 units

When price increases by 60 per cent, P_1=Rs.100+Rs.60=Rs.160

When quantity demanded reduces by 12 per cent, Q_1= (100-12) units = 88 units

Thus, Assumed initial expenditure =100☐100=Rs.10000

New expenditure (if initial expenditure=10000) = 88☐160=Rs.14080

New expenditure (if initial expenditure=100000=14080 $\times \dfrac{1000}{10000} = 1408$

New expenditure=Rs.1408

14. Price of the commodity increase form Rs. 10 to Rs.12 per unit and expenditure on the commodity increases by 20 per cent. Find elasticity of demand. Give a logical support to your answer.

Ans: Given that initial price = Rs.10, new price = Rs, 12, and increase in expenditure = 20 per cent, let assume that initial quantity =100. Accordingly, initial expenditure =10×100=1000, new expenditure =1000+20% of 1000 = Rs. 1200.

New quantity $= \dfrac{1200}{12} =100$

Thus, quantity demanded remains constant, even when a price rises from Rs.10 to Rs. 12. Implying that elasticity of demand = 0.

15. Price elasticity of demand is estimated to be 2. Price of the commodity happens to increase by 10 per cent. Find the change in quantity demanded when initially he was buying 120 units of the commodity.

Ans: Percentage change in price =10 percent

Or, $\dfrac{\Delta P}{P} = 0.1$, Q = 120, E_d =2

We know, Price elasticity of demand $(E_d) = -\dfrac{\Delta Q}{Q} \times \dfrac{p}{\Delta P}$

$2 = (-)\dfrac{\Delta Q}{120} \times \dfrac{1}{0.1}$

$2 = (-)\dfrac{\Delta Q}{12}$

$\Delta Q = -24$

$Q_1 = Q + \Delta Q = 120 + (-)24 = 96$

New quantity = 96 units.

16. From the following data calculate price elasticity of demand:

Price (Rs.)	Demand (units)
9	100
9	150

Ans: Given, P = Rs.9, P_1 = Rs.9, $\Delta P = P_1-P$ = Rs.9-Rs.9 = 0

Q=100 units, Q_1=150 units, $\Delta Q = Q_1-Q$ = (150-100) =50 units

Price elasticity of demand $(E_d) = -\dfrac{P}{Q} \times \dfrac{\Delta Q}{\Delta P} = \dfrac{9}{100} \times \dfrac{50}{0} = \dfrac{450}{0} = \infty$

Price elasticity of demand $(E_d) = \infty$

17. When price of good is Rs.7 per unit a consumer buys 12 units. When price falls to Rs.6 per unit he spends Rs.72 on the good. Calculate price elasticity of demand by using the percentage method. Comment on the likely shape of demand curve based on this measure of elasticity.

Ans: Given, P = Rs.7, P_1 = Rs.6, $\Delta P = P_1-P$ = Rs.6-Rs.7 = Rs.-1

Q= 12 units, $Q_1 = \dfrac{72}{6}$ = 12 units, $\Delta Q = Q_1-Q$ = (12-12) = 0 unit

Price elasticity of demand $(E_d) = -\dfrac{P}{Q} \times \dfrac{\Delta Q}{\Delta P} = -\dfrac{7}{12} \times \dfrac{0}{-1} = 0$

Price elasticity of demand = 0.

18. A consumer buys 14 units of a good at a price of Rs. 8 per unit. At price Rs. 7 per unit he spends Rs.98 on the good. Calculate price elasticity of demand by the percentage method. Comment upon the shape of demand curve based on this information.

Ans: Given, P=Rs.8, P_1=Rs.7, $\Delta P = P_1-P$ = Rs.7- Rs.8 = (-) 1

Q= 14 units, $Q_1 = \dfrac{98}{7}$ = 14 units, $\Delta Q = Q_1-Q$ = (14-14) = 0 unit

Price elasticity of demand $(E_d) = -\dfrac{P}{Q} \times \dfrac{\Delta Q}{\Delta P} = -\dfrac{8}{14} \times \dfrac{0}{-1} = 0$

Price elasticity of demand (E_d) = 0.

19. Price elasticity of demand for flowers and toys are respectively (-) 0.9 and (-) 0.5. Demand for which one is more elastic and why?

Ans: Demand for flowers will be more elastic than toys because percentage change in quantity demanded is more responsive to a given percentage change in price in the case of flowers than in the case of toys. Negative sign as a prefix to the elasticity of demand only signifies the inverse relationship between price and quantity demanded of a commodity.

20. A consumer buys 10 units of a good at a price of Rs. 11 per unit. When the price falls to Rs. 9 per unit, he spends Rs.90 on the good. Calculate price elasticity of demand using the percentage method. Also comment upon the shape of demand curve based on this information.

Ans: Given, P=Rs.11, P_1= Rs.9, ΔP= P_1-P = Rs.9- Rs.11 = Rs.-2

Q= 10 units, $Q_1 = \dfrac{90}{9}$ = 10 units, ΔQ= Q_1-Q= 10-10 = 0 unit

Price elasticity of demand $(E_d) = -\dfrac{P}{Q} \times \dfrac{\Delta Q}{\Delta P} = -\dfrac{11}{10} \times \dfrac{0}{-2} = 0$

Price elasticity of demand = 0.

21. A consumer buys 11 units of a good at a price of Rs.10 per unit. He can buy 13 units of the same by incurring an expenditure of Rs.130. Calculate the price elasticity of demand by percentage method. Also comment on the shape of the demand curve based on this information.

Ans: Given, P= Rs.10, P_1= Rs. $\dfrac{130}{13}$ = Rs. 10, ΔP=P_1-P = Rs.10- Rs.10 = Rs.0

Q= 11 units, Q_1= 13 units, ΔQ=Q_1-Q = 13-11 = 2units

$(E_d) = -\dfrac{P}{Q} \times \dfrac{\Delta Q}{\Delta P} = -\dfrac{10}{11} \times \dfrac{2}{0} = \dfrac{20}{0} = \infty$

Price elasticity of demand is infinity.

22. A consumer buys 13 units of a good at a price of Rs. 11 per unit. When price rises to Rs.13 per unit he buys 11 units. Use expenditure approach to find price elasticity of demand. Also comment on the shape of the demand curve based on this information.

Price	Demand	Total expenditure
11	13	143
13	11	143

Ans: Since total expenditure remains constant, price elasticity of demand is equal to unity.

Price elasticity of demand = 1

23. The demand for good rises by 20 per cent as a result of fall in its price. Its price elasticity of demand is (-) 0.8. Calculate the percentage fall in price.

Ans: Given, E_d= -0.8, Percentage change in quantity demanded = 20%

$(E_d) = \dfrac{\% \text{ Change in quantity deamnded}}{\% \text{Change in price}}$

$-0.8 = \dfrac{20\%}{\% \text{ Change in price}}$

Percentage change in price $= \dfrac{20\%}{-0.8} = 25\%$

Percentage fall in price = 25%

24. A 5 per cent fall in the price of good raises its demand form 300 units to 318 units. Calculate its price elasticity of demand.

Ans: Given, percentage change in price = -5%

Q=300 units, Q_1= 318 units, $\Delta Q = Q_1 - Q$= (318-300) units = 18 units

Percentage change in quantity demanded = $\dfrac{18}{300} \times 100 = 6\%$

Price elasticity of demand (E_d) = - (% change in demand/%change in price) = - (6%/-5%) = 1.2

25. A consumer buys 18 units of a good at a price of Rs.9 per unit. The price elasticity of demand for the good is (-) 1. How many units the consumer will buy at a price of Rs. 10 per unit?

Ans: Given, P=Rs.9, P_1=Rs.10, $\Delta P = P_1 - P$=Rs.10-Rs.9=1, Q=18units, Q_1=?, E_d=-1

Price elasticity of demand (E_d) $= \dfrac{P}{Q} \times \dfrac{\Delta Q}{\Delta P}$

$$-1 = \dfrac{9}{18} \times \dfrac{\Delta Q}{1}$$

$$\Delta Q = -2$$

$$Now, \Delta Q = Q_1 - 18$$

$$-2 = Q_1 - 18$$

$$Q_1 = 18 - 2 = 16$$

Consumer will buy 16 units at a price of Rs.10 per unit.

26. A consumer buys 30 units of a good at a price of Rs.10 per unit. Price elasticity of demand for the good is (-) 1. How many units the consumer will buy at a price of Rs. 9 per unit? Calculate. Ans: Given, P=Rs.10, P_1=Rs.9, $\Delta P = P_1 - P$=Rs.9-Rs.10=-1, Q=30units, Q_1=?, E_d=-1

Price elasticity of demand (E_d) $= \dfrac{P}{Q} \times \dfrac{\Delta Q}{\Delta P}$

$$-1 = \dfrac{10}{30} \times \dfrac{\Delta Q}{-1}$$

$$\Delta Q = 3$$

$$Now, \Delta Q = Q_1 - 30$$

$$3 = Q_1 - 30$$

$$Q_1 = 30 + 3 = 33$$

Consumer will buy 33 units at a price of Rs.9 per unit.

27. Price elasticity of demand of two goods A and B is (-) 2 and (-) 6 respectively. Which of the two goods has higher elasticity and why?

Ans: Given, price elasticity of demand (E_d) of Good- A= (-) 2, Price elasticity of demand (E_d) of Good-B= (-) 6, Price elasticity of Good-B is higher as compared to Good-A. This is because the negative sign just indicates the inverse relationship between price and demand. It does not relate to the value of elasticity of demand. Accordingly, in terms of elasticity of demand (-) 6 is to be treated as higher than (-) 2.

Exercise:

1. When demand curve is parallel to X-axis, elasticity of demand is: 1. Unity 2. Zero 3. Greater than unity 4. Infinity

2. On all points of rectangular hyperbola demand curve, elasticity of demand is: 1. Equal to one 2. Zero 3. Greater than unity 4. Less than unity

3. There is __________ relationship between elasticity of demand and slope of demand curve. 1. No 2. Positive 3. Negative 4. Both b & c

4. What will be the elasticity of demand when demand curve is parallel to Y-axis? 1. Unity 2. Zero 3. Less than unity 4. More than unity

5. In case of more availability of close substitutes, demand will be: 1. Less elastic 2. More elastic 3. Parallel to X-axis 4. Parallel to Y-axis

6. Price elasticity of demand at the mid-point of a straight line downward sloping demand curve is _______.1. Unity 2. Zero 3. Less than unity 4. More than unity

7. Elasticity of demand for salt is considered as: 1. More elastic 2. Less elastic 3. Unitary elastic 4. Infinite elastic

8. Which of the following indicates the higher elasticity? 1. Zero 2. -1, 3. -4 4. -3

9. What will elasticity of demand if lower segment of demand curve is twice than the upper segment of demand curve? 1. Unity 2. Zero 3. Less than unity 4. More than unity

10. Elasticity between tariff rates of electricity and home appliances is likely to be 1. Zero 2. Negative 3. Positive 4. None of the above

11. Which of the following is relevant concept if we want to measure elasticity between substitute or complementary goods? 1. Price elasticity of demand 2. Income elasticity of demand 3. Cross elasticity of demand 4. All of the above

12. Demand for medicines is _______. 1. Unity 2. Perfectly elastic 3. Inelastic 4. More than unity

13. What would be the elasticity of demand when AR>MR? 1. Unity 2. Elastic 3. Inelastic 4.
   All of the above

14. What would be the elasticity of demand when AR=MR? 1. Unity 2. Perfectly elastic 3. Inelastic 4. More than unity

15. Elasticity of demand of a straight line demand curve goes on increasing as you move downwards of it. Statement is true or false.

16. "Slope of demand curve and elasticity of demand are different concepts." Statement is true or false.

17. "There is inverse relationship between slope of demand curve and elasticity of demand." Statement is true or false.

18. "Demand will be more elastic in case of commodity has more substitutes." Statement is true or false.

19. Explain price elasticity of demand.

20. Consider the demand for a good. At price Rs.4, the demand for the good is 25 units. Suppose price of the good increases to Rs.5, and as a result, the demand for the good falls to 20 units. Calculate the price elasticity.

21. Suppose the price elasticity of demand for a good is -0.2. If there is a 5 per cent increase in the price of the good, by what percentage will the demand for the good go down?

Answers:

1. 4	2. 1	3. 3	4. 2	5. 2	6. 1
7. 2	8. 3	9. 4	10.2	11.3	12.3
13.4	14.1	15.F	16.T	17.T	18.T

Practice Numerical

1. When price of a good is Rs. 13 per unit, the consumer buys 11 units of that good. When price rises to Rs.15 per unit, the consumer continues to buy 11 units. Calculate price elasticity of demand. Ans: Perfectly elastic demand

2. When price of a good is Rs. 12 per unit, the consumer buys 24 units of that good. When price rises to Rs.14 per unit, the consumer buys 20 units. Calculate price elasticity of demand. Ans: 1

3. From the following data calculate the price elasticity of demand: Ans: Perfectly Inelastic demand

Price (Rs.)	Demand (units)
9	100
9	150

4. A consumer buys 17 units of a good at a price of Rs. 10 per unit. When price falls by Rs.8 per unit the consumer buys 23 units. Calculate price elasticity of demand using proportionate method. Ans: 0.44

5. A consumer buys 19 units of a good at a price of Rs. 11 per unit. When price rises to Rs.13 per unit the consumer buys 17 units. Using the expenditure

approach, what will you say about price elasticity of demand of the good? Ans: 0.58

6. A consumer buys 9 units of a good at a price of Rs. 11 per unit. When price falls by Rs.9 per unit the consumer buys 11 units. Using the expenditure approach, what will you say about price elasticity of demand of the good? Ans: 0.27

7. Due to 20% fall in price, demand for commodity rises by 2 units from 20 units. Calculate the elasticity of demand from this information. Ans: 0.5

8. Due to 20% fall in price, demand for commodity rises by 20% from initial 150 units. Calculate the elasticity of demand from this information. Ans: 1

9. Due to 40% fall in price, demand for commodity rises to 120 units from 20 units. Calculate the elasticity of demand from this information. Ans: 12.5

10. A consumer buys 10 units of a good at a price of Rs.10 per unit. He incurs an expenditure of Rs.200 when he buys 25 units. Calculate price elasticity of demand using the percentage method. Comment upon the likely shape of demand curve based on this information. Ans: 7

11. A consumer buys 14 units of a good at a price of Rs.8 per unit. At price Rs.7 per unit he spends Rs. 98 on the good. Calculate price elasticity of demand by percentage method. Comment upon the shape of demand curve based on this information. Ans: 0, Vertical

12. A consumer buys 13 units of a good at a price of Rs.11 per unit. When price rises to Rs.13 per unit he buys 11 units. Calculate price elasticity of demand through the expenditure approach. Comment upon the shape of demand curve based on this information. Ans: Less than one

13. If Ed = -0.2 and $\frac{\Delta P}{P}$ = 0.6, find new expenditure if initially it was Rs. 1000. Ans: 1408

14. If $\frac{\Delta P}{P}$ = - 0.2 and elasticity of demand = -0.5. Find quantity demanded after a fall in price when initially it was 60 units. Ans: 66

15. The price elasticity of demand for a good is -0.4. If its p rice increases by 5 percent, by what percentage will its demand fall? Calculate. Ans: 2% fall in quantity demanded

16. The demand for good rises by 20 percent as a result of all in its price. Its price elasticity of demand is (-) 0.8. Calculate the percentage fall in price. Ans: 25% fall in price

17. A 5 percent fall in the price of a good rises its demand from 300 units to 318 units. Calculate its price elasticity of demand. Ans: 1.2

18. When the price of commodity falls by 20 percent, its demand rises from 400 units to 500 units. Calculate its price elasticity of demand? Ans: 1.25

19. Price elasticity of demand of a good is -0.75. Calculate the percentage fall in its price that will result in 15 per cent rise in its demand. Ans: 20% fall in price

20. A 20 percent fall in the price of a good, raises its demand from 600 to 750 units. Calculate its price elasticity of demand. Ans: 1.25

21. A consumer buys 18 units of a good at a price of Rs. 9 per unit. The price elasticity of demand for the good is (-) 1. How many units the consumer will buy at a price of Rs. 10 per unit? Calculate. Ans: 16 units

22. Price elasticity of demand of a good is (-) 1. When its price per unit falls by one rupee, its demand rises from 16 to 18 units. Calculate the price before change. Ans: Rs. 8

23. A consumer buys 30 units of a good at a price of Rs.10 per unit. Price elasticity of demand for the good is (-) 1. How many units the consumer will buy at a price of Rs.9 per unit? Calculate. Ans: 33 units

24. When the price of a good falls from Rs.10 to Rs.8 per unit, its demand rises from 20 units to 24 units. What can you say about price elasticity of demand of the good through the 'expenditure approach'? Ans: Inelastic

25. When the price of a good rises from Rs.10 to Rs.12 per unit, its demand falls from 25 units to 20 units. What can you say about price elasticity of demand of the good through the 'expenditure approach'? Ans: Elastic

26. A consumer buys 27 units of a good at a price of Rs.10 per unit. When the price falls to Rs.9 per unit, the demand rises to 30 units. What can you say about price elasticity of demand of the good through the 'expenditure approach'? Ans: Unitary Elastic

27. When price of a good falls from Rs.15 to Rs.12 per unit, its demand rises by 25 per cent. Calculate price elasticity of demand. Ans: 1.25

28. Price elasticity of demand of a good is (-) 1. Calculate the percentage change in price that will raise the demand from 20 units to 30 units. Ans: 50% fall in price

29. What is meant by price elasticity of demand?

30. When is the demand for a good said to be perfectly inelastic?

31. When is the demand for a good said to be inelastic?

32. What is rectangular hyperbola shape of demand curve?

33. What is the difference between elasticity of demand and slope of demand curve?

34. How can we measure the price elasticity of demand?

35. How does point method measures elasticity of demand?

36. Why we have prefixed minus sign to the formula of elasticity of demand?

37. What are the different types of elasticity of demand?

38. Explain various degrees of price elasticity of demand.

39. "Elasticity of demand is constant along a straight line." Defend or Refute the statement

40. How is price elasticity of demand affected by: 1. Number of substitutes available for the good? 2. Nature of the good.

41. Explain any three factors that affect the price elasticity of demand. Give suitable examples.

CHAPTER 6

PRODUCTION FUNCTION

We have discussed the consumer behaviour in the previous chapters. We had discussion on how the rational consumer allocates his limited income on various commodities in order to get maximum satisfaction. In this chapter, we shall examine the behavior of a producer. We will see how firms or producers can produce efficiently and how their cost of production change with changes in both input prices and the level of output. A producer or a firm by utilizing different inputs produces output. This is called the process of production. It is though transformation of inputs into useful things. In other words, it is process of value addition or creation of utility. Firms or producers can turn inputs into outputs in various ways, using various combinations of inputs. We can express the relationship between the inputs into the production process and resulting output by a production function.

Production Function: *"The production function is purely a technical relation which connects factor inputs and output."*-**Koutsoyiannis**

"The rates of output of the products over their time of production depend on the rates of inputs of all the elements of production. This technical relationship, when presented in functional form for a given state of technology, is called a production function." – **Asimakopulos**

In mathematical terms, the production function can be expressed as below:

P=f(L, K) where L stands for Labour and K stands for Capital.

The production function of a firm is a relationship between inputs used and output produced by the firm. It shows the maximum quantity of a commodity that a firm can produce per unit of time with the given amount of inputs, and with given technological knowledge. The production function includes only those processes which are considered technically efficient. The choice of any particular technique out of various technical efficient methods is an economic choice.

Two things must be kept in mind when we discuss the production function.

I.   It must be considered with reference to a particular period of time.
II. It is determined by state of technology.

Short Run versus the Long Run:

Firm can increase the level of output either by increasing some of the factors or by increasing all factors. Now it is important to note that how firm will decide whether to increase level of output either by increasing some of the factors or by increasing all factors. The answer of this pertinent question requires the knowledge of short run or long run periods of time.

Short Run is period of time in which quantities of all factors cannot be changed. Only few of them can be changed. The factor which a firm can change is called variable factor and factor which cannot be changed is called the fixed factor. In other words, during short period firm can change only variable factors to increase production.

Long period is period of time that is required to change all the factors. In other words, firm can vary all its factors to increase production in long period. Long period may be different for different production processes.

Total Product (TP): TP is the sum total of output produced by all the units of the variable factor used in the process of production with other given factors. This is also called total return of the variable factor. When we change one factor of production and keep other factors of production as constant. Then for different units of that input, we get different quantities of output from the given production function. This relationship between the variable factor and output, keeping all other inputs constant, is often referred as Total Physical Output of the variable factor of production.

TP= $\sum$MP or AP*L (L=Units of variable factor)

Marginal Product (MP or MPP): MP is additional output as a result of employment of an additional unit of variable factor of production. **$MP_L = \Delta TP/\Delta L$ or $MP_K = \Delta TP/\Delta K$**

$MP_{nth} = TP_n - TP_{n-1}$

Average Product (AP or APP): AP refers to physical output per unit of the variable factor of production or input used in the process of production.

AP = TP/L or Average Product = Total product $\div$ Number of Units of variable factor

The average product is an indicator of productivity of the variable factor. The average product of labour measures the productivity of the firm's workforce in terms of how much output each worker produces on average.

Units of Labour	Total Product (TP)	Average Product (AP)	Marginal Product (MP)
1	2	2÷1= 2	2
2	5	5÷2=2.5	5-2=3
3	9	9÷3=3	9-5=4
4	12	12÷4=3	12-9=3
5	14	14÷5=2.8	14-12=2

Types of Production Function: As we already mentioned that production function expresses relationship between physical quantities of input and physical output. There are two broad categories of under which we study production functions. One is law of variable proportions and other is law of returns to scale.

The production of a firm can be studied by holding the quantities of some factors fixed, while varying the amount of other factors. This type of production function comes under the law of variable proportions and also known as variable proportion type production function. The production function can also be studied by varying the amounts of all factors. This behavior of production function is the subject matter of the law of returns to scale and also known as constant proportion type production function (under traditional theory). Now we shall examine the difference between these two production functions.

Difference between Law of Return to a Factor and Return to Scale

Basis of Difference	Laws of Returns to a Factor or Law of Variable Proportion Or Short Run Production Function	Laws of Returns to Scale Or Long Run Production Function
Meaning	The term return to a factor refers to change in output as a result of change in only one factor, keeping other factors as constant.	The term return to scale refers to the changes in output as all factors change by same proportion.
Time period	This law is relevant for *short period.*	This law is relevant for *long period.*
Scale	In this type of production function, *scale of production does not change.*	In this type of production function, *scale of production changes.*

Factor ratio	In this type of production function, factor ratio changes. So that's why this is known as *variable proportion* type production function.	In this type of production function (As per traditional approach), factor ratio remains constant. So that's why this is known as *constant proportion* type production function.

Law of Variable of Proportion or Law of Eventually Diminishing Marginal Physical Productivity

This law examines the input-output relation when the output is increased by varying the quantity of one input only. When the number of one factor is increased while all other factors remain constant, then the proportion between factors is changed. On account of change in the proportion of factors there will also be a change in total output at different rates. In economics, this tendency is called law of variable proportion.

Meaning: The law states that an increase in one factor by equal amount with fixed factors of production, cause marginal product to increase initially, but after a point marginal product of the variable factor must eventually decline.

Definition: " *The law of variable proportion states that if the input of one resources is increased by equal increments per unit of time while the inputs of other resources are held constant, total output will increase, but beyond some point the resulting output increase will become smaller and smaller.* "- **Leftwitch**

This law is based on the following assumptions."
1. The state of technology is assumed to be given and unchanged.
2. All units of variable factors are homogeneous.
3. Law applies in short period.
4. There is a possibility of varying the proportion between inputs

Explanation: Law of variable proportion can be explained with the help of table 1 and figure 1. In table 1 column one shows the units of the fixed factor and column two shows the amount of variable factor of production i.e. labour. Column 3, 4, 5 and 6 shows the TP, MP, AP and stages of production respectively. Table shows the classification of stages of production into increasing returns, diminishing returns and negative returns. The behaviour of TP, MP and AP is shown in the table and in the diagram is explained below.

Table: 1   Behavior of TP, MP and AP

Fixed factor (Land)	Variable factor (Labour)	TP	MP	AP = (TP/L)	Stages of production
1	1	2	2	2	
1	2	5	3	2.5	Stage 1 Increasing returns (MP)
1	3	9	4	3	
1	4	12	3	3	
1	5	14	2	2.8	Stage 2 Diminishing returns (MP)
1	6	15	1	2.5	
1	7	15	0	2.1	
1	8	14	-1	1.75	Stage 3 Negative Returns (MP)

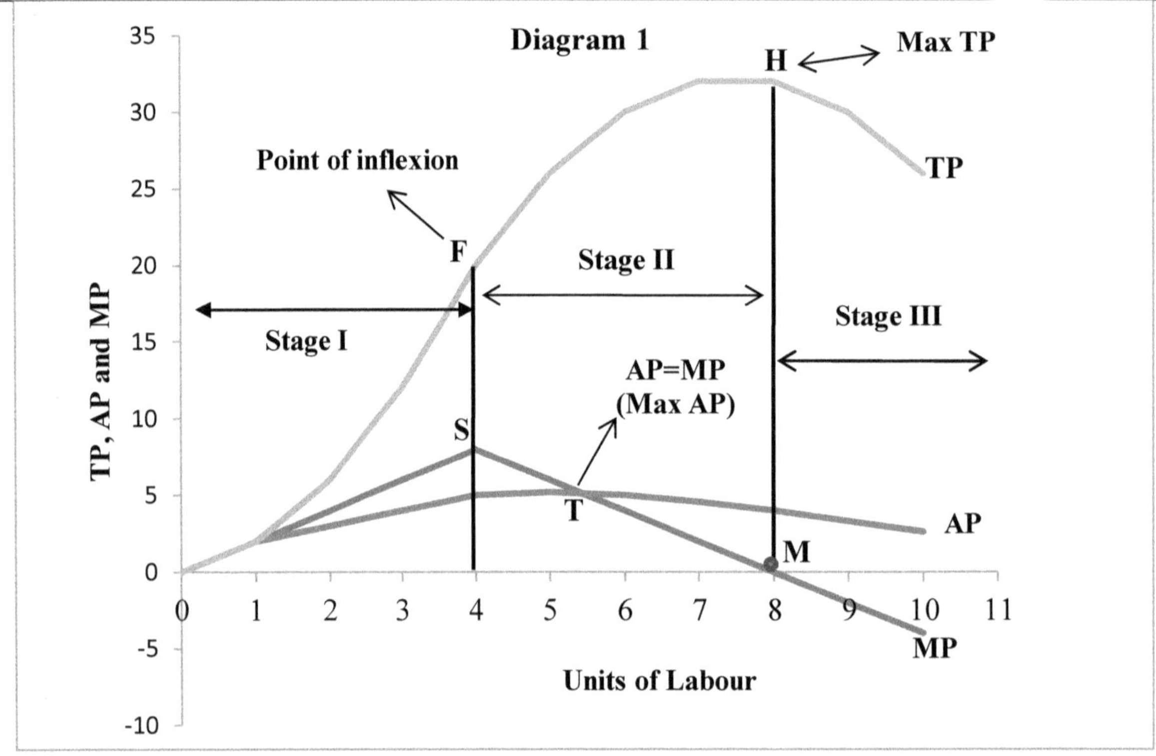

Diagram 1 shows the behaviour of TP, MP and AP curves as we increase the amount of variable factor with fixed factor and this behaviour is explained as follows.

Stage 1: Stage of Increasing Returns: In this stage TP is increasing at increasing rate up to point 'F' which means that marginal product is rising and from the point 'F' onwards the TP increases at diminishing rate i.e. MP is positive and falling. The point 'F' is the **'Point of Inflexion'** from where TP changes its rate of increase from increasing rate to diminishing rate. The Stage 1 ends where the average product curve reaches at its highest point. In 'Stage 1' marginal product of the variable factor is rising more than the increase in average product. 'Stage 1' is known as the stage of increasing return because average product of the variable factor increases throughout this stage.

Stage 2: Stage of Diminishing Return: In this stage the total product continues to increase at a diminishing rate (from 'F' to 'H') until it reaches its maximum point 'H' where the second stage ends. In this stage the marginal product starts declining and become zero at the end of second stage. Whereas, average product of the variable factor increase till point 'T' where it meets MP but after that it starts falling slower than the fall of MP. At the end of the second stage, marginal product of the variable factor becomes zero. This stage is known as the stage of diminishing returns as both the average and marginal product of the variable factor finally falling in this stage.

Stage 3: Stage of Negative Return: In this stage total product starts declining and as a result of this marginal product of the variable factor turns negative and the marginal product curve MP goes below the X- axis. In this stage, variable factor is too much relative to the fixed factor. This stage is called the stage of negative return due to negative marginal product of the variable factor.

Table: Three Stages of Production

Stage	TP	AP	MP
I	In this stage TP is increasing at increasing rate up to point 'F'.	AP increases in this stage but lies below MP i.e. AP<MP.	Increases from 'O' to 'S', and reaches at its maximum point.
II	From the point 'F' onwards the TP increases at diminishing rate and continues to increase at a diminishing rate until it reaches its maximum point 'H'.	AP increases and reaches its maximum at point 'T' and AP=MP. After this point AP begins to diminish but AP>MP.	It begins to diminish and becomes zero at 'M'.
III	It starts declining and TP curve slopes downward.	AP continuous to diminish in this stage and AP>MP.	Turned negative.

Causes of Increasing Returns to a Factor

1. **Fuller Utilisation of the Fixed Factor**: In the initial stages, fixed factor remains underutilized. Its fuller utilisation calls for greater application of the variable factor. Hence, initially, additional units of the variable factor add more and more units to total output.
2. **Increased Efficiency of the Variable Factor and Division of Labour**: Additional application of the variable factor causes process based division of labour that raises efficiency of the factor. Accordingly MP of the factor tends to rise.
3. **Better Co-Ordination between the Factors**: So long as fixed factor remains underutilized, additional application of the variable factor tends to improve the degree of co-ordination between the fixed and variable factors. As a result, output increases at the increasing rate.

Causes of Diminishing Returns to a Factor

1. **Fixity of the factor**: Fixity of the factor is the principal cause that explains the occurrence of the law of diminishing returns. As more and more units of the variable factor continue to be combined with the fixed factor, the latter gets over utilised. Hence, the diminishing returns occur.
2. **Imperfect factor substitutability**: According to Mrs. Joan Robinson factors of production are imperfect substitute of each other. More and more of labour cannot be used in place of land that is a fixed factor. Accordingly, diminishing returns to the variable factor become inevitable.
3. **Poor co-ordination between the factors**: Continues increasing application of the variable factor along with fixed factor disturbs the ideal factor ratio. This results poor co-ordination between the fixed and variable factors and diminishing returns to a factor happens.

Causes of Negative Returns to a Factor

1. Negative returns occur due to excessive application of variable factor with fixed factor, even after the complete exhaustion of fixed factor.

Rational Stage of Production/ Stage of Operation: A rational producer always seek to produce in stage 2, where MP is zero and TP is at maximum point and producer is making maximum use of his resources.

Stage 2 is the Rational Stage of Production

A rational producer will never choose to produce in **Stage 1 and 3**. Because in Stage 1 the fixed factors are too much relative to the variable factor therefore MP of the fixed factor is negative. In Stage 3 variable factors is the much relative to the fixed factor, therefore MP of the variable factor is negative. Stage 1 and 3 represent non economic region in production function.

Relationship between TP, AP and MP

Total Product (TP): TP is the sum total of output produced by all the units of the variable factor used in the process of production with other given factors.

TP= $\sum$MP or

TP= AP×L (L=Units of variable factor)

Marginal Product (MP or MPP): MP is additional output as a result of employment of an additional unit of variable factor of production.

$MP_{nth} = TP_n - TP_{n-1}$

Average Product (AP or APP): AP refers to physical output per unit of the variable factor of production or input used in the process of production.

$$AP = \frac{TP}{L}$$

I.   We can determine the value of other two if the value of one is given, from the following relationship

TP= $\sum$MP or AP×L (L=Units of variable factor), $MP_{nth} = TP_n - TP_{n-1}$,

$$AP = \frac{TP}{L}$$

II. As long as MP is positive and rising TP increases at increasing rate and AP is also increasing but MP>AP.

III. As long as MP is positive and falling TP increases at decreasing rate and AP is also increasing but AP>MP.

IV. When MP becomes zero, TP reaches at its maximum point, and AP is declining but AP>MP

V.   When MP turned negative, TP starts falling, and AP continues to diminish but AP>MP.

Relation between TP and MP	Relation between AP and MP
As long as MP is positive and rising, TP increases at increasing rate. MP is at its highest point corresponding to point of inflexion.	As long as AP is rising MP>AP and as long as AP is decreasing, AP>MP. There is a range of output where MP starts falling and AP is still rising, this just happens purely due to mathematical relationship between MP and AP. Because, being a rate of change MP rapidly increases and rapidly falls as compared to AP.
As long as MP is positive and falling, TP increases at decreasing rate.	AP becomes equal to MP when AP reaches at its maximum point. MP cuts AP at its highest point, or MP is falling when AP=MP.
When MP becomes zero, TP reaches at its maximum point, when MP turned negative, TP starts falling.	When MP turned negative, AP continues to diminish but remain positive.

Returns to a Factor: When a producer effects a change in his production by increasing or decreasing only one factor and as a result there is change in the proportion of combination of factors of production, then this proportional relationship between production and factors of production is referred as law of returns to a factor.

Increasing Returns to a Factor (Diminishing Cost): Increasing returns to a factor refers to a situation in which total output tends to increase at increasing rate when more of the variable factor is combined with the fixed factors of production

L	K	TP	MP	TC	AC
1	1	2	2	100	50
2	1	5	3	200	40
3	1	9	4	300	33
4	1	14	5	400	29
5	1	20	6	500	25

Constant Returns to a Factor (Constant Cost): Constant returns to a factor refers to a situation in which total output tends to increase at constant rate when more of the variable factor is combined with the fixed factors of production

L	K	TP	MP	TC	AC
1	1	5	5	100	20
2	1	10	5	200	20
3	1	15	5	300	20
4	1	20	5	400	20
5	1	25	5	500	20

Diminishing Returns to a Factor (Increasing Cost): Diminishing returns to a factor refer to a situation in which total output tends to increase at diminishing rate when more of the variable factor is combined with the fixed factors of production.

L	K	TP	MP	TC	AC
1	1	5	5	100	20
2	1	9	4	200	22
3	1	12	3	300	25
4	1	14	2	400	28
5	1	15	1	500	33

****

Exercise:

1. When MP is falling, TPP will be 1. Convex, 2. Concave, 3. Straight line 4. Horizontal line
2. Which of the following can be used to measure TPP? 1. AP*L 2. ΣMP 3. Both I&II 4. None of the above
3. Which of the following can be negative? 1. TP 2. APP 3. AP 4. MPP
4. Which of the following is considered as 'Rational stage of production'? 1. First 2. Second 3. Third 4. None of the above
5. In case of increasing returns, which of the following is true? I. MP>AP II. TP increases at increasing rate III. Both I&II IV. None of the above
6. Point of inflexion refers to that point where: 1. TP starts increasing 2. TP stops increasing 3. MP = 0 4. TP starts increasing at diminishing rate from increasing rate
7. Marginal product curve is a: 1. Inverted S-shaped 2. Inverted U-shaped 3. Rectangular hyperbola 4. None of these
8. Production function shows the _______ relationship between physical inputs and physical output. 1. Behavioural 2. Economic 3. Technical 4. None of the above
9. Total output is maximum when marginal product is _______. 1. Zero 2. Negative 3. Positive 4. None of the above
10. Law of variable proportions operates only if factor ratio happens to change. Statement is true or false.
11. MP curve makes an inverted-U because of the operation of law of variable proportions. Statement is true or false.
12. AP is maximum where MP = 0. Statement is true or false.
13. Average cost will increase in case of 1. Increasing returns 2. Diminishing returns 3. Constant returns 4. None of above
14. When TP increases, then MP will 1. Increase 2. Decrease 3. Both 1&2 4. Constant
15. In short period only labour is fixed factor. Statement is true or false.

Answers

1. 2	2. 3	3. 4	4. 2	5. 3
6. 4	7. 2	8. 3	9. 1	10.T
11.T	12.F	13.2	14.3	15.F

NCERT QUESTIONS:

1. What is the total product of an input?

2. What is the average product of an input?
3. What is the marginal product of an input?
4. Explain the concept of production function.
5. Explain the relationship between the marginal product and the total product of an input.
6. Explains the concepts of the short run and the long run.
7. What is law of diminishing marginal product?
8. What is law of variable proportions?
9. The following table gives the total product schedule of labour. Find the corresponding average product and marginal product schedules of labour.

L	0	1	2	3	4	5
AP_L	0	15	35	50	40	48

10. The following table gives the average product schedule of labour. Find the total product and marginal product schedules. It is given that the total product is zero at zero level of labour employment.

L	1	2	3	4	5	6
AP_L	2	3	4	4.25	4	3.5

11. The following table gives the marginal product schedule of labour. It is also given that total product of labour is zero at zero level of employment. Calculate the total and average product schedules of labour.

L	1	2	3	4	5	6
AP_L	3	5	7	5	3	1

12. Let the production function of a firm be: $Q = 5L^{\frac{1}{2}}K^{\frac{1}{2}}$. Find out the maximum possible output that the firm can produce with 100 units of L and 100 units of K. (Ans: 500)

13. Let the production function of a firm be: $Q = 2L^2K^2$. Find out the maximum possible output that the firm can produce with 5 units of L and 2 units of K. (Ans: 200)

14. Find out the maximum possible output for a firm with 10 units of L and 10 units of K when its production function is: Q=5L+2K (Ans: 70)

Schedules

1. The following table gives the total product schedule of labour. Find the corresponding average product and marginal product schedule of labour.

Labour	0	1	2	3	4	5
TP_L	0	15	35	50	40	48

2. Calculate the APPs and MPPs of a factor from the following table of its TPP schedule:

Labour	0	1	2	3	4	5	6	7
TPP	0	5	12	20	28	35	40	42

3. Calculate the total and average product from the given schedules.

Labour	1	2	3	4	5	6
MP_L	3	5	7	5	3	1

4. The following tables gives the APP of a factor, it is also known that the TPP at zero level of labour is zero. Determine its TPP and MPP schedule:

Units of labour	1	2	3	4	5
APP	50	45	40	35	30

5. Identify the different phases of the law of variable proportions from the following schedule. Give reasons for your answer.

Units of variable inputs	1	2	3	4	5
TPP units	4	9	13	15	12

6. Identify the three phases of the law of variable proportion from the following and also give reasons behind each phase:

Units of variable inputs	1	2	3	4	5
TPP units	10	22	30	35	30

7. Complete the following table assuming that there is increasing returns to a factor throughout and also find MPP.

Units of variable inputs	1	2	3	4
TPP units	100			

8. Complete the following table assuming that there are constant returns to a factor throughout and draw the TPP and MPP on graph and comment on their shapes.

Units of variable inputs	1	2	3	4
TPP units	50			

9. Complete the following table assuming that there is decreasing returns to a factor throughout and draw the TPP and MPP on graph and comment on their shapes.

Units of variable inputs	1	2	3	4
TPP units	10			

10. Complete the following table:

Units of labour	0	1	2	3	4	5	6
TPP	0	20			88		
MPP			22			17	
APP	-			22			20

11. Complete the following table:

Units of labour	1	2	3	4	5	6
APP	8	10	-	9	-	7
MPP	-	-	10	-	4	-

Answers

1. The following table gives the total product schedule of labour. Find the corresponding average product and marginal product schedule of labour.

Labour	0	1	2	3	4	5
TP_L	0	15	35	50	40	48
MP_L	-	15	20	15	10	8
AP_L	-	15	17.5	25	20	24

2. Calculate the APPs and MPPs of a factor from the following table of its TPP schedule:

Labour	0	1	2	3	4	5	6	7
TPP	0	5	12	20	28	35	40	42
MP_L	-	5	7	8	8	7	5	2
AP_L	-	5	6	6.33	7	7	6.67	6

3. Calculate the total and average product from the given schedules.

Labour	1	2	3	4	5	6
MP_L	3	5	7	5	3	1
TP_L	3	8	15	20	23	24
AP_L	3	4	5	5	4.6	4

4. The following tables gives the APP of a factor, it is also known that the TPP at zero level of labour is zero. Determine its TPP and MPP schedule:

Units of Labour	1	2	3	4	5
APP	50	45	40	35	30
TP_L	50	90	120	140	150
MP_L	50	40	30	20	10

5. Identify the different phases of the law of variable proportions from the following schedule. Give reasons for your answer. (IR: Increasing Returns, DR: Diminishing Returns, NR: Negative Returns)

Units of variable inputs	1	2	3	4	5
TPP units	4	9	13	15	12
MPP	4 (IR)	5 (IR)	4 (DR)	2 (DR)	-3 (NR)

6. Identify the three phases of the law of variable proportion from the following and also give reasons behind each phase:

Units of variable inputs	1	2	3	4	5
TPP units	10	22	30	35	30
MPP	10 (IR)	12 (IR)	8 (DR)	5 (DR)	-5 (NR)

7. Complete the following table assuming that there is increasing returns to a factor throughout and also find MPP.

Units of variable inputs	1	2	3	4
TPP units	100	210	330	460
MPP	100	110	120	130

8. Complete the following table assuming that there are constant returns to a factor throughout and draw the TPP and MPP on graph and comment on their shapes.

Units of variable inputs	1	2	3	4
TPP units	50	100	150	200
MPP	50	50	50	50

9. Complete the following table assuming that there is decreasing returns to a factor throughout and draw the TPP and MPP on graph and comment on their shapes.

Units of variable inputs	1	2	3	4
TPP units	10	18	24	28
MPP	10	8	6	4

10. Complete the following table:

Units of labour	0	1	2	3	4	5	6
TPP	0	20	42	66	88	105	120
MPP		20	22	24	22	17	15
APP	-	20	21	22	22	21	20

11. Complete the following table:

Units of labour	1	2	3	4	5	6
APP	8	10	10	9	8	7
MPP	8	12	10	6	4	2
TPP	8	20	30	36	40	42

Practice Questions:

1. Define production function. What are its types?
2. What is short and long run in context of production function?
3. Define marginal product and average product. Explain their relationship in case of increasing returns to a factor.
4. Giving reason, explain the behaviour of total product under the law of variable proportions. Use diagram.
5. Explain the law of variable proportion with the help of schedule and diagram.
6. Explain the relationship between TP, AP and MP.
7. Explain the diminishing return to factor with behaviour of TP and MP.
8. Explain the law of variable proportions with the help of TPP and MMP curves.
9. Difference between 'returns to a factor' and returns to scale.

10.Explain the relationship between TP and MP in all stages of production.

11.State the behaviour of marginal product in the law of variable proportions. Explain the causes of this behaviour.

12.Giving reasons, explain the 'law of variable proportions'.

13.Explain the various stages of law of variable proportion. Which stage is considered as rational stage of production?

14.Why second stage is considered as rational stage?

CHAPTER 7

CONCEPT OF REVENUE

Revenue is an important concept to study producer's behaviour. Without measuring it producer won't be able to ascertain his profits or market share of his product or services. Revenue refers to the money that producer receives by selling goods and services in the market. It is also known as sale proceeds. Size of revenue that producer obtained from selling the goods and services depends mainly upon the demand of that good or service in the market, assuming other factors as constant more demand means more revenue and vice versa.

There are three concepts of revenue

Total Revenue/Gross Revenue (TR): Total amount of money received by the firm from the sale of a certain quantity of output is called total receipts or revenue. Total revenue depends upon the quantity of output sold in the market. It is calculated by multiplying price (P) with quantity sold (Q). **TR= P*Q**

> **Total Revenue = Price × Quantity Sold**

For example if firm sells 50 units of a commodity at Rs. 20 per unit, then total revenue will be 50*20= Rs. 1000

Profit: It is the surplus income obtained by subtracting cost from revenue. Keeping other things constant there is direct relationship between profit and revenue. Higher revenues lead to higher profit and vice versa provided there is no change in per unit cost.

> **Profit = Revenue - Cost**

Average Revenue (AR): Average revenue is the amount of revenue earned per unit of the product sold. It is calculated by dividing the total revenue by number of units of the product sold. **AR= TR/Q or PQ/Q =P**

If all units of a commodity sold at the same price, then average revenue is equal to the price of the commodity.

For example, if firm sells 50 units of a commodity for Rs. 1000, then per unit revenue will be Rs.1000÷50= Rs. 20 per unit.

Marginal Revenue (MR): MR refers to the change in total revenue which results from the sale of one extra or one less unit of a commodity.

$$\text{MR}_{nth} = \text{TR}_n - \text{TR}_{n-1} \text{ or MR} = \frac{\text{Change in TR}}{\text{Change in Quantity}} \text{ or MR} = \frac{\Delta \text{TR}}{\Delta \text{Q}}$$

For example if total revenue received by firm from sale of 10 units of a commodity is Rs. 1000 and from 11 units it is Rs. 1020. Then MR of 11th unit will be the change in total revenue caused by sale of additional unit of a commodity i.e. Rs.1020- Rs.1000= Rs. 20

Relationship between TR, AR and MR

1. TR, AR and MR can be calculated from each other if value of one of them is given. $\textbf{TR= AR} \times \textbf{Q}$, $\textbf{AR=} \dfrac{\textbf{TR}}{\textbf{Q}}$, $\textbf{MR}_{\textbf{nth}} = \textbf{TR}_\textbf{n} \textbf{-TR}_{\textbf{n-1}}$, $\textbf{TR =} \sum \textbf{MR}$

Relationship and Nature of Revenue Curves When Price is Constant

The following observations are obtained from table 1 regarding the nature and shapes of revenues curves when price remains constant for any quantity sold. This type of relationship between various revenues curves is found in perfect competition.

1. TR increases at constant rate as long as MR is positive and constant.
2. **AR=MR**
3. Both AR and MR are constant.

Table 1				
Quantity Sold (Q)	**Price** (P)	(TR= P×Q)	(AR=TR/Q)	(MR= ΔTR/ΔQ)
0	5	0	-	-
1	5	5	5	5
2	5	10	5	5
3	5	15	5	5
4	5	20	5	5

Diagram 1

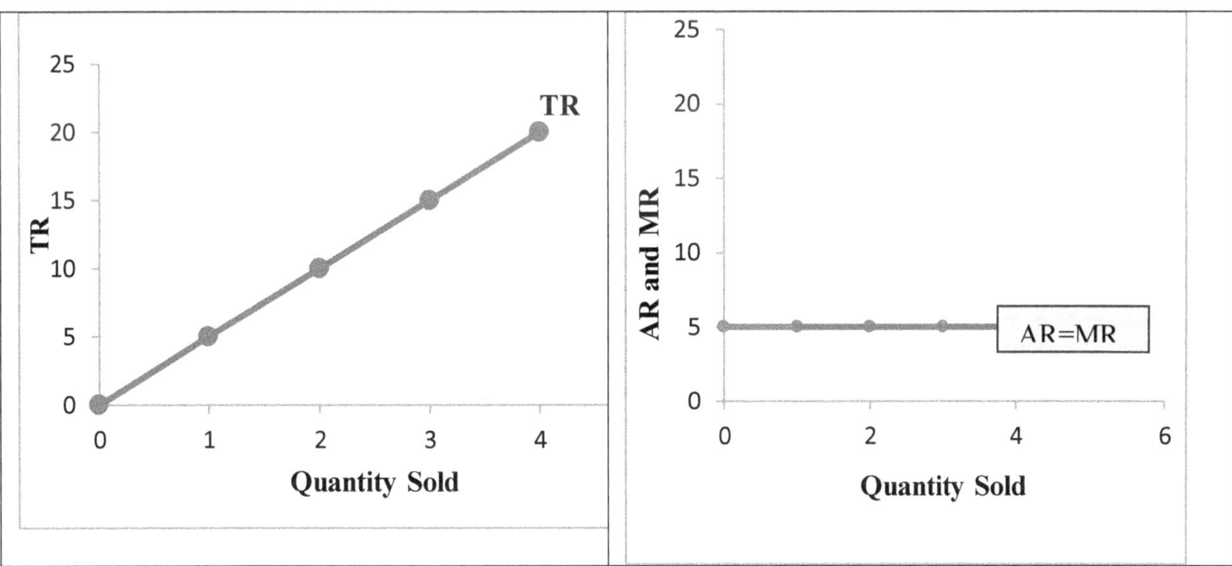

Relationship and Nature of Revenue Curves When Price Varies

The following observations are obtained from table 2 regarding the nature and shapes of revenues curves when price is reduced to increase the sale of a product. These curves are found in monopoly and monopolistic competition.

1. TR increases at diminishing rate as long as MR is positive and falling.
2. TR attains its maximum point corresponding to zero value of MR.
3. TR starts falling when MR becomes negative.
4. Area under the MR curve is TR.
5. Both AR and MR are downward sloping straight lines, such that AR>MR.
6. The slope of MR curve is twice of the slope of AR curve, due to which MR curve is equi-distant from Y-axis and AR curve.

Table 2				
Quantity Sold (Q)	**Price** (P)	(TR= PQ)	(AR=TR/Q)	(MR= ΔTR/ΔQ)
0	11	0	-	-
1	10	10	10	10
2	9	18	9	8
3	8	24	8	6
4	7	28	7	4
5	6	30	6	2
6	5	30	5	0
7	4	28	4	-2

Diagram 2

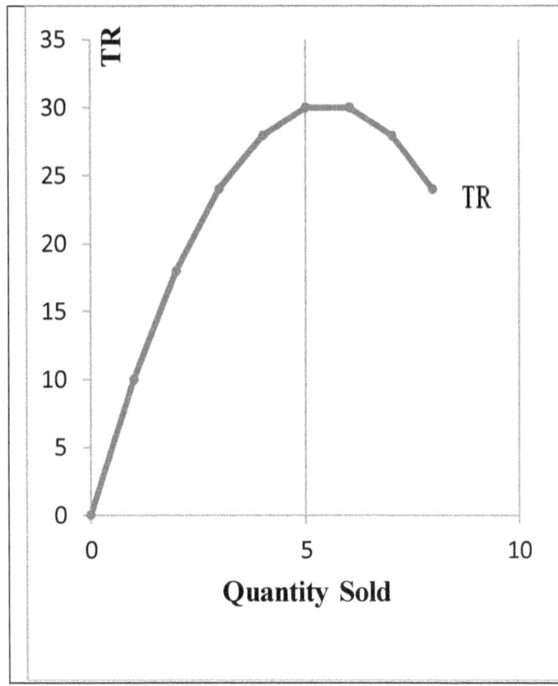

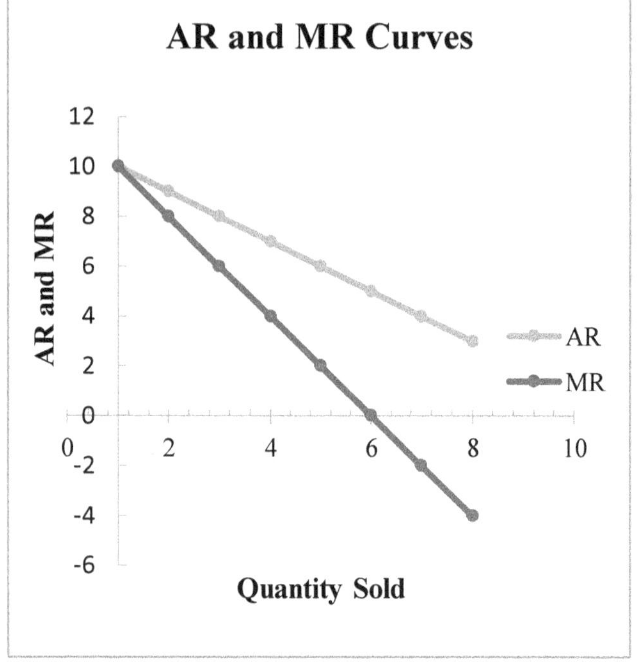

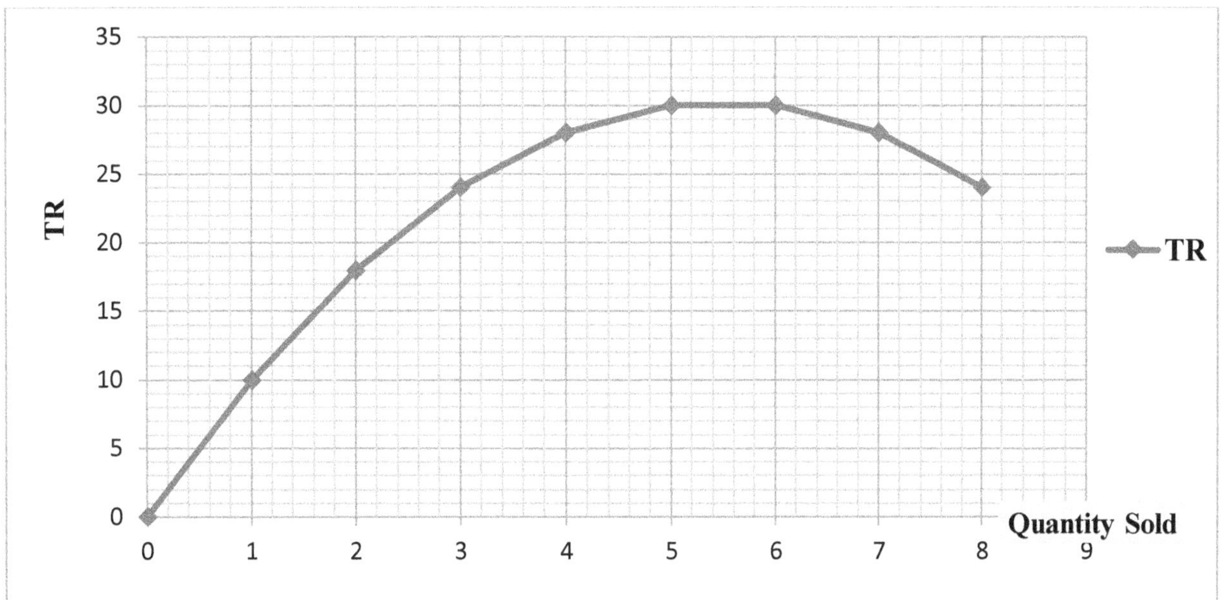

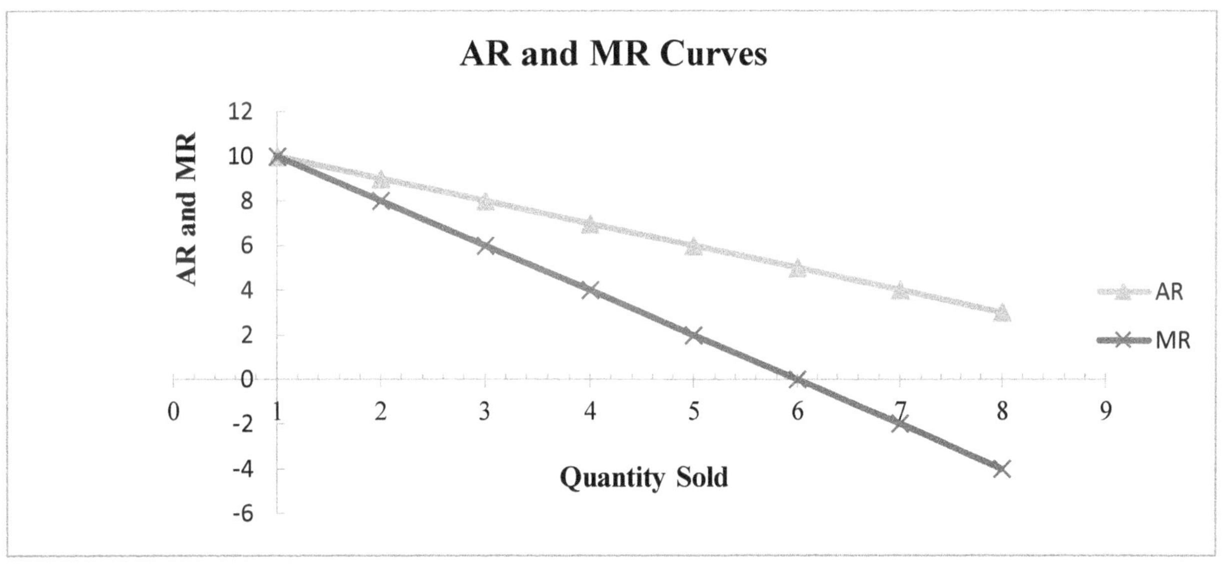

****

Exercise

1. Revenue = 1. Costs – Profit 2. Costs + Profit 3. Costs × Profit 4. Costs ÷ Profit
2. For a perfectly competitive firm, price is: 1. Greater than MR 2. Equal to TR 3. Equal to MR 4. Less than MR
3. Select the correct option: 1. TR=ΣAR 2. TR = ΣMR 3. AR= MR*Q 4. TR = MR*Q
4. Under monopoly, MR can be negative only when: 1. AR is increasing 2. AR is decreasing 3. AR is constant 4. AR is Zero
5. When TR is increases at constant rate, MR should be: 1. Increasing 2. Decreasing 3. Constant 4. Zero

6. MR is below the AR under: 1. Perfect competition 2. Monopoly 3. Monopolistic competition 4. Both 2 & 3

7. Firm's AR curve is the same as: 1. Budget line 2. PPC 3. Firm's supply curve 4. Firm's demand curve

8. Area under the MR curve shows the 1. TR 2. AR 3. Gross Profit 4. Net Profit

9. In case of perfect competition TR always increases with increase in sale. Statement is true or false.

10. $\Sigma MR = AR*Q$ always true. Statement is true or false.

Answers:

1. 2	2. 3	3. 2	4. 2	5. 3
6. 4	7. 4	8. 1	9. T	10.T

Schedule:

1. Complete the following table:

Price (in Rs.)	Output (in units)	Total Revenue (in Rs.)	Marginal Revenue (in Rs.)
	1	6	
4			2
	3	6	
1			-2

2. Complete the following table when each unit of a commodity can be sold at Rs.5.

Quantity Sold	1	2	3	4	5	6	8
TR							
MR							
AR							

3. The demand schedule facing a monopoly is given below. Derive its TR, AR and MR schedules.

Price	0	10	20	30	40	50	60	70
Quantity demanded (in units)	8	7	6	5	4	3	2	1

4. Derive the TR and AR schedules

Qty	0	1	2	3	4	5	6	7
MR	-	14	10	7	5	0	-3	-5

5. A trader can sell 3 smart phones at Rs.1000 per set. If he sells 4 phones, his marginal revenue is Rs.850. At what price will he sell all the four?

6. Complete the following table:

Output	4	5	7	8
TR			56	
AR		10	8	6
MR		2		

7. Complete the following table:

Output (in units)	1	2	3	4	5
AR	10		8		
MR	10	8		0	
TR	10				20

8. Complete the TR, MR and AR schedule in the following table. Market price of each unit of good is Rs.10.

Output (in units)	1	2	3	4	5	6
TR						
MR						
AR						

9. Complete the following table:

Price	Output (units)	Total Revenue (Rs.)	Marginal Revenue (Rs.)
10	1		
	2	14	4
4		12	
	4		-4

10. Complete the following table:

Price	Output (units)	Total Revenue (Rs.)	Marginal Revenue (Rs.)
7		7	
	2	10	
	3		-1
1			-5

Answers

1. Complete the following table:

Price	Output	Total Revenue	Marginal Revenue
6	1	6	6
4	2	8	2
2	3	6	2
1	4	4	-2

2. Complete the following table when each unit of a commodity can be sold at Rs.5.

Quantity Sold	1	2	3	4	5	6	8
TR	5	10	15	20	25	30	40
MR	5	5	5	5	5	5	10/2
AR	5	5	5	5	5	5	5

3. The demand schedule facing a monopoly is given below. Derive its TR, AR and MR schedules.

Price (AR)	0	10	20	30	40	50	60	70

Quantity Demanded	8	7	6	5	4	3	2	1
TR	0	70	120	150	160	150	120	70
MR		-70	-50	-30	-10	10	30	50	70

4. Derive the TR and AR schedules

Qty	0	1	2	3	4	5	6	7
MR	-	14	10	7	5	0	-3	-5
TR	0	14	24	31	36	36	33	28
AR	-	14	12	10.33	9	7.2	5.5	4

5. A trader can sell 3 smart phones at Rs.1000 per set. If he sells 4 phones, his marginal revenue is Rs.850. At what price will he sell all the four? (Ans: 962.5)

6. Complete the following table:

Output (in units)	4	5	7	8
TR	48	50	56	48
AR	12	10	8	6
MR	-	2	6	-8

7. Complete the following table:

Output (in units)	1	2	3	4	5
AR	10	9	8	6	4
MR	10	8	6	0	-4
TR	10	18	24	24	20

8. Complete the TR, MR and AR schedule in the following table. Market price of each unit of good is Rs.10.

Output (in units)	1	2	3	4	5	6
TR	10	20	30	40	50	60
MR	10	10	10	10	10	10
AR	10	10	10	10	10	10

9. Complete the following table:

Price (Rs.)	Output (units)	Total Revenue (Rs.)	Marginal Revenue (Rs.)
10	1	10	10
7	2	14	4
4	3	12	-2
2	4	8	-4

10. Complete the following table:

Price	Output (units)	Total Revenue (Rs.)	Marginal Revenue (Rs.)
7	1	7	7
5	2	10	3
3	3	9	-1
1	4	4	-5

1. What is revenue?
2. What is difference between revenue and profit?
3. Explain the relationship between TR, AR and MR under perfect competition.
4. Explain the relationship between TR, AR and MR under imperfect competition.
5. Explain the relationship between TR, AR and MR when price is constant.
6. How are the total revenue of a firm, market price, and the quantity sold by the firm related to each other?
7. Explain with the help of schedule and diagram that TR= ΣMR.
8. Why is the total revenue curve of a price taking firm an upward sloping straight line? Why does the curve pass through the origin?
9. What is the relation between market price and average revenue of a price taking firm?
10. What is the relation between market price and marginal revenue of a price taking firm?
11. Comment on the shape of the MR curve in case the TR curve is:
    a) A positively sloped straight line passing through the origin
    b) A horizontal line

CHAPTER 8

CONCEPTS OF COST

As we have discussed in previous chapter, the input-output relations in terms of physical quantities of input and output. However, the decisions of producer about quantum of production are taken on the basis of money value of the inputs and outputs. Generally, producers are willing to produce those levels of output corresponding to which the gap between cost of production and revenue is maximum. This chapter pertains to the study of cost-output relationship and various concepts of costs that are vital part of the study of producer behavior.

Cost of Production and Cost function

Cost of Production refers to the total amount spent on acquiring the services of factor inputs (Land, Labour, Capital and Entrepreneur) and non factor inputs (Raw material etc.).

Cost Function expresses the relationship between cost and level of output. Symbolically, $C=f(Q)$. Here, C is cost of production and Q is level of output.

Explicit and Implicit Costs

Explicit costs are those cash payments which firms make to outsiders for their services and goods. For example, payments made to suppliers of raw materials, interest paid to bank on loan, payments to transport companies, salaries and wages to workers, payments of taxes to the government, payment of insurance (fire or theft) premiums, depreciation charges, rent paid for hired land or building etc. The explicit costs are also known as accounting costs.

Implicit costs are imputed costs of owner's own factors or resources used in the process of production. According to Leftwitch, "Implicit costs of production are costs of self owned, self employed resources." For example, Interest on owners own capital, rent for owners own land, wages of his own labour and normal profits for his entrepreneurial functions etc.

Total Economic Cost: It is the sum of explicit and implicit costs.

> ### Total Economic Cost = Explicit Cost + Implicit Cost

Short Run Nature of Costs: Short Run is period of time in which quantities of all factors cannot be changed. The factor which a firm can change is called variable factor and factor which cannot be changed is called the fixed factor. Accordingly, short run costs have two components. **I. Fixed Costs (FC or TFC)**

II. Variable Costs (VC or TVC)

> **Short Run Total Cost = Fixed Cost + Variable Cost**

Fixed/Supplementary/Overhead/ Indirect/Unavoidable costs: These are costs which remain fixed even when output changes. In the words of Benham, "The fixed costs are those costs that do not vary with the size of its output." If the production is zero, fixed costs remain same as shown in Table 1. Total fixed cost curve is a horizontal line parallel to X-axis. Examples of fixed costs are salary of permanent staff, interest on fixed capital, licence fee, insurance premiums etc.

Table 1. Total Fixed Cost		Diagram 1
Output	**TFC**	
0	10	
1	10	
2	10	
3	10	
4	10	
5	10	

Variable/Prime/Direct/Avoidable Cost: These are costs which vary as the level of output varies. They are directly related with output. They rise with increase in output and fall with decrease in output. When production is zero, variable cost is

Table 2. Total Variable Cost		Diagram 2
Output	**TVC**	
0	0	
1	10	
2	18	
3	24	
4	28	
5	32	
6	38	
7	46	
8	56	
9	68	
10	82	

also zero. It is cost which is incurred on the use of variable factor and non factor inputs. For example, expenditure on raw materials, wages to temporary workers, electricity expenses (without minimum charges), taxes, depreciation etc. The shape of TVC curve is inverted 'S' as shown in diagram 2.

Why TVC curve looks like inverted 'S' shaped?

Initially, TVC increases at diminishing rate, then at constant rate and finally at increasing rate. This behavior of TVC made its appearance like inverted 'S'. The rate of increases of TVC is determined by the three stages of returns to a factor, viz. increasing returns, constant returns, and decreasing returns. TVC increases at a diminishing rate when law of increasing returns to a factor is operating. It starts increasing at constant rate and increasing rate corresponding to operation of law of constant returns and increasing returns to a factor respectively.

Total Cost: In the short run, total cost is the sum total of fixed cost and variable cost (**TC =TFC+TVC). The** behavior of TC curve is shown by the schedule 3 and diagram 3.

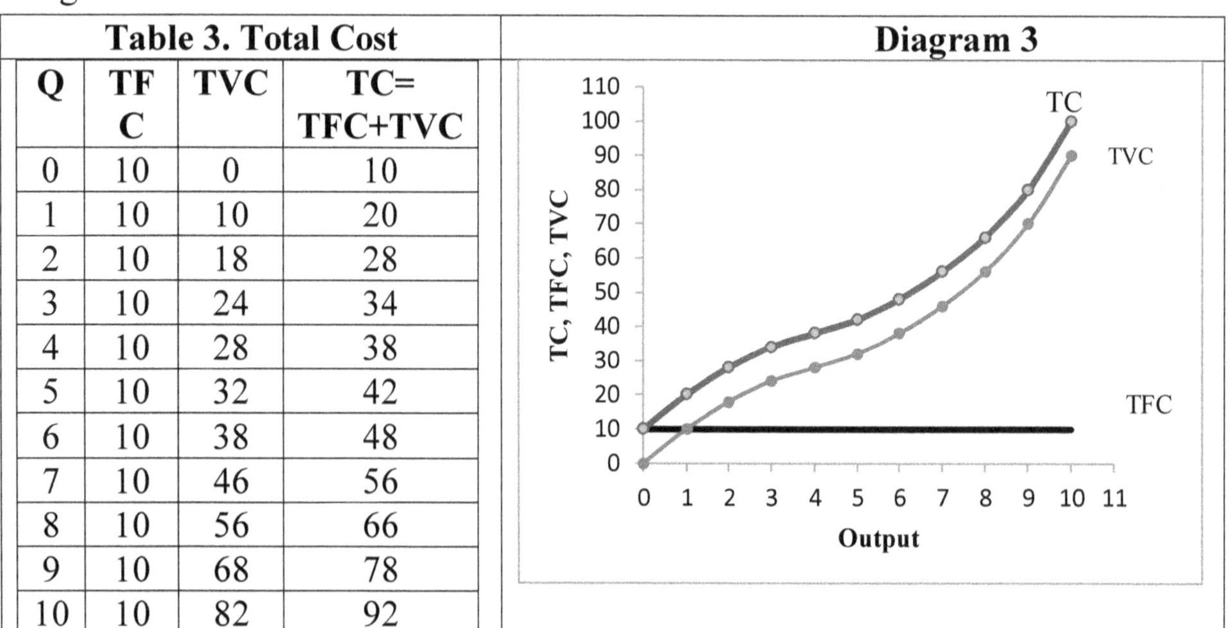

Table 3. Total Cost			
Q	TFC	TVC	TC= TFC+TVC
0	10	0	10
1	10	10	20
2	10	18	28
3	10	24	34
4	10	28	38
5	10	32	42
6	10	38	48
7	10	46	56
8	10	56	66
9	10	68	78
10	10	82	92

TC starts from the Y axis i.e. from where fixed cost starts. This means that when output is zero TC is equal to TFC. Both TC and TVC are of inverted 'S' shaped. The difference between total cost and variable cost remains constant. Hence, TC and TVC are always parallel to each other as shown in diagram 2.

Average Fixed Cost (AFC): It is fixed cost per unit of output. It is calculated by dividing total fixed cost by total output. AFC = TFC/Q. AFC falls as level of output increases. Initially, AFC falls rapidly, after that its fall becomes gradual.

Graphically, AFC curve is downward sloping curve and never touches X-axis (Asymptotic to base line, as Q→∞, AFC→0). It is a rectangular hyperbola. This shows that TFC remains constant at all levels of output.

Table: 4	
Output	**AFC**
0	∞
1	10.0
2	5.0
3	3.3
4	2.5
5	2.0
6	1.7
7	1.4
8	1.3
9	1.1

Diagram: 4

Average Variable Cost (AVC): It is fixed cost per unit of output. It is calculated by dividing total variable cost by total output (AVC = TVC/Q). Graphically, AVC is U shaped. Initially, AVC falls due to operation of law of increasing return to a factor, and then it falls gradually and reaches at lowest point due to operation of law of constant returns to a factor as shown in table 5 and diagram 5. Finally, AVC rises in accordance with diminishing returns to a factor. AVC looks like U, because of the operation of law of variable proportion.

Table: 5	
Output	**AVC**
0	-
1	10.0
2	9.0
3	8.0
4	7.0
5	6.4
6	6.3
7	6.6
8	7.0
9	7.8
10	9.0

Diagram: 5

Average Cost is defined as the cost per unit of output. It is calculated by dividing total cost by total output as shown in table 6 and 7. AC curve is also 'U' shaped as shown in diagram 6 and 7.

[AC=TC/Q or (TFC+TVC)/Q or AC=AFC+AVC]

Table: 6	
Output	**AC**
0	-
1	20
2	14
3	11
4	10
5	8
6	8
7	8
8	8
9	9
10	10

Diagram: 6

Table: 7			
Q	**AFC**	**AVC**	**AC**
0	∞	-	-
1	10.0	10.0	20
2	5.0	9.0	14
3	3.3	8.0	11
4	2.5	7.0	10
5	2.0	6.4	8
6	1.7	6.3	8
7	1.4	6.6	8
8	1.3	7.0	8
9	1.1	7.8	9
10	1.0	9.0	10

Diagram: 7

Marginal Cost is the change in total cost/total variable cost due to the addition of one unit of output as shown in table 8. MC curve is also 'U' shaped as shown in diagram 8.

$MC = \Delta TC/\Delta Q$ or $\Delta TVC/\Delta Q$, $MC_{nth} = TC_n - TC_{n-1}$ or $TVC_n - TVC_{n-1}$,

Here, ΔTC = Change in total cost, ΔQ = Change in output, MC_{nth} = MC of nth unit of output, TC_n = Total cost of 'n' units of output, TC_{n-1} = Total cost of 'n-1' units of output.

For example: Total cost of producing 2 units of output is Rs. 28 and of 3 units it is Rs. 34. Marginal cost of 3rd unit will be the change in TC i.e. 34-28= Rs. 6.

Feature of MC:

1. It is a variable cost and independent of fixed cost.

2. It can be calculated from TC and TVC as shown in table 9.
3. Its summation is equal to TVC i.e. **∑MC= TVC (See table 9).**
4. It is U-shaped as shown in diagram 4.

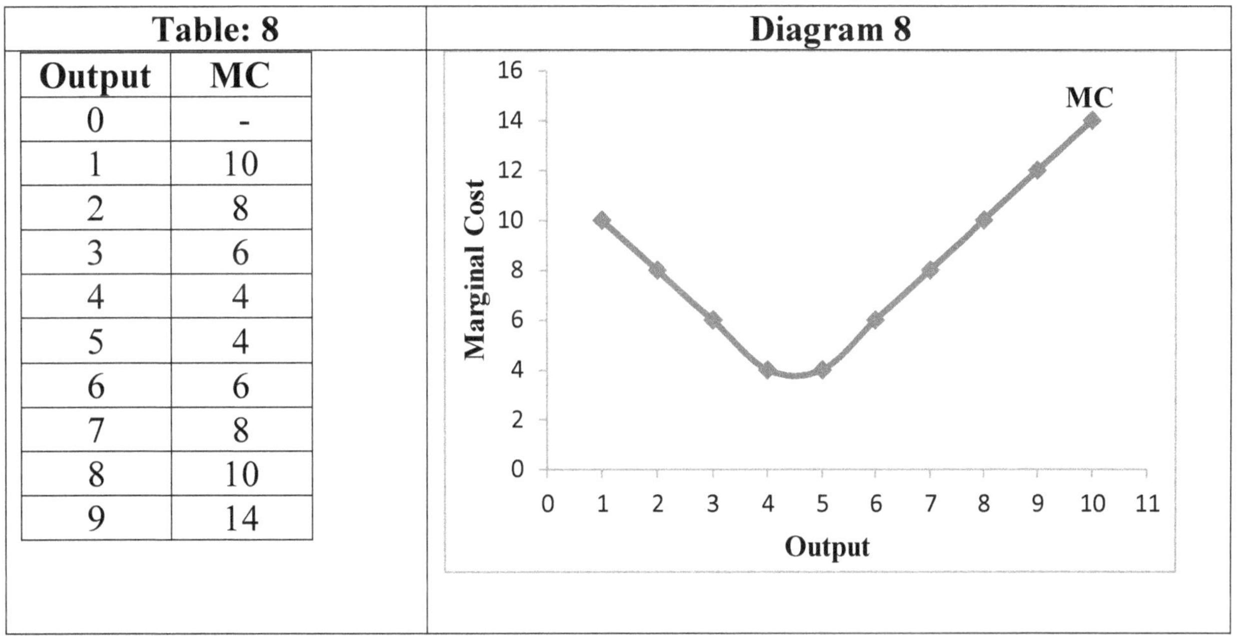

Output	MC
0	-
1	10
2	8
3	6
4	4
5	4
6	6
7	8
8	10
9	14

Relationship between AC and MC

We had discussion on the estimation and behavior of various cost curves. Now, we are going to discuss the relationship between these cost curves. The relationship between AC and MC is explained with the help of table 9 and diagram 9.

Relationship between AC and MC

1. Both AC and MC are calculated from TC i.e. **MC = ΔTC/ΔQ, AC=TC/Q** as shown in table 9.
2. As long AC falls, MC is lower than AC (AC>MC).
3. As long AC rises, MC is greater than AC (AC<MC).
4. When AC reaches at its lowest point, then AC=MC. In other words, MC cut AC at its minimum point.
5. There is a range of output where MC is rising and AC is falling.

There is mutual attraction between AC and MC. When AC falls, MC falls faster than AC, when AC is constant MC becomes equal to AC and MC rises at faster rate with increase in AC. Being a rate of change MC sharply falls and rises as compared to AC. It attains its lowest point earlier than AC and cuts AC at its lowest point when it is rising as shown in diagram 9.

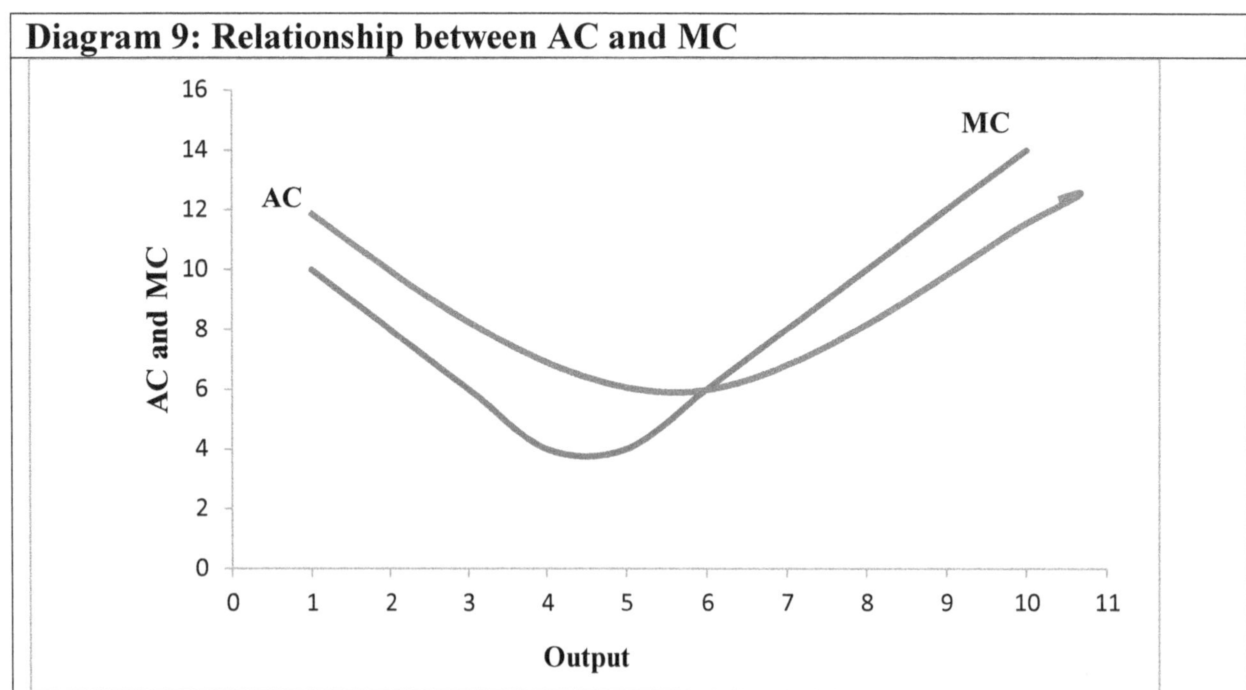

Diagram 9: Relationship between AC and MC

Table 9. Various Concepts of Cost

Q	TFC	TVC	TC=TFC+TVC	AFC= FC/Q	AVC=AVC/Q	AC	MC	∑MC=TVC
0	10	0	10	∞	-	-	-	0
1	10	10	20	10.0	10.0	20	10	10
2	10	18	28	5.0	9.0	14	8	18
3	10	24	34	3.3	8.0	11	6	24
4	10	28	38	2.5	7.0	10	4	28
5	10	32	42	2.0	6.4	8	4	32
6	10	38	48	1.7	6.3	8	6	38
7	10	46	56	1.4	6.6	8	8	46
8	10	56	66	1.3	7.0	8	10	56
9	10	70	80	1.1	7.8	9	14	70
10	10	90	100	1.0	9.0	10	20	90

Relationship between AVC and MC

The relationship between AVC and MC is similar to the relationship between AC and MC.

1. Both AVC and MC are calculated from TVC i.e. **MC = ΔTVC/ΔQ, AVC=TVC/Q**
2. As long AVC falls, MC is lower than AVC (AVC>MC).
3. As long AVC rises, MC is greater than AVC (AVC<MC).
4. When AVC reaches at its lowest point, then AVC=MC. In other words, MC cut AVC at its minimum point.

Relationship between TVC and AVC

The relationship between TVC and AVC is that, AVC is per unit variable cost while TVC is total variable cost. Initially, TVC increase at a diminishing rate in accordance with operation of law of increasing returns to a factor (when MP is rising) and corresponding to that stretch of TVC, AVC is falling. Finally, TVC increases at increasing rate due to application of law of diminishing returns and corresponding to that stretch AVC is rising.

Relationship between TC and AC

The relationship between TC and MC is similar to the relationship between TVC and AVC. AC is per unit variable cost while TC is total cost. Initially, TC increase at a diminishing rate in accordance with operation of law of increasing returns to a factor (A stage when MP is rising) and corresponding to that stretch of TC, AC is falling. Finally, TC increases at increasing rate due to application of law of diminishing returns (A stage when MP is falling) and corresponding to that stretch AC is rising.

Relationship between TC and MC

The relationship between TC and MC is such that MC is slope of TC. MC is obtained from TC as the change in total cost due to the addition of one unit of output. When MC is falling, TC rises at a diminishing rate. When MC is rising, TC increases at an increasing rate. Corresponding to lowest point of MC, TC changes its curvature, it stops increasing at diminishing rate and starts increasing at increasing rate.

Why AC curve or ATC curve is U shaped?

The AC curve initially slopes downward from left to right but finally it slopes upwards from left to right. This makes AC to look like U shaped. The reasons behind this bahvaiour are as under.

1. **AC is summation of AVC and AFC:** AFC always decline as output rises and AVC initially falls and eventually starts rising due to operation of law of variable proportion. AC reflects the shapes of both AFC and AVC. As output increases AFC tends to fall rapidly and AVC also falls due to increasing returns to a factor. At higher levels of output AFC falls very slowly and AVC rises due to diminishing returns to a factor. The increase in AVC becomes dominant force as a result AC starts rising. The relative strength of AFC and AVC generates the U-shaped ATC.

2. **Basis of law of variable proportion:** `According to law of variable proportion, in short period, initially marginal product (MP) of variable factor increases

(increasing returns) and finally starts falling (diminishing returns). U-shaped AC is in accordance with behavior of MP. There is inverse relationship between per unit cost and MP. The AC tends to fall because of increasing returns to a factor and finally tends to rise because of diminishing returns.

Production Cost versus Selling Cost

Production costs may be defined as those costs which a firm incurs on the production of a product and varies with quantity of production. These are incurred for creating utilities and contribute to economic welfare of the country by increasing availability of goods and services. It affects the supply curve of industry.

Selling costs are incurred for the promotion of sales and their volume depends upon nature of competition. In the words of Robert Awh, "Selling costs includes all expenses incurred to increase the demand for goods." In general, selling costs do not contribute to the welfare of the community. It affects the demand curve.

Schedules

1. Prepare cost schedule (Calculate AFC, ATC and MC) from 0 to 5 units of output. Assume TFC =Rs. 50 and per unit variable cost is Rs. 4

Answer:

Output	0	1	2	3	4	5
AFC	-	50	25	16.67	12.5	10
ATC	-	54	29	20.67	16.5	14
MC	-	4	4	4	4	4

2. Complete the following table:

Output	Total Cost	Total Variable Cost	Marginal Cost
0	12		
1	18		
2	21		

Answer:

Output	Total Cost	Total Variable Cost	Marginal Cost
0	12	-	-
1	18	18-12=6	18-12=6
2	21	21-12=9	21-18=3

3. From the information given below find out: AFC of producing 3 units, AVC of producing 4 units, Least AC level of output, MC of producing 5th unit, and TVC of producing 6 units.

Output (units)	0	1	2	3	4	5	6
Total cost (Rs.)	150	300	420	600	790	1000	1260

Answer:

Output	TC	TFC	AFC	TVC	AVC	MC	AC
0	150	150	∞	-	-	-	∞
1	300	150	150	150	150	150	300
2	420	150	75	270	135	120	210
3	600	150	50	450	150	180	200
4	790	150	37.5	640	160	190	197.5
5	1000	150	30	850	170	210	200
6	1260	150	25	1110	185	260	210

AFC of producing 3 units=Rs. 50, AVC of producing 4 units = Rs.160, Least AC level of output = Rs. 4, MC of producing 5th unit = Rs. 210, TVC of producing 6 units = Rs. 1110

4. Complete the following table:

Output	Total Cost	Average Variable Cost	Marginal Cost
0	60	-	-
1	140	-	-
2	190	-	-
3	240	-	-

Answer:

Output	TC	TFC	TVC	AVC	MC
0	60	60	0	0	-
1	140	60	80	80	80
2	190	60	130	65	50
3	240	60	180	60	50

5. Complete the following table:

Output	AFC	TFC	TVC	MC
0	-	50	-	-
1	-	-	-	10
2	-	-	18	-
3	-	-	-	6
4	-	-	20	-

Answer:

Output	AFC	TFC	TVC	MC
0	∞	50	-	-
1	50	50	10	10
2	25	50	18	8
3	16.67	50	24	6
4	12.5	50	20	-4

6. Calculate MC and AFC from the given information.

Output	Total Variable Cost	Total Fixed Cost

0	-	500
1	400	-
5	1600	-

Answer:

Output	TVC	TFC	MC	AFC
0	-	500	-	
1	400	500	400	500
5	1600	500	$\dfrac{1600-400}{5-1}=\dfrac{1200}{4}$ $=300$	100

7. Complete the following table:

Output	TVC	AVC	MC
1	10	-	-
-	-	8	6
3	27	-	-
-	-	10	13

Answer:

Output	TVC	AVC	MC
1	10	10	10
2	16	8	6
3	27	9	11
4	40	10	13

8. Find out explicit cost, and implicit cost from the following:

Particulars	Amount (in 000'Rs.)
Investment in fixed assets	2000
Borrowings at 10% interest per annum	1500
Wages paid during the year	120
Annual rental value of the owners factory building	100
Annual depreciation	100
Estimated annual value of the management services of the owner	320

Answer: Explicit Cost= Interest on borrowing + Wages paid during the year + Annual depreciation [150+120+100 = Rs.370 thousand]

Implicit Cost= Imputed interest on own investment + Annual rental value + Estimated annual value of the management services [50+100+320 = Rs.470 thousand]

9. Complete the following table:

Output	Average Cost	Marginal Cost

1	12	-
2	10	-
3	-	10
4	10.5	-
5	11	-
6	-	17

Answer:

Output	Average Cost	Marginal Cost	Total Cost
1	12	12	12
2	10	8	20
3	10	10	30
4	10.5	12	42
5	11	13	55
6	12	17	72

****

Exercise

1. Which of the following indicates fixed costs? 1. Licence fee 2. Interest on fixed capital 3. Both 1 &2 4. Wages of daily workers
2. When production is zero, total cost will be 1. Zero 2. Equal to variable cost 3. Equal to fixed cost 4. Equal to marginal cost
3. Which of the following is true about Average fixed cost (AFC)? 1. Rectangular hyperbola 2. Never touches X Axis 3. Always fall with increase in output4. All of the above
4. What happens to ATC when MC>ATC? 1. ATC will rise 2. ATC will fall 3. ATC will remain constant 4. None of these
5. Average cost is the vertical summation of 1. AFC and TVC 2. AFC and AVC 3. AVC and MC 4. None of these
6. Expenditure incurred by the producer on the purchase of inputs from the market is known as _____.
7. Which of the following is true about MC? 1. It is a variable cost 2. It is U shaped 3. MC=AC, where AC is lowest 4. All of the above
8. Implicit costs are costs of self-owned and self-employed resources. Statement is true or false.
9. Marginal cost can never be constant. Statement is true or false.
10. Area under MC curve is equal to TC. Statement is True or False.
11. The difference between ATC and AVC will _________ as output falls? 1. Increase 2. Decrease 3. Constant 4. Both 1 &2
12. Does TC always start from Y-axis? Statement is true or false.

13.AC and AVC never meet each other. Statement is true or false.

14.The shape of TVC is _____ shaped. 1. S 2. U 3. Inverted S 4. Rectangular hyperbola

15.Normal profit is related to _______ cost.

Answers:

1. 3	2. 3	3. 4	4. 1	5. 2
6. Explicit	7. 4	8. T	9. F	10.F
11.1	12.F	13.T	14.3	15.Implicit

NCERT Questions:

1. Briefly explain the concept of the cost function.

2. What are the total fixed cost, total variable cost and total cost of a firm? How are they related?

3. What are the AFC, AVC and AC of a firm? How are they related?

4. Can there be some fixed cost in the long run? If not, why?

5. What does the average fixed cost curve look like? Why does it look so?

6. What do the short run marginal cost, AVC and short run AC curves look like?

7. Why does the SMC curve cut the AVC curve at the minimum point of the AVC curve?

8. At which point does the SMC curve cut the SAC curve? Give reason in support of your answer.

9. Why is the short run marginal cost curve 'U' shaped?

10.The following table shows the total cost schedule of a firm. What is the total fixed cost schedule of this firm? Calculate the TVC, AVC, AFC, SAC and SMC schedule of the firm.

Q	0	1	2	3	4	5	6
TC	10	30	45	55	70	90	120

11.The following table gives the total cost schedule of a firm. It is also given that the average fixed cost at 4 units of output is Rs.5. Find the TVC, TFC, AVC, AFC, SAC and SMC schedules of the firm for the corresponding values of output.

Q	1	2	3	4	5	6
TC	50	65	75	95	130	185

12.A firm SMC schedule is shown in the following table. The total fixed cost of the firm is Rs. 100. Find the TVC, TC, AVC and SAC schedules of the firm.

Q	0	1	2	3	4	5	6
SMC	-	500	300	200	300	500	800

14.Complete the following table:

Q	1	2	3	4	5	6
AC	12	10	-	10.5	11	-
MC	-	-	10	-	-	17

Practice Questions

1. What is economic cost?
2. What is fixed and variable cost? Give two examples of each.
3. Distinguish between explicit cost and implicit cost and give examples.
4. Define marginal cost. Explain its relation with average cost.
5. Define variable cost. Explain the behaviour of total variable cost as output increases.
6. Giving examples, distinguish between fixed cost and variable cost.
7. What is the behaviour of average fixed cost as output increases?
8. Draw average variable cost, average total cost and marginal cost curves in a single diagram.
9. Draw total variable cost, total cost, and total fixed cost curves in a single diagram.
10. An individual is both the owner and the manager of a shop taken on rent. Identify implicit and explicit cost from this information. Explain.
11. A product invests his own savings in starting a business and employs a manager to look after the business. Identify the implicit and explicit costs from this information. Explain.
12. A producer starts a business by investing his own savings and hiring the labour. Identify implicit and explicit costs from this information. Explain.
13. A farmer takes a farm on rent and carries on farming with the help of family members. Identify implicit and explicit costs from this information. Explain.
14. Show with the help of a numerical example that AC is constant when MC is equal to it.
15. State the relation between total cost and marginal cost.

CHAPTER 9

PRODUCER'S EQUILIBRIUM

In an earlier chapter, we have explained consumer's equilibrium. In this chapter, we analyse producer's equilibrium or firm's equilibrium. A firm is defined as an economic entity which employs factors of production to produce commodities that it sells to other people. A firm is said to be in equilibrium when it selects a particular level of output at which the profit is maximized. There is no incentive for it to increase or decrease output from that level.

Firm: It is an economic entity which uses his factors of production to produce commodities to earn profit by selling them.

How does a firm decide the profit-maximisation level of output?

We combine the cost and revenue curves to study how firms take decisions with regard to output and prices under different types of markets. Profits are defined as the difference between the revenue that the firm earns from selling its output and the cost of producing that output, i.e., $\pi = TR - TC$ where, Greek letter π (pi) shows total profits, TR shows total revenue, TC shows total costs. When the difference between TR and TC is maximum, profit would be maximised. A profit maximizing firm will produce that output which maximizes the difference between TR and TC or AR and AC.

Normal profits refer to the minimum return that a firm should earn to keep his resources in present occupation. It is the implicit cost of the functions of an entrepreneur. Normal profits are the pure returns on capital and risk premium needed to compensate the entrepreneur for the risks involved in production. Normal profits are considered a part of cost of production and are included in the cost. **Excess of revenue over costs is what we call pure profits or economic profits in economics.**

Equilibrium of Firm or Producer

There are two approaches to find out equilibrium of the firm or producer.
1. **Total Revenue (TR) and Total Cost (TC) approach**
2. **Marginal Revenue (MR) and Marginal Cost (MC) approach**

TR and TC approach

We use graph and schedule to explain TR and TC approach of producer's equilibrium. According to this approach producer will attain his equilibrium position corresponding to that level of output where the total profit is maximum. Total profit is defined as the excess of total revenue (TR) over total cost (TC). Therefore, profit is maximised when difference between TR & TC is maximum or where slope of TR (MR) is equal to slope of TC (MC). Firm's total revenue curve TR and short-run total cost curve TC of the firm are depicted in diagram 1. TR curve is a straight line starts from origin. Short-run TC curve starts from point 'A'

Table 1: Producer's Equilibrium with the help of TR & TC approach

Output	0	1	2	3	4	5	6	7	8	9	10	11
TR	0	10	20	30	40	50	60	**70**	80	90	100	110
TC	10	20	29	37	44	50	56	**63**	75	90	110	135
Profit	-10	-10	-9	-7	-4	0	4	**7**	5	0	-10	-25
Remarks	L	L	L	L	L	BEP	P	**Eq**	P	BEP	L	L

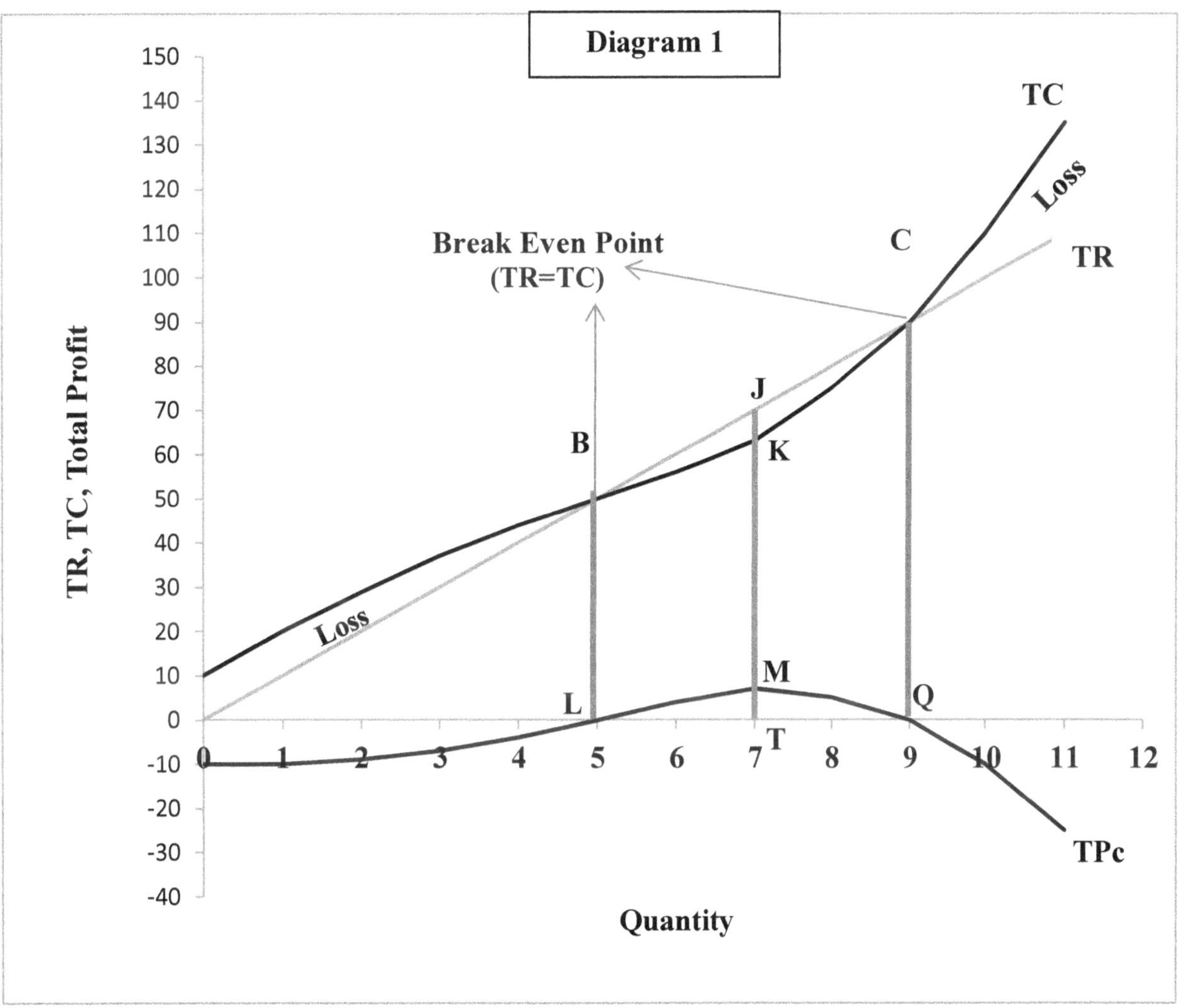

on the Y-axis. It is clear from diagram 1 that up to 5 units of output, TC curve lies above TR curve. The firm is therefore, incurring losses to the extent of difference between TC & TR. The points B & C corresponding to 5 & 9 units of output respectively are called the break-even points (BEP). Beyond 5 units, total revenue becomes larger than total cost and the firm begins to earn profits till its output reaches 9 units. Beyond, 9 units TC overtakes TR, and the firm starts incurring losses again. It means that the firm's profitable range of output lies between 5 units and 9 units. Profit maximising level of output is corresponding to 7 units of output where the vertical difference between TR and TC is maximum i.e. Rs. 7 (or JK). Producer's equilibrium will struck corresponding to 7 units of output as shown in the diagram 1.

It is also clear that the firm will neither produce more than nor less than 7 units of output. The profit-maximising level of output can also be identified by directly drawing total profit curve (TPC) by taking the vertical difference between total revenue (TR) and total cost (TC) at various levels of output. Total profit curve starts from −Y axis, showing loss at 0 units and meet X- axis at 5 units. After 5 units TPC shows profit till 9 units. The highest profit is shown by TPC at 7 units. The profits earned at 7 units of output are equal to '**MT**' or '**JK**'.

MR and MC Approach

According to this approach producer will attain his equilibrium position or his profit will be maximised when the following two conditions are satisfied:

1. **MR=MC**, and
2. **MC is rising or MC must cut MR from below**

Let us understand the significance of these conditions with the help of Table 2 and diagram 2. As per this table and diagram both conditions of MR and MC approach are fulfilled corresponding to 9th unit of output and there is maximum amount of total profit at Rs. 23. Corresponding to the first unit of output only first condition is fulfilled i.e. MR=MC but second condition is not satisfied because MC is falling. It is evident from the table 2 & diagram 2 that between 1st unit and 9th unit MR>MC. The excess of MR over MC indicates profit from intra marginal units that induces producer to produce more units of output. The producer will stop at 9th unit because corresponding to that level of output MR =MC and profit is jumped to maximum level or equal to 'area ABE'. There is no incentive for the producer to produce more than 9 units of output because after that level of output MC>MR and his profit will fall from the maximum level. It is evident from the diagram 2 that producer will neither produce an extra unit of output nor one unit less of the equilibrium level of output. If he will produce one unit less than the equilibrium output his profits would reduce to 'area ABCD' from maximum profit 'area ABE' (ABE-CED). On the other side, if he tries to produce one unit more than the equilibrium output his profits would reduce by area EFG from maximum profit area ABE (ABE-EFG) as shown in diagram 2. Hence, producer has no incentive either to produce more than or less than the equilibrium level of output. We should be very clear about that maximisation of profit implies equilibrium, but equilibrium does not always imply maximisation of profit. Because sometimes corresponding to equilibrium level of output there may be loss to the firm. Equilibrium always refers to the best level of output out of various levels of output under given circumstances. If there are losses everywhere then equilibrium will show that level of output where loss is minimum, and when there is profit then it will show that level of output where profit is maximum.

Table 1. MR, MC and Producer's Equilibrium

Output (in units)	MR (in Rs.)	MC (in Rs.)	Profit (Intra Marginal Units)	Total Profit
1	12	12	0	0
2	12	10	2	2
3	12	9	3	5
4	12	8	4	9
5	12	7	5	14
6	12	8	4	18
7	12	9	3	21
8	12	10	2	23
9	12	12	0	23
10	12	15	-3	20

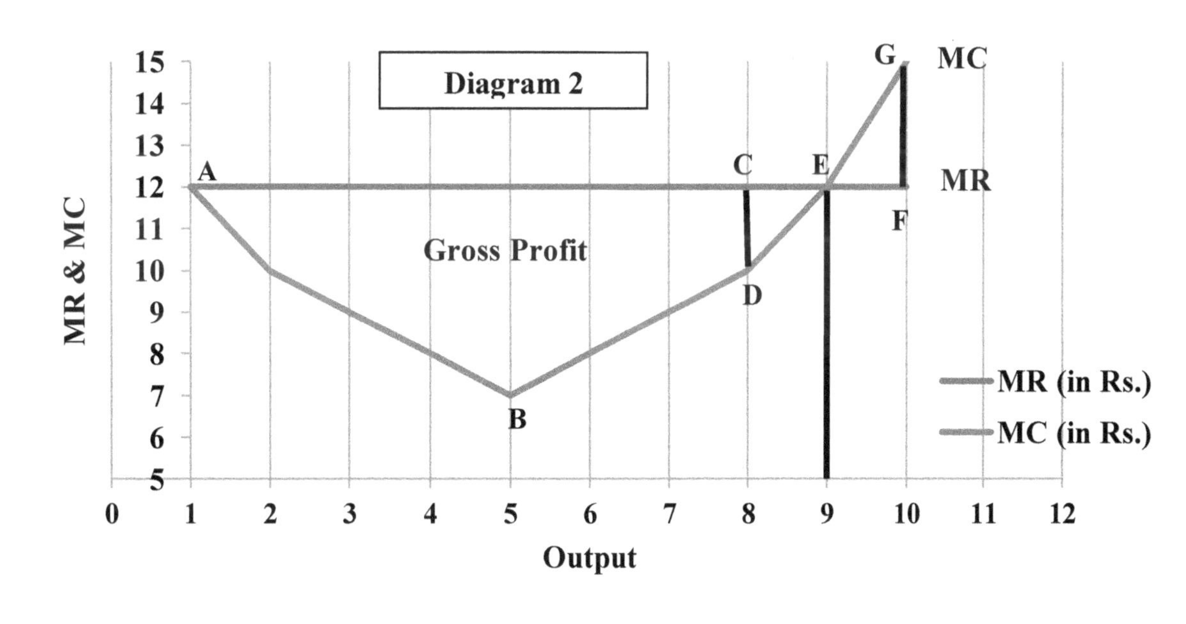

In diagram 2, we have shown the gross profit instead of net profit. Because in MR and MC approach, to find profit we use ΣMR to obtain TR and ΣMC for cost i.e. TVC. The difference between TR and TVC is Gross profit, whereas difference between TR and TC is Net Profit.

Gross Profit = Total Revenue – Total Variable Cost

Net Profit = Total Revenue – Total Cost or Gross Profit – Fixed Cost

Shut Down Rule: The firm should down if the price of the product is less than the average variable cost of production at the profit maximizing output. In general Shut Down Point is where AR = AVC. Firm will certainly stop producing when AR<AVC, because it is losing money on every unit it produces.

****

Exercise:

1. Difference between TR and TC is maximum when: 1. AR=MR 2. MR=MC 3. MR=AC 4. MC=AC
2. Normal profit is a part of: 1. Total revenue 2. Total cost 3. Marginal revenue 4. Average revenue
3. A firm reaches shut down point when: 1. TR=TVC 2. TR=TC 3. TC=AVC 4. MC=AC
4. Production may continue so long as: 1. TR ≥ TC 2. TR ≥ TVC 3. TR ≥ TFC 4. None of these
5. Accounting Profits are: 1. TR-TC 2. TR-TVC 3. TR-Explicit costs 4. TR-Implicit costs
6. According to MR and MC approach equilibrium will struck where: 1. MR=MC 2. MC must be rising 3. TR= TVC 4. Both a & b
7. Equilibrium is never struck if the producer is in losses. True or False
8. Break-even point always indicates maximisation of profit. True or False
9. If MR>MC, it is always better situation than if MR=MC for profits to be maximised. True or False
10. The producer strikes his equilibrium only when MP is diminishing. True or False
11. When output is beyond the point of equilibrium, profits are maximised. True or False
12. Normal profit is a part of total cost. True or False

Answers

1. 2	2. 2	3. 1	4. 2	5. 3
6. 4	7. F	8. F	9. F	10.T
11.F	12.T			

NCERT & Practice Questions:

1. Why equilibrium is not struck when MR>MC?

2. The following table shows the total revenue and total cost schedules of a competitive firm. Calculate the profit at each output level. Determine also the market price of a good.

Quantity Sold	TR	TC	Profit
0	0	5	
1	5	7	
2	10	10	
3	15	12	
4	20	15	
5	25	23	
6	30	33	
7	35	40	

Ans: [-5, -2, 0, 3, 5, 2, -3, -5] Price = Rs. 5

3. The following table shows the total cost schedule of a competitive firm. It is given that the price of the good is Rs. 10. Calculate the profit at each output levels. Find the profit maximizing level of output.

Q	0	1	2	3	4	5	6	7	8	9	10
TC (Rs.)	5	15	22	27	31	38	49	63	81	101	123

Ans: [-5, -5, -2, 3, 9, 12, 11, 7, -1, -11, -23] 5 units

4. What is producer's equilibrium? Explain the conditions of producer's equilibrium through the 'marginal cost and marginal revenue' approach. Use diagram.

5. Explain the conditions of producer's equilibrium with the help of a numerical example.

6. What is normal profit, net profit and gross profit?

7. What is shut down rule?

8. Give the meaning of producer equilibrium. A producer produces that quantity of his product at which marginal cost and marginal revenue are equal. Is he earning maximum profits? Give reasons for your answer.

9. "Maximisation of profit implies equilibrium, but equilibrium does not always imply maximisation of profit." Do you agree with the statement? (Hint Agree)

10. Explain the rationale behind the conditions of equilibrium of a producer.

11. Why a producer will not be in equilibrium if the conditions of equilibrium are not met?

12. What is shut down point? Should producer be discontinued when AR =AVC?

13. As per MR and MC approach only gross profits are maximised. Why? Explain with schedule and diagram.

14. Why firms never strike its equilibrium in state when MC is falling? Explain with schedule and diagram.

15. From the following table, find out the level of output at which the producer will be in equilibrium. Give reasons for your answer.

Output (units)	Marginal Revenue (Rs.)	Marginal Cost (Rs.)
1	8	10
2	8	8
3	8	7
4	8	8
5	8	9

Ans: Corresponding to 4 units where MR=MC and MC is rising

16. From the following table, find out the level of output at which the producer will be in equilibrium. Give reasons for your answer.

Output (units)	Marginal Cost (Rs.)	Total Revenue (Rs.)
1	12	10
2	10	20
3	8	30
4	10	40
5	12	50

Ans: Corresponding to 4 units where MR=MC and MC is rising [Hint: Find MR from TR]

17. From the following information about a firm, find the firm's equilibrium output in terms of marginal cost and marginal revenue. Give reasons. Also find profit at this output.

Output (units)	Total Revenue (Rs.)	Total Cost (Rs.)
1	7	8
2	14	15
3	21	21
4	28	28
5	35	36

Ans: Corresponding to 4 units where MR=MC & MC is rising, Profit = 0 [Hint: Find MR & MC]

18. From the following information about a firm, find the firm's equilibrium output in terms of marginal cost and marginal revenue. Give reasons. Also find profit at this output.

Output (units)	Total Revenue (Rs.)	Total Cost (Rs.)
1	6	7
2	12	13
3	18	17
4	24	23
5	30	31

Ans: Corresponding to 4 units where MR=MC & MC is rising, Profit = 1 [Hint: Find MR & MC]

CHAPTER 10

THEORY OF SUPPLY

Theory of Supply is an important and integral part of the price theory as like theory of supply. It studies the producer's behaviour in the market. As we know that price is determined by both, the supply and supply of the product. In present chapter, we shall have discussion on concept of supply.

Meaning of Supply

Supply means the quantity of a commodity which its producers or sellers offer for sale at a given price, per unit of time.

*"We may define supply as a schedule of the amount of a good that would be offered for sale at all possible prices, of any one instant of time or during any one period of time." -***Meyers**

There are three important aspects of supply.

1. Supply is a desired quantity, i.e., how much producers are willing to sell and not how much they actually sold.
2. The second thing to note about supply is that supply is always expressed with reference to price. With a change in the price of a commodity, its supply will also change.
3. Supply is a flow variable. Therefore, supply refers to the amount which producers or sellers are willing to sell during a specific period of time-per day, per week, per month or per year.

Difference between Stock and Supply

Supply should not be confused with the **'Stock'** of the commodity. Stock of a commodity is the total amount of the commodity available with the producers at any given time. Supply of a commodity does not comprise the entire stock of the commodity, but only that part of it which the producers are willing to bring into the market and offer for sale at a particular price. Thus, the stock of a commodity is the actual amount of it with the producers, while supply is that part of the stock which is offered for sale at any given time (intended supply) in the market.

Quantity Supplied: Quantity supplied refers to specific amount of a commodity

Supply Schedule

It is table showing relationship between price and quantity supplied. It is classified as ***Individual Supply Schedule and Market Supply Schedule.***

Individual Supply Schedule: This schedule shows the quantity of a commodity that is offered for sale at various prices by a single seller as shown in table 1. It is clear from the table that a seller is willing to sell 10 kg of X- commodity at Rs. 10, 20 kg at Rs. 20 and 30 kg at Rs. 30.

Table 1: Individual Supply Schedule for X-Commodity

Price of X- Commodity (Rs. Per Kg)	Quantity Supplied of X-Commodity (Kg)
10	10
20	20
30	30

commodity corresponding to Rs. 10 per Kg, 20 kg of X-commodity corresponding to Rs. 20 per kg, and30 kg of X-commodity corresponding to Rs. 30 per kg.

Market Supply Schedule: Market supply is the sum of supplies of a commodity made by all individual sellers as shown in table 2. It is clear from the table that all the sellers are willing to sell 90 kg of X- commodity corresponding to Rs. 30 per kg, 60 kg of X-commodity corresponding to Rs. 20 per kg, and 30 kg of X-commodity corresponding to Rs. 10 per kg.

Table 2: Market Supply Schedule for X-Commodity

Price of X-Commodity (Rs. Per Kg)	Quantities Supplied of X-Commodity (Kg)			
	Buyer Mr. Lal (S2)	Buyer Mr. Bal (S1)	Buyer Mr. Pal (S3)	Market Supply (MS)
30	30	20	40	30+20+40=90
20	20	10	30	20+10+30=60
10	10	0	20	10+0+20=30

Supply Curve

Supply curve is diagrammatic presentation of the supply schedule. It shows the relationship between price and quantity supplied of a commodity graphically. According to relationship supply curve is positively sloped. Like supply schedule, supply curve is also classified as Individual Supply Curve and Market Supply Curve.

Individual Supply Curve: It is defined as the curve which displays various quantities of a given commodity which an individual seller is ready to sell at various prices at given time, other things being constant. It is positively sloped shown by curve 'S' in diagram 1.

Market Supply Curve: It is usually upward sloping curve which displays various quantities of a given commodity which all sellers are willing to sell at different prices at given time, other things being constant. It is obtained by horizontal summation of supply curves of all individual sellers S1, S2 and S3 in the market and shown by curve 'MS' in diagram 2. It is clear from the diagram 1 & 2 that sellers are not willing to sell any quantity at price below Rs. 10 per unit. The price below which the sellers are not willing to sell their goods is known as the '**Reserve Price'**.

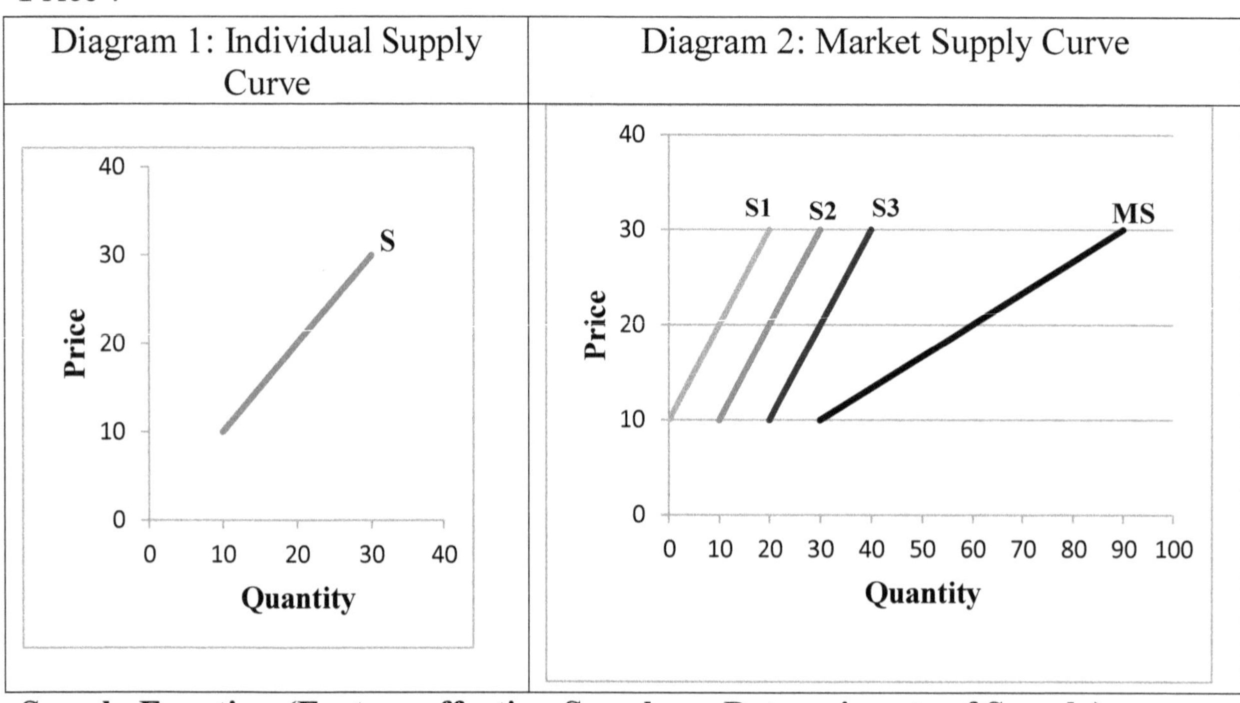

Supply Function (Factors affecting Supply or Determinants of Supply)

Supply function studies the functional relationship between supply for a commodity and its various determinants. Supply is a function of several factors expressed in the form of the following equation.

$$Q_x = f (P_x, P_r, P_f, N_f, P_e, G_p, TS, G_f, T)$$

It is very difficult to analyze the effect of simultaneous change in all factors on supply, that's why we study the effect of one factor at one time by assuming other factors as constant. The important factors which determine the supply of commodity are as follows:

1. **Price of the Commodity (P_x):** The most important determinant of the supply of commodity is its own price. Assuming other factors constant, quantity supplied falls with decrease in price of the commodity and vice versa. This relationship, which shows positive relation between supply of a commodity and the price of it, also known as Law of supply.

2. **Price of Related Goods (P_r):** The supply of a commodity is also affected by changes in price of its related goods. There is inverse relationship between supplies of a commodity in question to the price of its related (Substitute) good. For example a farmer can produce rice or cotton on his land. If the price of cotton rises, farmer will increase the supply of cotton by producing more of cotton in place of rice.

3. **Price of the Inputs (P_f):** Change in price of inputs like price of raw material, wages etc. affects the supply of a commodity. Increase in price of inputs will increase the cost of production and there will be decrease in supply of a commodity at same price. Decrease in price of inputs will decrease the cost of production and there will be increase in supply of a commodity at same price.

4. **Number of Firms/Sellers (N_f):** The supply of a commodity also depends upon number of sellers or firms selling that commodity. Entry of more sellers will increase and the exit will decrease and the supply of commodity at same price.

5. **Price Expectations (P_e):** Changes in price expectations also affects the supply of a commodity. If the sellers fear that the trend of fall in price will continue in future also, they will be willing to increase supply of commodity at same price or there will be a chance of panic-selling by some sellers. On the other hand, expectations of rise in future prices will induce them to withhold the supply and, thereby, there will be decrease in supply.

6. **Government Policies (G_p):** The policies of the governments are also important determinants of supply. A reduction in quotes and tariffs on foreign goods will open up the market to foreign producers and will tend to increase the supply. On the other side, the policy of protection will reduce the supply. The economic policies like policy of liberalization and privatization will also have favourable effect on supply.

7. **Taxation & Subsidies (TS):** The supply of a commodity is heavily influenced by the existing tax rates and subsidies. Higher rate of taxation and lower subsidies will lower the cost of production that encourages the producers to increase the supply of goods. On the other side, lower rate of taxation and higher subsidies will increase the cost of production that discourages the producers to decrease the supply of goods.

8. **Goal or Objective of the Firms (G_f):** Supply of a commodity depends upon the goals of the firms producing that commodity. The supply of goods would be larger in the market if the goal of the firm is to maximise sales rather than profit. On the other side, if firm wants to maximise profits then supply of goods would be relatively less as in case of sales maximisation.

9. **Technology (T):** Technology play important role in determining the supply of goods. Improvement in the techniques of production, innovations and discoveries helps to increase the productivity and lowers the cost of production and in turn increase the supply of goods.

Law of Supply

Law of supply studies the relationship between price and supply of a commodity. *Law of supply states that sellers will sell more at higher prices and sell less at lower prices, ceteris paribus or other things remaining the same as shown in table 3 and diagram 3.*

Table 3: Supply Schedule		Diagram 3: Supply Curve
Price	**Quantity Supplied**	
10	10	
20	20	
30	30	

Why does the supply curve slopes upward? Why more quantity is supplied at higher price or why less quantity is supplied at lower price?

Supply curve is positively sloped or more quantity is offered for sale at higher price due the following reasons:

1. **Maximisation of Profit:** The main objective of the seller is to maximise his profits. To achieve this objective he always tries to sell more quantity at higher price keeping other things constant. This makes supply curve to look like a positively sloped curve.

2. **Law of Increasing Cost:** The second reason behind the positively sloped curve is the operation of law of diminishing returns or law of increasing cost. Under law of increasing cost per unit cost of production increases with increase in production. To keep the margin or profit per unit stable producer always tries to sell more quantity only when he is offered with higher price.

Exceptions to the Law of Supply

There are certain cases where law of supply doesn't apply.

1. **Price Expectations:** An important exception to the law of supply is 'price expectations'. If the sellers fear that in future price will fall rapidly, they may resort to 'panic-selling' and try to clear his stock at falling price. On the other hand, if the prices show an upward trend, the sellers may expect prices to rise

further. In this situation, they will try to withhold or hoard stock of goods. This hoarding means less is offered for sale even at higher prices.

2. **Agriculture Products:** The law may not apply in case of agricultural products, whose supply is governed by natural factors. If due to poor monsoon the production of food grains (Rice) is low, their supply will not increase, howsoever the price may be high.

3. **Rare Paintings:** It may quite happen that the supply is more or less fixed, as in the case of rare paintings by same renowned painter and will not vary with changes in price.

4. **Perishable Goods:** Sellers will be ready to sell more units of perishable commodities although their prices may be falling.

5. **Auction and Clearance Sales:** The law of supply also does not hold well in case of auction and clearance sales. In case of clearance sales supply is increased at the reduced prices.

Change in Quantity Supplied or Movement along the Supply Curve

Change in quantity supplied occurs when the quantity supplied of the commodity changes due to change in its own price, keeping other things as constant (Cetris Paribus). It is indicated by a movement along a particular supply curve and it is of two types:

Extension of Supply or Increase in Quantity Supplied: When quantity supplied of a commodity rises due to increase in its own price, other things being constant, it is called extension in supply.

Price (X-commodity)	Quantity Supplied (X-commodity)
5	10
10	20

Table shows that when price of X commodity rises from Rs. 5 to Rs. 10 its supply rises from 10 units to 20 units. This is called extension in supply and it is shown by upward movement along the supply curve 'SS' from point 'A' to point 'B' as shown in figure I.

Contraction of Supply or Decrease in Quantity Supplied: When quantity supplied of a commodity falls due to fall in its own price, cetris paribus, it is called contraction of supply.

Price (X-commodity)	Quantity Supplied (X-commodity)
10	20
5	10

Table 2 shows that when price of X commodity falls from Rs. 10 to Rs. 5 its supply falls from 20 units to 10 units. This is called contraction of supply and it is shown by downward movement along the supply curve 'SS' from point 'B' to point 'A' as shown in figure II

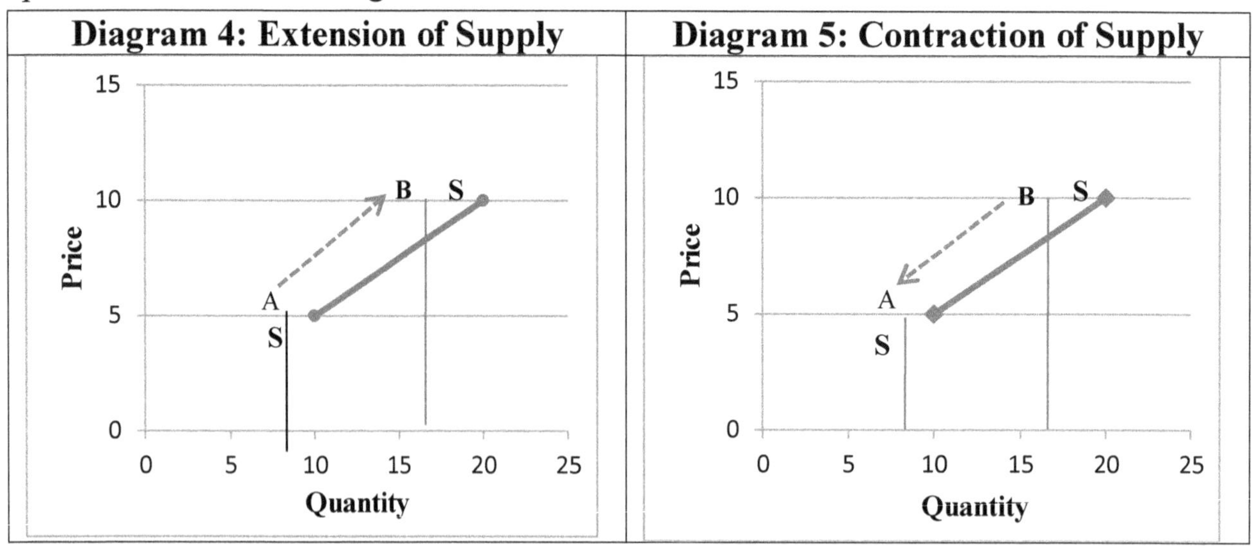

Change in Supply (Shifting of the Supply Curve)

Change in supply refers to either leftward shifting or rightward shifting of the supply curve. In other words it means either increase or decrease in quantity supplied of a commodity at same price due to change in determinants of supply function other than the own price of commodity. It is caused by change in other factors like change in price of related goods, goal of the firm, number of firms, prices of inputs etc. Change in supply is classified as increase in supply and decrease in supply.

Increase in Supply: Increase in supply implies a rightward shift of the supply curve, displaying that sellers are willing to sell more quantity of a commodity at same price, due to favourable change in other determinants of supply function like, decrease in prices of related goods and inputs, improvement in technology, decrease in taxes, increase in subsidies, increase in number of firms etc. It is shown by rightward shift in supply curve from 'SS' to 'S_1S_1' in diagram.

Decrease in Supply: Decrease in supply implies a leftward shift of the supply curve, displaying that sellers are willing to sell less quantity of a commodity at same price, due to unfavourable change in other determinants of supply function like increase in prices of related goods and inputs, increase in taxes, decrease in subsidies, decrease in number of firms etc. It is shown by leftward shift in supply curve from 'SS' to 'S_1S_1' in diagram.

<table>
<tr><th>Diagram 6: Increase in Supply</th><th>Diagram 7: Decrease in Supply</th></tr>
<tr><td>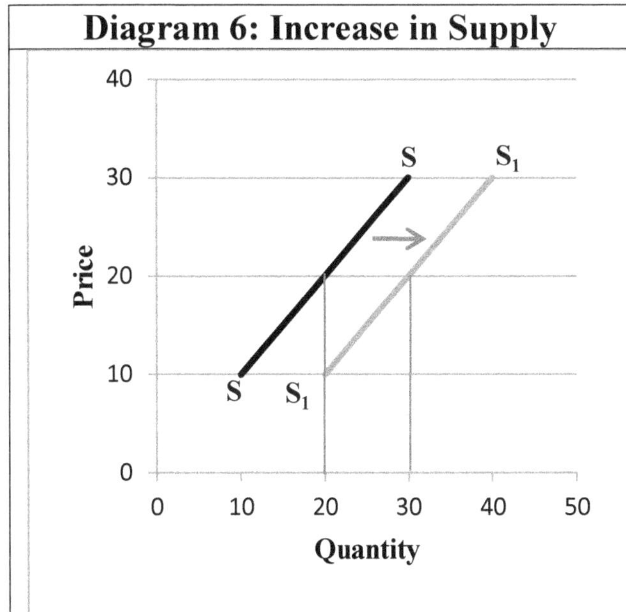</td><td>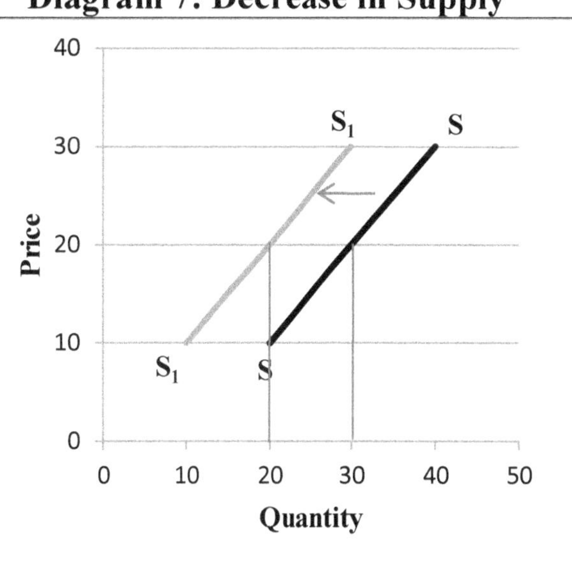</td></tr>
</table>

Difference between Extension in Supply and Increase in Supply

Extension in Supply	Increase in Supply
Extension in supply refers to increase in quantity supplied of a commodity due to increase in its own price, other things being constant.	Increase in supply implies a rightward shift of the supply curve, displaying that sellers are willing to sell more quantity of a commodity at same price.
It is caused by increase in price of the commodity.	It is caused by decrease in price of related goods, price of inputs, improvement in technology, decrease in taxes, increase in subsidies, increase in number of firms etc.
It is shown by upward movement along the supply curve 'SS' from point 'A' to point 'B' as shown in diagram	It is shown by rightward shift in supply curve from 'SS' to 'S₁S₁' as shown in diagram.
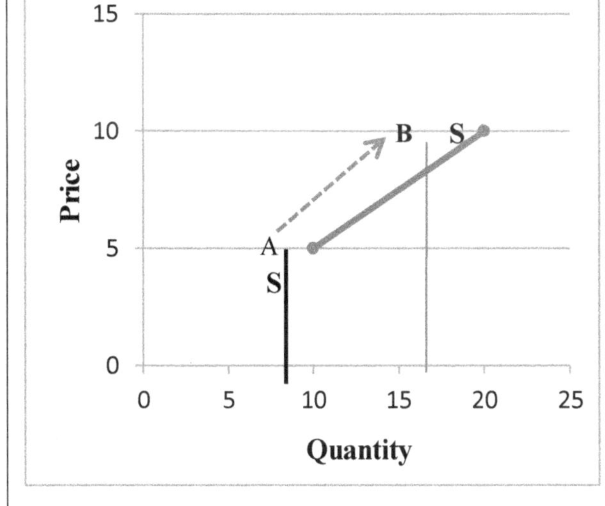	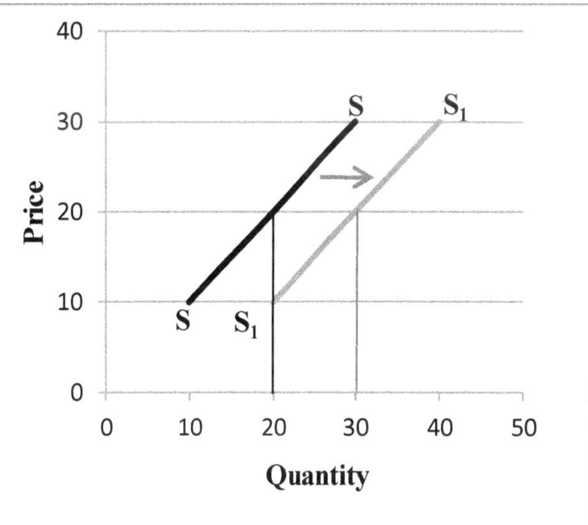

Difference between Contraction in Supply and Decrease in Supply

Contraction in Supply	Decrease in Supply
Contraction in supply refers to decrease in quantity supplied of a commodity due to decrease in its own price, other things being constant.	Decrease in supply implies a leftward shift of the supply curve, displaying that buyers are willing to sell less quantity of a commodity at same price.
It is caused by fall in price of the commodity.	It is caused by increase in prices of related goods, price of inputs, increase in taxes, decrease in subsidies, decrease in number of firms etc.
It is shown by downward movement along the supply curve SS from point B to point A as shown in diagram.	It is shown by leftward shift in supply curve from SS to S_1S_1 as shown in diagram.

Difference between Change in Quantity Supplied and Change in Supply

Change in Quantity Supplied	Change in Supply
Change in quantity supplied occurs when the quantity supplied of the commodity changes due to change in its own price, keeping other things as constant.	Change in supply refers to either increase or decrease in quantity supplied of a commodity at same price due to change in determinants of supply function other than the own price of commodity.
It is caused by change in price of the commodity alone.	It is caused by change in other factors like change in price of related goods, goal of the firm, number of firms, price of inputs etc.
It is indicated by a movement along a	It is indicated by shifting of the supply

particular supply curve either upward or downward.	curve either leftward or rightward.
It is classified as *extension in supply and contraction in supply*.	It is classified as *increase in supply and decrease in supply*.
Extension of supply occurs when quantity supplied of a commodity rises due to increase in its own price	**Increase in supply** implies a rightward shift of the supply curve, displaying that sellers are willing to sell more quantity of a commodity at same price as shown in diagram from SS to S_1S_1.
Contraction of supply occurs when quantity supplied of a commodity falls due to decrease in its own price.	**Decrease in supply** implies a leftward shift of the supply curve, displaying that buyers are willing to sell less quantity of a commodity at same price as shown in diagram from S_1S_1 to SS.

Elasticity of Supply

Price elasticity of supply measures the responsiveness of quantity supplied to change in its own price. $\mathbf{Es} = \dfrac{\textbf{\% Change in Quantity Supplied of a Commodity X}}{\textbf{\% Change in Price of a Commodity X}}$

Degrees of price elasticity of supply

1. **Perfectly Elastic Supply (E=∞):** It is the situation where in very small change in price produces infinite change in quantity supplied. A very small decrease in price cause supply to extend to infinity and the same fall in price causes the supply to contracts to zero. In this case supply curve will be a horizontal line as shown in figure 1, and will be parallel to X- axis.

2. **Perfectly Inelastic Supply (E=0):** In this case consumer will buy a fixed quantity of a good regardless of its price, that is to say whatever change in price, the supply remains the same. In other words, there will be no change in quantity supplied due to change in price. In this case supply curve will be vertical line as shown in figure 2.

Diagram 8: Perfectly Elastic Supply (E= ∞)	Diagram 9: Perfectly Inelastic Supply (E=0)
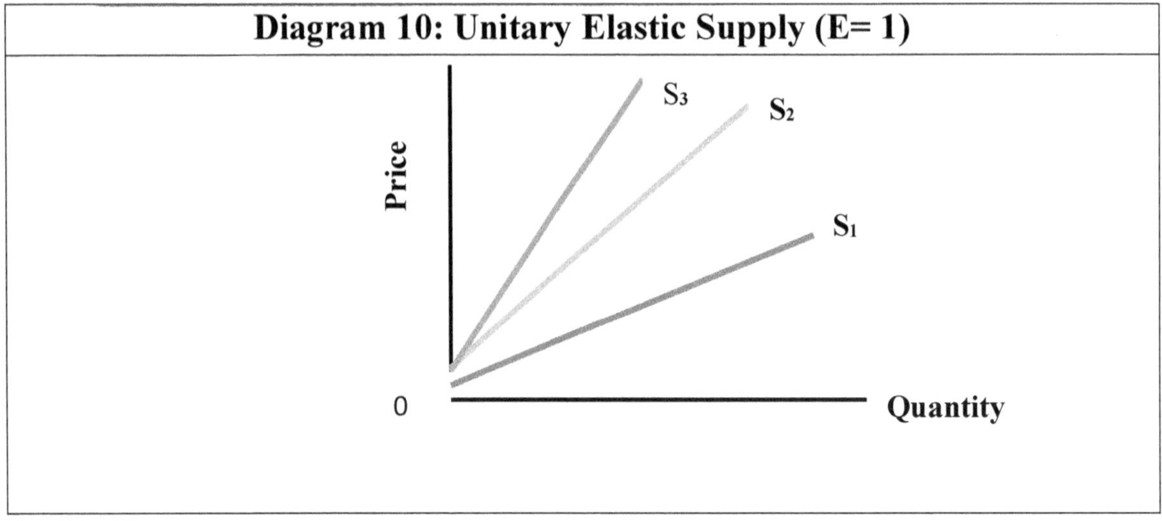	

3. **Unitary Elastic Supply (E=1):** Supply is said to be unitary elastic when change in price produces equi-proportionate change in quantity supplied i.e. $\frac{\Delta Q}{Q} = \frac{\Delta P}{P}$. In other words, it is case where % change in quantity supplied is exactly equal to % change in price. In this case supply curve will pass through point of origin as shown in diagram 10. Supply curves S_1, S_2 and S_3 are passing through point of origin

Diagram 10: Unitary Elastic Supply (E= 1)

4. **More than Unitary Elastic Supply/Elastic Supply (E>1):** Supply is said to be more than unitary elastic when proportionate change in quantity supplied is more than proportionate change in price. i.e. $\frac{\Delta Q}{Q} > \frac{\Delta P}{P}$. In other words, it is case where % change in quantity supplied is greater than % change in price. In this case supply curve will be flatter and starts from Y-axis as shown in diagram 11.

5. **Less than Unitary Elastic Supply/Inelastic Supply (E<1):** i.e. $\frac{\Delta Q}{Q} < \frac{\Delta P}{P}$. Supply is said to be less than unitary elastic when proportionate change in quantity supplied is more than proportionate change in price. In other words, it is case where % change in quantity supplied is less than % change in price. In this case supply curve will be steeper as shown in diagram 12 and starts from X-axis.

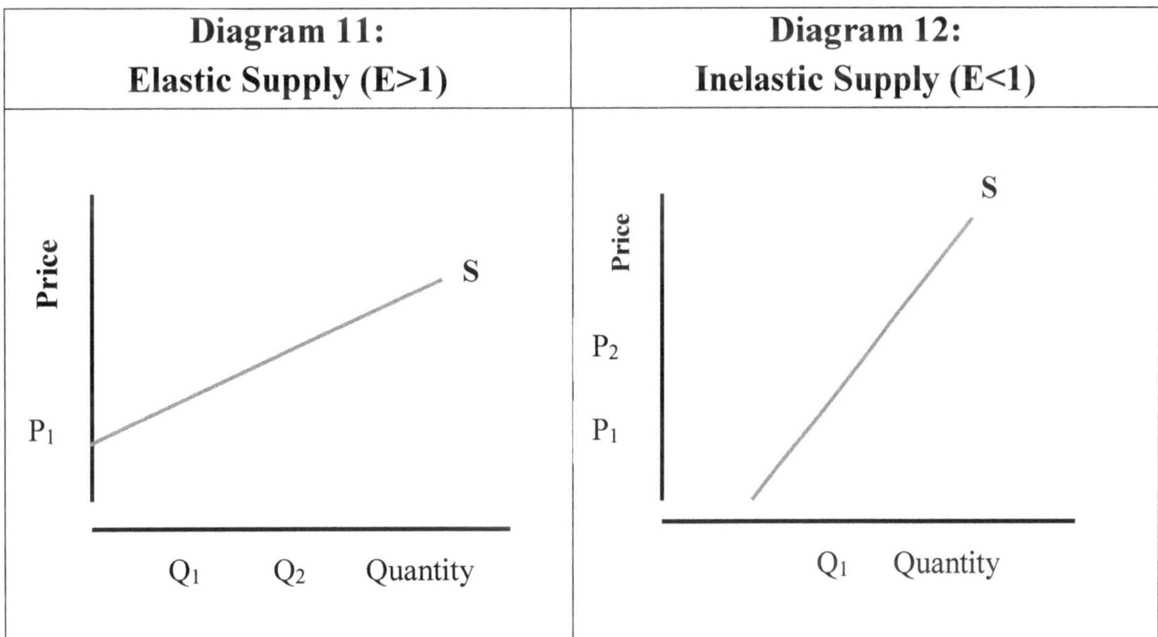

Measurement of Price Elasticity of Supply

There are two methods of measuring price elasticity of supply.

1. **Percentage or Proportionate Method:** This method measures the price elasticity of supply by using the following formula

$$E_S = \frac{\text{% Change in Quantity Supplied}}{\text{% Change in price}}$$

% Change in Quantity Supplied $= \frac{\Delta Q}{Q} \times 100$ (Where $\Delta Q = Q_1 - Q$, Q_1 is the final quantity and Q is initial quantity)

% Change in Price $= \frac{\Delta P}{P} \times 100$ (where $\Delta P = P_1 - P$, P_1 is the final price and P is initial price)

Or $E_S = \frac{\Delta Q}{\Delta P} \times \frac{P}{Q}$

2. **Graphical Method:** This method measures the price elasticity of supply by noticing the point from where linear supply curve originates. The horizontal shape of supply curve or supply curve parallel to X-axis (As shown in diagram 8) shows perfectly elastic supply ($E=\infty$). The vertical shape of supply curve or supply curve parallel to Y-axis (As shown in diagram 9) shows perfectly inelastic supply ($E=0$). Supply curve originates from point of origin shows unitary elastic supply (As shown in diagram 10), supply curve which starts from Y-axis shows elastic supply (As shown in diagram 11) and supply curve starts from X-axis shows inelastic supply (As shown in diagram 12).

Factors Influencing Elasticity of Supply:

1. **Nature of the Commodity:** Elasticity of supply depends upon the nature of the commodity. Commodities on the basis of their nature can be classified as 1. Perishable and 2. Durable. Perishable products cannot be stored for long time and their supply does not respond to change in their price. Hence, their supply is inelastic. Durable products on the other hand, can be stored, hence their supply is generally elastic i.e., supply responds to the change in prices.
2. **Laws of Cost of Production:** Elasticity of supply is also influenced by the laws of returns (Laws of cost of production). If production is subject to law of diminishing returns (Law of increasing cost), then the supply of such goods will be less elastic. The response of supply to increase in price will be poor because it is difficult to extend supply due to increase in cost of production. On the contrary if production obeys the law of increasing returns (Law of decreasing costs) then supply will be elastic.
3. **Techniques of Production:** Supply of the commodity will be elastic where production of such commodities involves the use of simple techniques of production. Simple techniques are usually less expensive in nature and are easy to use. On the other hand, if the techniques of production of a commodity are

cumbersome, complex, expensive and time-consuming in nature, then supply of such commodities would generally be less elastic.

4. **Time:** The element of time exercises an important influence on elasticity of supply. The longer the period of time the more elastic is the supply. On the other hand, shorter the time period lesser will be the elasticity of supply. In analyzing the impact of time upon elasticity of supply, economists distinguish between:

   a) Very short period or Market period: In very short period the supply can be increased upto existing stock only. This makes supply as perfectly inelastic supply because supply cannot be increased beyond the stock even with increase in price.

   b) Short period: In short period the supply can be increased upto the capacity of the plant. This makes supply relatively elastic as compared to very short period.

   c) Long period: In long period, time is long enough to enable the fullest adjustment to be made in the supply position, and this makes supply curve more elastic.

5. **Nature of Inputs:** The elasticity of supply heavily depends upon the nature of inputs used for the production. If the production of a commodity uses inputs that are ubiquitous and the most common then their supply will be more elastic. On the other side, if inputs are localized or rarely available for making the products then their supply will be relatively inelastic.

6. **Ability to Take Risk:** The elasticity of supply is also influenced by risk-taking capacity of the entrepreneurs. The supply will be more elastic, if entrepreneurs are willing to take risk. On the other hand, if entrepreneurs hesitate to take risks, the supply will be inelastic.

7. **Natural Factors:** The role of natural factors is very important in influencing the elasticity of supply. If the production of commodity is more depended upon the natural factors like rain, temperature etc then its supply will be inelastic. E.g. Agriculture products. On the other hand, if the production of commodity has no relation with natural factors or has less dependence on these factors, then its supply will be elastic. E.g. production of washing machine (Manufactured products).

Numerical of Price Elasticity of Supply

1. Price of a commodity increases from Rs.10 to Rs.12. As a result, its supply rises from 35 units to 42 units. Find out elasticity of supply. Ans. $E_s=1$

2. As a result of 15 per cent rise in the price of a commodity, its supply increases from 25 to 30 units. Calculate elasticity of supply. Ans. E_s=1.33

3. The price of a commodity is Rs.12 per unit and its quantity supplied is 500 units. When its price rises to Rs. 15 per unit, its quantity supplied rises to 650 units. Calculate its price elasticity of supply. Is supply elastic? Ans. E_s=1.2, yes, Supply is elastic.

4. Price elasticity of supply for a product is 'unity'. A firm supplies 25 units of this product at a price of Rs.5 per unit. If the price of product rises to Rs.6 per unit. How much quantity of the product will be supplied by the firm? Ans. New quantity=30 units.

5. When price of the commodity falls from Rs.10 per unit to Rs.9 per unit, its quantity supplied falls by 20 per cent. Calculate its price elasticity of supply. Is its supply elastic? Ans. E_s=2, yes, Supply is elastic

6. The quantity supplied of a commodity at a price of Rs.8 per unit is 400 units. Its price elasticity of supply is 2. Calculate the price at which its quantity supplied will be 600 units. Ans. New price =Rs.10

7. When the price of a commodity rises from Rs.10 to Rs.11 per unit, its quantity supplied rises by 100 units. Its price elasticity of supply is 2. Calculate its quantity at the increased price. Ans. Quantity supplied = 600 units

8. The price elasticity of supply of a commodity is 2. When its price falls from Rs.10 to Rs.8 per unit, its quantity supplied falls by 500 units. Calculate the quantity supplied at the reduced price. Ans. Quantity supplied =750 units.

9. For a commodity, if E_s =1.4 and $\frac{\Delta P}{P} = 0.6,$ find the percentage change in quantity supplied. Ans. 84%

10. The market price of a good change from Rs.5 to Rs.20. As a result, the quantity supplied by the firm increases by 15 units. The price elasticity of supply is 0.5. Find the initial and final output levels of the firm. Ans. 10 units and 25 units

One Mark Questions

1. The entire schedule showing various quantities offered for sale by all firms at different possible prices in the market of the commodity is called: 1. Quantity supplied 2. Market supply 3. Individual supply 4. None of these

2. Law of supply states that: 1. There is positive relation between supply and price 2. There is negative relation between supply and price 3. There is constant relation between supply and price 4. There is no relation between supply and price

3. Movement along the supply curve is caused by: 1. Decrease in price of the commodity 2. Increase in price of the commodity 3. Both (a) and (b) 4. Decrease in the price of competing product

4. Upward movement along the supply curve occurs due to: 1. Increase in own price of the commodity 2. Decrease in own price of the commodity 3. Factors other than own price of the commodity 4. Both (a) and (b)

5. In case of contraction of supply, we move: 1. To right on the another supply curve 2. From lower point to upper point 3. From upper point to lower point 4. Both (a) and (b)

6. Due to increase in GST rate, supply curve will: 1. Shift to the right 2. Shift to the left 3. Both (a) and (b) 4. None of these

7. Due to decrease in rate of interest and wages, supply curve will: 1. Shift to the right 2. Shift to the left 3. Both (a) and (b) 4. None of these

8. Government in its new industrial policy allowed private firms to produce urea, then supply curve of urea will: 1. Shift to the right 2. Shift to the left 3. Both (a) and (b) 4. None of these

9. What will be the reaction of supply curve if the goal of the firm is shifted to 'Sales Maximisation'? 1. There will be more supply at higher price 2. Supply curve will remain intact 3. There will be more supply at same price 4. None of these

10. There will be rightward shift of supply curve of 'X commodity' in a country if: 1. Govt. lift a ban on import of 'X commodity' 2. Govt. lift a ban on export of 'X commodity' 3. Increase in excise duty on production of 'X commodity' 4. Price of 'X commodity' rises

11. Price elasticity of supply will be more elastic if; 1. Production of that commodity obeys law of increasing cost 2. Producer is risk averter 3. Production of that commodity obeys law of increasing returns 4. Production of that commodity is governed by natural factors

12. GOI raises the FDI limit for the food processing sector, then what will be the effect of this move on the supply curve of processed food in India. 1. Rightward shift of supply curve 2. Leftward shift of supply curve 3. No change in supply curve 4. Extension of supply curve

13. Supply is a; 1. Flow 2. Stock 3. Both (a) and (b) 4. None of the above

14. What will be the effect on supply of Paddy if GOI offers MSP on Cotton along with subsidy? 1. Contraction in supply 2. Increase in supply 3. Extension in supply 4. Decrease in supply

15. A straight line supply curve passing through the origin forming an angle of 40° indicates: 1. $E_s=0$ 2. $E_s=1$ 3. $E_s>1$ 4. $E_s<1$

16. When supply curve is parallel to Y-axis, then elasticity of supply is: 1. Unity 2. Infinity 3. Zero 4. Negative

17. In perfect competition the rising segment of MC curve acts as firm's; 1. Demand Curve 2. Supply Curve 3. Both (a) and (b) 4. Profit Curve

18. Compared to long period supply curve, short period supply curve is: 1. More Elastic 2. Less Elastic 3. Unitary Elastic 4. Perfectly Inelastic

19. Market supply curve is: 1. Horizontal summation of supply curves 2. Vertical summation of supply curves 3. Both (a) and (b) 4. None of the above

20. Elasticity of supply on a straight line upward sloping curve, starting from the origin $=1$, even when it does not form a 45° angle. (True/False)

21. Market supply schedule is the supply schedule of the single firm in the industry. (True/False)

22. Change in supply always means a forward shift in supply curve. (True/False)

23. The supply curve is positively sloped due to operation of law of increasing cost. (True/False)

24. Supply curve will be a horizontal line when slope of supply curve is zero. (True/False)

Answers

1. 2	2. 1	3. 3	4. 1	5. 3	6. 2
7. 1	8. 1	9. 3	10.1	11.3	12.1
13.1	14.4	15.2	16.3	17.2	18.2
19.1	20.T	21.F	22.F	23.T	24.T

Exercise

1. Define supply.
2. Difference between stock and supply.
3. What is meant by 'increase 'in supply?
4. What is reserve price?
5. Define 'market supply'. What is the effect on the supply of a good when government imposes a tax on the production of that good? Explain.
6. What is supply schedule? What is the effect on the supply of a good when government gives a subsidy on the production of that good? Explain.
7. What is decrease in supply?
8. Give meaning of 'change in quantity supplied'.

9. What is a supply schedule? Explain how change in technology of producing a good affects the supply of that good.

10. Define supply curve. How does fall in price of an input affect the supply of a good using that input?

11. Explain how changes in prices of other products influence the supply of a given product.

12. Explain how changes in prices of inputs influence the supply of a product.

13. Explain the distinction between "Increase in supply" and "Extension in supply". Use diagrams.

14. Explain the distinction between "Decrease in supply" and "Contraction in supply". Use diagram.

15. Explain the distinction between "Change in quantity supplied" and "Change in supply". Use diagram.

16. Draw supply curves showing price elasticity of supply equal to 1. Zero 2. One 3. Infinity throughout

17. How the change in tax on a product does influences the supply of that product? Explain.

18. How does technological progress affect the supply curve of a firm?

19. How does the imposition of GST affect the supply curve of a firm?

20. How does an increase in the price of an input affect the supply curve of a firm?

21. How does an increase in the number of firms in a market affect the market supply curve?

22. What does the price elasticity of supply mean? How do we measure it?

23. Explain the various factors that influence the elasticity of supply.

24. What are exceptions of law of supply?

25. What is the shape of supply curve of a firm in the short run?

26. What is the shape of supply curve of a firm in the long run?

27. Consider the market with two firms. The following table shows the supply schedule of the two firms: the SS_1 column gives the supply schedule of firm 1 and the SS_2 column gives the supply schedules of firm 2. Compute the market supply schedule.

Price		0	1	2	3	4	5	6
Firm 1 (Supply)		0	0	0	1	2	3	4
Firm 2 (Supply)		0	0	0	1	2	3	4

28. There are 3 identical firms in the market. The following table shows the supply schedule of firm1. Compute the market supply schedule.

Price	0	1	2	3	4	5	6	7	8
SS_1	0	0	2	4	6	8	10	12	14

29. When the price of a good rises from Rs. 20 per unit to Rs.30 unit, the revenue of the firm producing this good rises from Rs.100 to Rs.300. Calculate the price elasticity of supply.

30. A firm's revenue rises from Rs.400 to Rs.500 when the price of its product rises from Rs.20 per unit to Rs.25 per unit. Calculate the price elasticity of supply.

31. The price elasticity of supply of a good is 0.8. Its price rises by 50 per cent. Calculate the percentage increase in its supply.

32. Give one reason for an "increase" in supply of a commodity.

33. Give one reason for a "decrease" in supply of a commodity.

34. Give the meaning of market supply.

35. A firm supplies 10 units of a good at a price of Rs.5 per unit. Price elasticity of supply is 1.25. What quantity will the firm supply at a price of Rs.7 per unit?

36. The price elasticity of supply of a commodity is2.0. A firm supplies 200 units of it at a price of Rs.8 per unit. At what price will it supply 250 units?

37. 15 per cent rise in the price of a commodity raises its supply from 300 units to 345 units. Calculate its price elasticity of supply.

38. When is supply of a good said to be inelastic?

39. Total revenue of a firm rises from Rs.400 to Rs.500 when the price of its product rises from Rs.8 per unit to Rs.10 per unit. Calculate the price elasticity of supply.

40. A fall in the price of a firm's product results in a fall in its supply by 40 per cent. Its price elasticity of supply is 1.6. Calculate the percentage fall in its price.

41. Price elasticity of supply of a good is 2. By what percentage should its price rise so that its supply rises by 30 per cent?

CHAPTER 11

FORMS OF MARKET

In common parlance, the term market means a particular place or locality, where goods are bought and sold. For example: Dhobi bazaar, Post office bazaar, Sirki bazaar in Bathinda, Nai Sarak, Chandni Chowk bazaar in Delhi etc.

In economics, the term market is used in broader sense. It refers to a complex set of activities by which actual and potential buyers as well as sellers are in such close contact with one another other that the price of commodity as well as its output is determined. Thus, market determines who the buyers and sellers are, what the prices will be and what quantities will be bought and sold.

"Economists understand by the term market not any particular market place in which things are bought and sold, but the whole of any region in which buyers and sellers are in such free intercourse with one another that the price of the same goods tends to equality easily and quickly."- Cournot

Features of Market:

1. Does not mean any particular area or place, rather it means the entire area over which buyers and sellers are spread and have close contact with each other.
2. Both buyers and sellers are needed in the market.
3. There must be at least one commodity to be transacted.

Forms of Market: Markets are generally classified into three categories

I. **Perfect Competition**
II. **Monopoly**
III. **Imperfect Competition (Monopolistic Competition, Oligopoly)**

Perfect Competition

Perfectly competitive is a market in which all firms (large number) produce an identical product and each is so small in relation to the industry that its production decisions have no effect on market price. New firms can easily enter the industry if they perceive a potential for profit, and existing firms can exit if they start making losses.

"Perfect competition is a market situation in which there are large number of buyers and sellers. The seller sell homogeneous product at single uniform price. The price is determined not by the firm but by industry." **– Boulding**

Characteristics/Feature of Perfect Competition:

1. **Large Numbers of Small Sellers & Buyers**: In perfect competitive market includes large number of small sellers and buyers. Each individual firm produces a small part of the market supply and its production decisions have no effect on market price. On the other side buyers are also in large number. Each buyer demanded a very small portion of market demand. Under these conditions neither a seller nor a buyer alone can affect the price prevailing in the market by changing its quantity supplied or quantity demanded respectively.

2. **Homogenous Products:** Products of all of the firms in a market are perfectly substitutable with one another. There is no way in which buyer could differentiate among the products of different firms. The technical characteristics of the product as well as the services associated with its sale and delivery are same. The assumptions of large numbers of sellers and of product homogeneity imply that individual firm is price taker not maker.

3. **Firm is Price Taker Not Maker:** Each individual firm sells a very small proportion of total market output; its decisions have no impact on market price. Each firm takes market price as given. The existence of large number of sellers and product homogeneity imply that perfectly competitive firm is price taker. Demand curve faced by an individual firm is perfectly elastic which indicates that firm can sell any amount of output at the prevailing market price.

4. **Free Entry & Exit of Firms:** The entry and exit of the firms is free of any barriers. Firms have full freedom to enter or leave the industry according to their choice. This assumption implies that firms will earn only normal profits (AR=LAC) in the long period. In case of super normal profits are earned by existing firms, new firms will enter the industry. This will increase the market supply and price will start falling. The entry of new firms will continue till super normal profits become zero. In case of losses some of the existing firms will leave the industry. This will decrease the market supply and price will start rising. The exit of firms will continue till the losses are disappeared.

5. **Profit Maximization:** The only objective is assumed to maximization of profits. No other objectives are pursued by the firm.

6. **No Government Regulations:** There is any restriction on buyer and seller with regard to their buying and selling of any product. Tariffs, subsidies, rationing of production or demand and so on are assumed to be absent.

7. **Perfect Mobility:** The factors of production are free to move from one firm to another that they like. It is assumed that workers can move between different jobs, which imply skills can be learned easily. No factor of production is assumed to be monopolized. Goods and services can be sold at any place where they likely to get better price.

8. **Perfect Knowledge:** It is assumed that all sellers and buyers have complete knowledge of the conditions prevailing in the market. They have free access to information regarding the same. There is no uncertainty about future developments in the market.

9. **No Selling Cost:** There is no advertisement and selling cost in perfect competition. This is due to homogenous products of sellers, and small share of individual sellers in the market supply with no control over price.

10. **Bahaviour of Revenue curves under perfect competition:** In case of perfect competition firm is price taker not maker. Price is determined by industry and an individual seller has no power to influence the prevailing price in the market. As the price remains constant, TR will increase at constant rate and will be an upward sloping straight line. AR and MR curves are horizontal lines (Parallel to X-axis) and are equal (AR=MR) as shown in diagram 1. AR curve is demand curve under perfect competition and it is perfectly elastic (e=∞).

Diagram 1

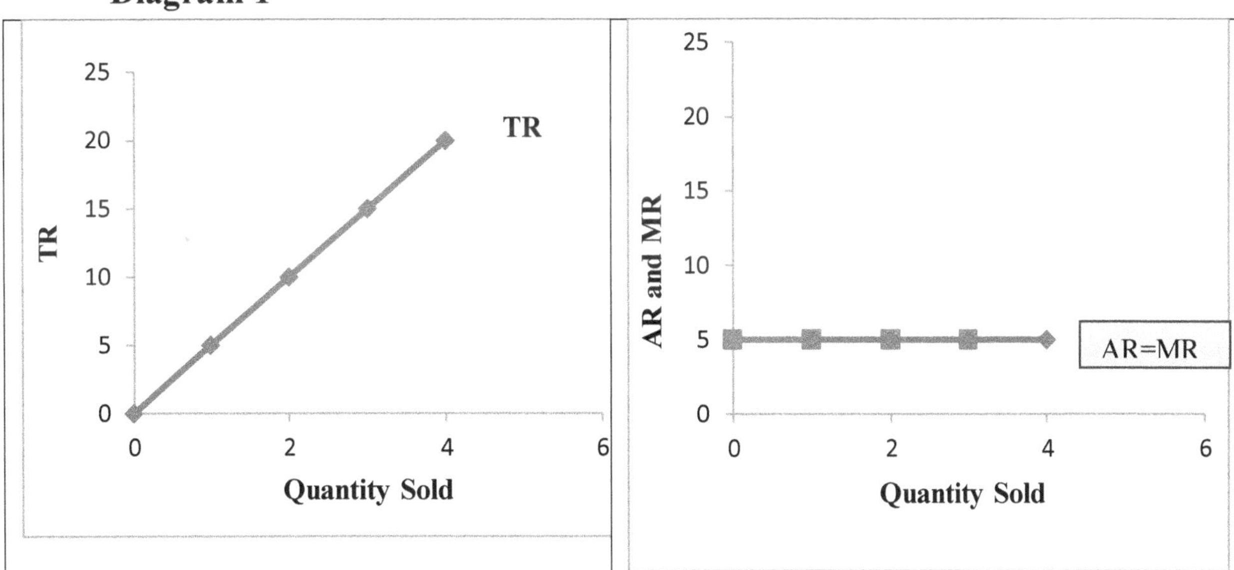

Monopoly: This form of market is polar opposite of perfect competition. A monopoly is a market that has only one seller and many buyers. The word monopoly comes from the Greek words **mono** for ***"One"*** and **polist** for ***"Seller."*** A monopolist is the only firm producing in its industry, and there is no other seller producing a close substitute products. In real world true or pure monopoly markets are rare. Their existence may be seen because of some form of government regulation or protection. However practically, the firm with dominant share in the industry and others having negligible share is considered as monopoly market. E.g. Railway in India, RBI has monopoly to issue notes.

"Monopoly is a market situation in which there is single seller, there are no close substitutes for commodity it produces, and there are barriers to entry."- ***Koutsoyiannis***

Absolute or Pure Monopoly: It is a form of market which is controlled by a single producer and has full control over the market supply of product which has no substitute, not even a remote one. It is a theoretical concept and rare phenomena in reality.

Relative Monopoly or Imperfect Monopoly: It refers to a situation when the supply of product is concentrated in few hands. This type implies absence of close substitutes.

Characteristics/Feature of Monopoly:
1. **Single Seller with Many Buyers:** It is a market with single seller and many buyers. A single seller may be a sole proprietor, a partnership firm or joint stock company.
2. **No Close Substitutes:** According to Boulding, "A pure monopoly firm is one that produces such a commodity as has no effective substitute in the production of other firms." There is no close substitute of the product produced by monopolist.
3. **Monopoly is also an Industry:** The difference between firm and industry doesn't exist in monopoly because it is a market with single seller with no close substitute available in the market.
4. **Restrictions on Entry of New Firms:** There are restrictions on the entry of new firms in the monopoly. Restrictions may be in the form technical barriers, government regulations etc. According to Bains, "A firm assumes monopoly situation when it has no close rival."
5. **Possibility of Price Discrimination:** Monopolist may also indulge in price discrimination. It is practice of selling same good at different prices to different buyers by monopolist.

6. **Firm is Price Maker & Taker**: Under monopoly, firm is price taker as well maker. Being a single seller in the market, monopolist has full control over price. However, demand curve faced by monopolist is negatively sloped. He can sell more quantity of a commodity by reducing the price.

7. **Revenue Curves Under Monopoly:** A monopolist can sell more quantity of the product by lowering its price and faces downward sloping demand curve. AR curve which represents industry's demand curve is downward sloping straight line under monopoly. MR curve is also a downward sloping straight line in such a way that it is equi-distant from AR curve and Y axis. While total revenue curve is concave shaped and increases at diminishing rate as long as MR is positive and attains its maximum point when MR is zero as shown in diagram 2. AR and MR curves are less elastic in monopoly while it is more elastic in monopolistic competition. It means that under monopoly, any increase in price causes relatively less decrease in demand for its product.

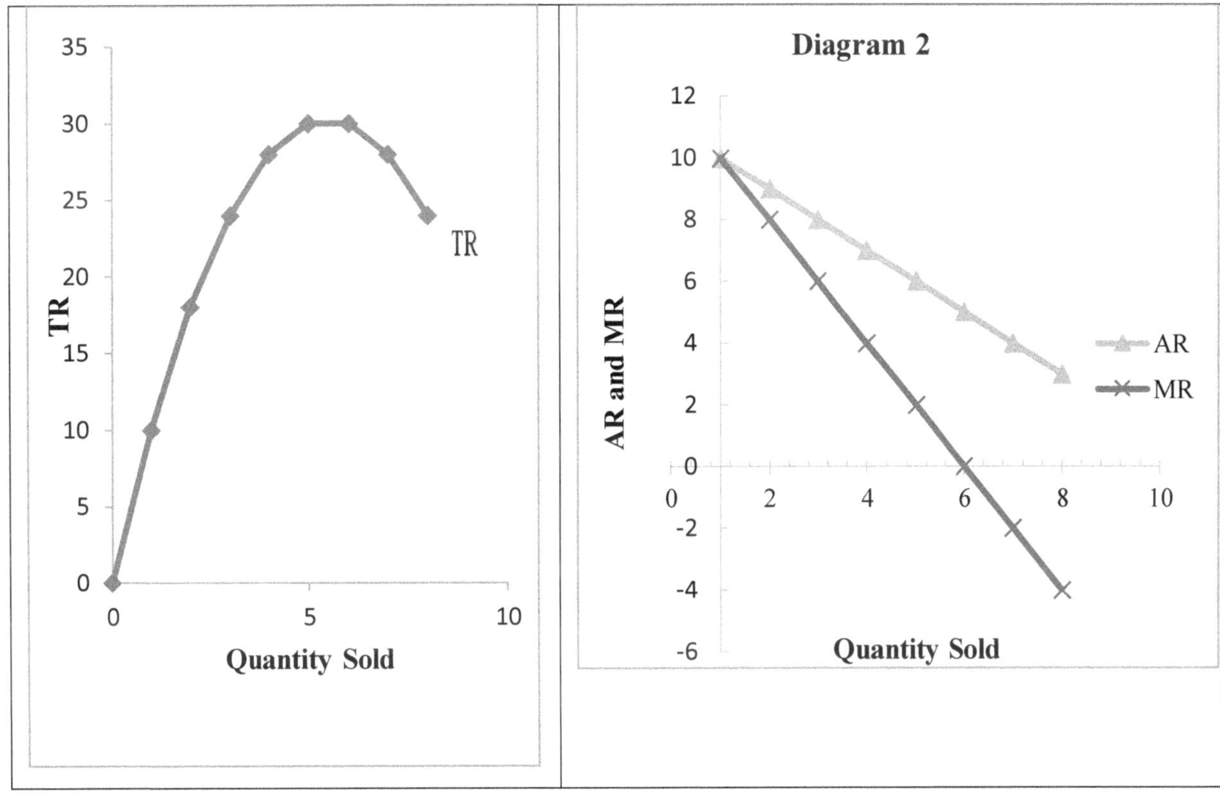

Why Monopolies Arise? What are Sources of Monopoly or Causes of Emergence of Monopoly?

The fundamental cause behind the monopoly is barriers to entry of new firms. For this reason, monopoly remains the only seller in the market without any competition. There are following main sources of barriers to entry.

1. **Government Created Monopolies**
    I. **Patents and Copy Rights:** Patents rights and copy rights are two exclusive rights offered to original producer by the government. Patent or copy right holder get exclusive rights to manufacture and sell the product or service for some specified period (Patent life). During that period nobody else can produce or sell product or service without the permission of patent holder.
    II. **License:** Monopolies can arise when government grants an exclusive right or permission to produce some good or service to a single firm. For example, government of India gives rights to Indian Railways to control and manage entire rail network in India.
2. **Monopoly Resources:** When a single firm owned a key resources or input required for production of a commodity. Such type of exclusive ownership of a key input is the main cause of emergence of monopoly.
3. **The Production Process:** Monopoly can also be emerged when a single firm can produce or supply a good or service to entire market at a lower cost than other producers. It is a case of natural monopoly. Such a monopoly arises when a firm is enjoying economies of scale over the relevant range of output.
4. **Limit Pricing Policy:** It is important source of monopoly. It is policy adopted by existing seller to set price just below the minimum long run average cost of potential entrants to avoid their entry.
5. **Mergers and Acquisitions:** Some times through merger and acquisition monopoly arises.

Monopolistic Competition:

Perfect competition and pure monopoly are two extremes and imperfect competition comes in the mid of these two forms of markets. Prof. E.H. Chamberlin and Mrs. Joan Robinson developed a scientific and systematic approach to this concept in their respective books viz. *"The Theory of Monopolistic Competition"* and *"The Economics of Imperfect competition"* respectively in 1933. Monopolistic is one form of the imperfect competition which is commonly visible in reality.

Monopolistic competition retains some elements of monopoly and perfect competition. It includes large number of sellers and buyers as in perfect competition. Each seller sells different but close substitute product and have control over price like in monopoly which directly varies with degree of product differentiation. Firms selling bathing soaps, toothpastes, biscuits, washing powders, services at barber shops etc. are examples of monopolistic competition. There are many sellers of single product with slight difference from each other's product. For example in case of bathing soaps firms are offering different brands like Lux, Vivel, Godrej, Ganga, Patanjali, Nirma, Dettol, Savlon, Margo, Neem etc.

"Monopolistic competition is found in the industry where there is large number of small sellers, selling differentiated products but close substitute products."-**J.S. Bains**

Characteristics/Features of Monopolistic Competition

1. **Large Number of Small Sellers and Many Buyers**: The number of sellers and buyers are very large in monopolistic competition. There may be 25, 30, 50 or 70 sellers in the market for single product. Generally, each seller have small share in the total market supply. Hence, reactions of the rival firms are not bothered by individual sellers. They can follow an independent price and output policy.

2. **Product Differentiation:** It is an important feature of monopolistic competition. According to this features each firm produces a product that is at least slightly different from those of other firms. In other words, products of various sellers are not homogeneous but are close substitutes of each other. Products may either differ in physical characteristics such as difference in quality, size design, colour, packing, brand name, raw material used etc., or conditions surrounding the sale of product like location of the seller, reputation, courtesy, credit facility, trustworthiness etc. product differentiation is the hall mark of monopolistic competition. This feature offers an individual seller some monopoly of its own differentiated product.

3. **Free Entry & Exit of Firms:** In monopolistic competition firms are free to enter and leave the group. The new entrants cannot copy the brand name, trade mark, design of the product of other seller. However, they are free to produce close substitute to the product produce by rival firms.

4. **Important Role of Selling Cost:** Selling costs play important role in monopolistic competition. Each firm incurs heavy amount on advertisement and promoting its products. They try their best to attract consumers towards their brands with most appropriate selling techniques.

5. **Imperfect Knowledge:** In monopolistic competition buyers and sellers do not have perfect knowledge about the price of the product and other market

conditions. It is not possible to compare products of different sellers with each other due to product differentiation.

6. **Imperfect Mobility:** Factors of production are not free to move from one firm to another or from one occupation to other occupation. There exist some constraints on the free movement of factors of production.

7. **Non Price Competition:** In monopolistic competition firms try to gain customers by offering free gifts, lucky coupons, buy one get one free offers, without indulging in price war. Such a competition is called non-price competition.

8. **Firm is Price Taker & Maker:** Each firm has its own price policy. Individual firm can decide price of the product independently. Demand curve faced by the individual seller under monopolistic competition is downward sloping. Firm can sell more quantity of a commodity by reducing the price.

9. **Partial Control Over Price:** Under monopolistic competition each firm has partial control over price due availability of close substitutes in the market. Degree of control over price depends upon the degree of product differentiation.

10. **Revenue Curves Under Monopolistic Competition:** Under monopolistic competition revenues curves are similar to monopoly. These revenues curves are more elastic in monopolistic competition while it is less elastic in monopoly as shown in diagram 3. It means that under monopolistic competition, any increase in price causes relatively more decrease in demand for its product.

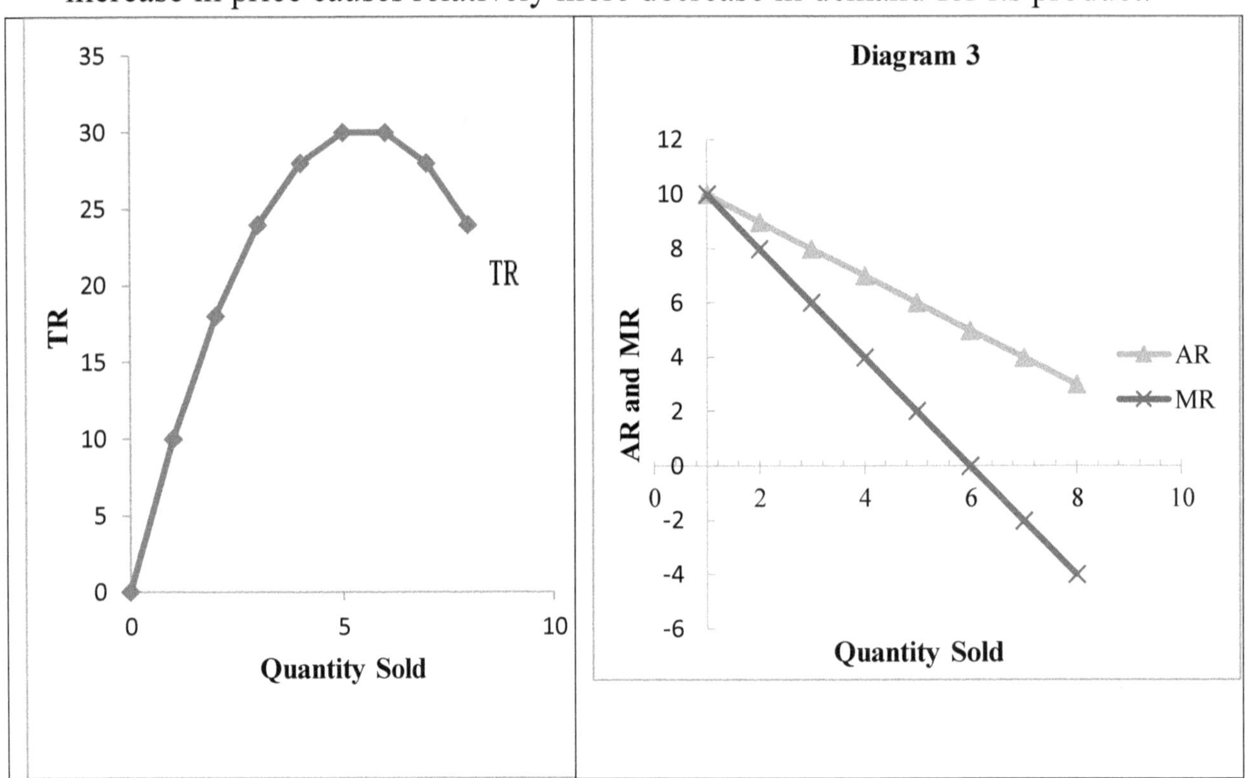

Oligopoly: This word is derived from two Greek words Oligo means 'few' and pollen means 'to sell'. Oligopoly is an important form of imperfect competition. It is market structure in which only a few sellers offers similar or slightly differentiated products. Examples of oligopolistic markets include automobiles, steel, petrochemicals, telecom and computers.

"Oligopoly is a market situation in which number of firms in an industry is, so small that each must consider the reactions of rivals in formulating its price policy."- **McConnel**

Characteristics/Features of Oligopoly

1. **Few Sellers/Firms and Many Buyers:** Oligopoly is a market structure in which only few sellers dominate the industry. However, there may be lack of uniformity in the size of the firms. Some firms have large share and others may have small share in the market. The products sold by them are either homogeneous or slightly differentiated.

2. **Mutual Interdependence:** In oligopoly there is high degree of interdependence among firms in respect of decision making. Any change in price and output by one firm is closely watched by the rival firms. Therefore, while taking any decision a firm has to take into account the impact of its decision on competing firms and reaction of the other firms. In other words, any action by a firm will call for a reaction by its rival firms. For example, free internet data usage given by Jio to its customers, initiated counter moves by Airtel, Idea and they also offered similar services to offset the impact of Jio. Such interdependence prevails due to high cross elasticity of demand of oligopoly products.

3. **Indeterminate Demand Curve:** Demand curve is indeterminate under oligopoly. A demand curve shows the amounts of product a firm can sell at various prices. It is possible to draw demand curve in case of perfect competition, monopoly and monopolistic competition due to lack of uncertainty regarding reactions of rival firms. Because any change in price by one firm has negligible effect on rival firms. In case of oligopoly any change in price by one firm may result change in prices by rival firms and no certain prediction about reaction pattern of rival firms can be made. Therefore, demand curve of an oligopolist is indeterminate.

4. **Barriers to Entry:** Under oligopoly there exist some barriers to entry of new firms. Economies of scale, patent rights, expertise in the field of production,

cost advantage, control over key inputs are some common examples of barriers to entry.

5. **Cut throat Competition or Keen Competition:** There is very high degree of competition among rival firms. Each firm keeps close watch on the actions of rival firms. Any change in price by one firm may result change in prices by rival firms. Sometimes these actions and reactions may lead to price war between firms.

6. **Advertisement:** Selling costs have important role to play in oligopoly. Heavy expenditure is incurred to imprint brand image on consumer's minds or to persuade buyers. In this Prof. Baumol remarks that "It is only under oligopoly that advertisement comes fully into its own." It is a matter of life and death under oligopoly, firm which fails to keep up with advertising budget of its rivals may find its customers drifting off to rival products.

7. **Uncertainty:** Under oligopoly it is not possible to predict accurately the behavior of rival firms. Any change in price or output by a firm will have direct effect on the working of rivals.

8. **Price Rigidity:** In oligopoly price remain rigid. Because, any change in price by oligopolist firm will not benefit the firm. If firm tries to reduce the price the rival firms also reduce their prices. Likewise if a firm tries to raise its price, other firms will not do so.

9. **Non Price Competition:** In oligopoly firms try to gain customers by offering free gifts, lucky coupons, buy one get one free offers, after sale services without indulging in price war. Such a competition is called non-price competition.

Duopoly: It is a special case of oligopoly. It is market in which there are two sellers.

Perfect /Pure Oligopoly: Oligopoly without product differentiation is known as Perfect /Pure Oligopoly. All rival firms produce identical products. E.g. cement, steel, aluminum etc.

Impure /Differentiated /Imperfect Oligopoly: Oligopoly with product differentiation is known as Impure /Differentiated /Imperfect Oligopoly. All rival firms produce differentiated products. E.g. Cigarettes, Air Conditioners etc.

Collusive or Cooperative Oligopoly: A collusive oligopoly implies presence of explicit or implicit agreement or understanding among the firms to avoid competition. All firms cooperate with each other with regard to their price and output decisions. Firms do not engaged in price wars; rather they jointly maximize their profits. Due to cooperation firms may achieve a stable price-output equilibrium.

Cartel: A cartel is a combination of firms whose object is to limit the scope of competitive forces within a market. It is formed to avoid competition and to maximise profits jointly.

"A cartel is a group of firms acting together to coordinate output decisions and control prices as if they were a single monopoly."- **D.N. Hyman**

Non Collusive or Non-cooperative Oligopoly: A non collusive oligopoly implies absence of explicit or implicit agreement or understanding among the firms. All firms act independently and compete with each other. There is a cut throat competition and heavy expenditure is incurred by firms to develop brand image. Firms often engaged in price wars. The failure of the market to reach a price-output equilibrium is the most important feature of models dealing with non- collusive oligopoly.

Partial Oligopoly: It refers to the market situation, where a large firm dominates the market and other firms follows him with regard to their price policy. Dominant firm acts as price leader.

Full Oligopoly: It refers to a market situation where all firms are of almost equal size, there is no dominant firm enough to play the role of a price leader.

****

Exercise:
1. In which kind of market, a firm is a price taker not maker? 1. Perfect competition 2. Monopoly 3. Monopolistic competition 4. Oligopolistic competition
2. 'A firm can sell more only at a lower price.' This is the feature of ________ 1. Perfect Competition 2. Monopoly 3. Oligopoly 4. Duopoly
3. Charging different prices from different buyers for the same good is called: 1. Price ceiling 2. Price floor 3. Price discrimination 4. Price control
4. Cartels are closely related to_____ 1. Perfect competition 2. Monopoly 3. Oligopoly 4. None of these
5. Compared with monopolistic competition, a firm's demand curve under monopoly is______1. Unitary elastic 2. Less elastic 3. More elastic 4. Infinitely elastic
6. Product differentiation is the main feature of _____. 1 Perfect Competition 2. Monopoly 3. Oligopoly 4. Monopolistic Competition
7. The difference between firm and industry disappears in monopoly. Statement is true or false.

8. Under perfect competition firms are indulged in heavy advertisements. Statement is true or false.
9. Under monopoly AR=MR. Statement is true or false.
10. A monopoly producer cannot control both prices as well as quantity of his product. Statement is true or false.

Answers:

1. 1	2. 2	3. 3	4. 3	5. 2
6. 4	7. T	8. F	9. F	10.T

Practice Questions:
1. What is market? What are its various types?
2. What perfect competition?
3. What is monopoly?
4. What is price discrimination?
5. What is product differentiation?
6. What is non price competition?
7. What is perfect oligopoly?
8. What is imperfect oligopoly?
9. What is meant by collusive oligopoly?
10. What is the behaviour of revenue curves under monopolistic competition?
11. What is the behaviour of revenue curves under perfect competition?
12. Why there is no need of selling cost in perfect competition?
13. Give four points of difference between perfect competition and monopolistic competition.
14. What are the characteristics of a perfectly competitive market?
15. Why firm is price taker in perfect competition, but not the price maker?
16. Explain why the demand curve facing a firm under monopolistic competition is negatively sloped.
17. What would be the shape of the demand curve so that the total revenue curve is a positively sloped straight line passing through the origin?
18. Explain the implication of 'freedom of entry and exit to the firms' under perfect competition.
19. Explain the implication of 'perfect knowledge about market' under perfect competition.
20. Distinguish between collusive and non-collusive oligopoly. Explain how the oligopoly firms are interdependent in taking price and output decisions.

21. Explain the implications of the feature 'large number of buyers' in a perfectly competitive market.

22. Explain the implications of the feature 'homogenous products' in a perfectly competitive market.

23. Explain the implications of the feature 'large number of sellers' under perfect competition.

24. Distinguish between 'cooperative' and 'non-cooperative' oligopoly.

25. Explain why firms are mutually interdependent in an oligopoly market.

26. Explain why there are only a few firms in an oligopoly market.

27. Explain the implications of 'differentiated product' in monopolistic competition.

28. Explain 'large number of buyers and sellers' features of a perfectly competitive market.

29. Explain any two features of monopoly market.

30. Explain "freedom of entry and exit to firms in industry" feature of monopolistic competition.

31. Why can a firm not earn abnormal profits under perfect competition in the long run? Explain.

32. Why is the demand curve of a firm under monopolistic competition more elastic than under monopoly?

33. Give the meaning of 'collusive' oligopoly. Explain the any two features of oligopoly.

CHAPTER 12
MARKET EQUILIBRIUM

We have discussed the theory of demand and theory of supply in previous chapters. Now, we are going to discuss about the determination of price and output equilibrium. In this chapter, we will explain how the forces of demand and supply interact to determine equilibrium price? How the equilibrium price is changed with shifts in demand and supply? We will also discuss the applications of demand and supply that are considered to be important for framing the policies by the government, especially in the field of price control.

Determination of Market Equilibrium (Equilibrium Price and Equilibrium Quantity):

The equilibrium price and quantity is determined by the market forces of demand and supply. Market equilibrium is a situation where market demand and market supply are equal or where market demand and market supply intersect each other. This equilibrium implies the equilibrium price and equilibrium quantity.

Equilibrium Price: The price at which the quantity demanded and quantity supplied are equal to each other. It is price where market clears, meaning that market demand (MD) is equal to market supply (MS). It is determined by the market demand and market supply of a commodity as shown in table 1 and diagram 1.

Equilibrium Quantity: It is a quantity of a commodity bought and sold by buyers and sellers respectively in a market corresponding to equilibrium price as shown in table 1 and diagram 1.

Explanation: Demand for and supply of X-commodity is measured on the X-axis and price on the Y-axis. The demand curve for X-commodity is shown by 'DD' and it is negatively sloped. The supply curve of X-commodity is shown by 'SS' and it is positively sloped. Both these curves intersect at point 'E' corresponding to price Rs. 30 (Equilibrium Price), and quantity demanded and supplied in market is 30 (Equilibrium Quantity) as shown in diagram 1. Below the equilibrium price, there is a situation of excess demand and above the equilibrium price; there is a situation of excess supply.

Table 1: Demand and Supply of X-commodity against various prices

Price (in Rs.)	Supply of X-commodity (in Kg)	Demand for X-commodity (in Kg)	Situation
10	10	50	Excess Demand
20	20	40	Excess Demand
30	**30**	**30**	*Equilibrium*
40	40	20	Excess Supply
50	50	10	Excess Supply

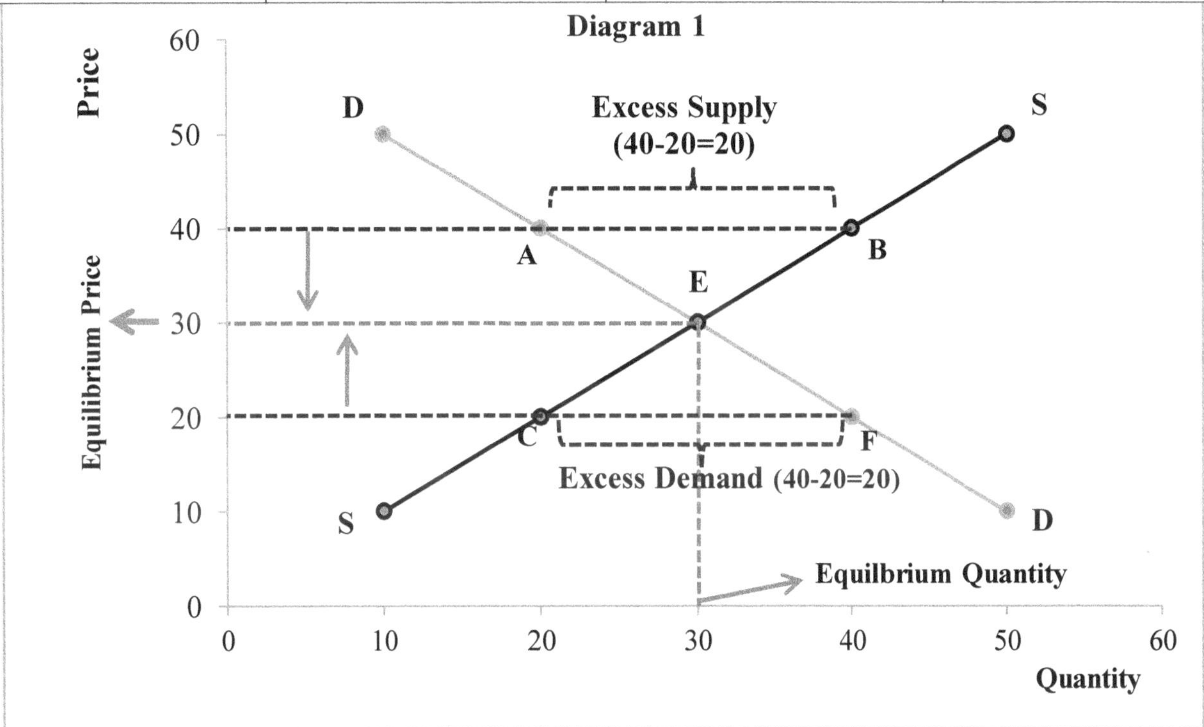

The situation of excess demand and excess supply will no longer exist in the market, because there is inherent tendency in market mechanism that will keep market in equilibrium. In situation of excess demand, price will begin to increase (from Rs. 20 to Rs. 30) and will cause contraction in demand (from 'F' to 'E' on demand curve DD) and extension in supply (from 'C' to 'E' on Supply curve SS) as shown in diagram 1. This process of contraction in demand and extension in supply will continue till the existence of excess demand. As and when excess demand is exhausted price will stop rising and equilibrium is restored. In situation of excess supply, price will begin to fall (from Rs. 40 to Rs. 30) and will cause extension in demand (from 'A' to 'E' on demand curve 'DD') and contraction in supply (from 'B' to 'E' on Supply curve 'SS') as shown in diagram 1. This process of extension in demand and contraction in supply will continue till the existence of excess supply. As and when excess supply is over price will stop falling and equilibrium is restored.

Effect of Change in Demand of X-commodity on Equilibrium Price and Quantity: Change in demand implies increase or decrease in demand of X-commodity. We shall discuss the effects of increase or decrease in demand on equilibrium price and quantity.

Increase in Demand: Demand for X- commodity may increase due to increase in income, increase in price of substitute goods, decrease in price of complementary goods, expectation of increase in prices in future, favourable change in tastes, fair distribution of income and increase in population. This will cause rightward shift in the demand curve of X-commodity from DD to DD_1 to right as shown in diagram 2. As result of shift in demand curve to the right, there will be excess demand (EA as shown in diagram 2) in the market for X-commodity. The excess demand will cause the price of X- commodity to increase from Rs. 30 to Rs. 40, quantity from 1500 units to 2000 units and shifts market equilibrium from E to E_1. The increase in price will continue as long as there is presence of excess demand, and will stop rising where excess demand is completely exhausted. Excess demand contracts to zero due to contraction in demand from A to E_1 and extension in supply from E to E_1, triggered by increase in price.

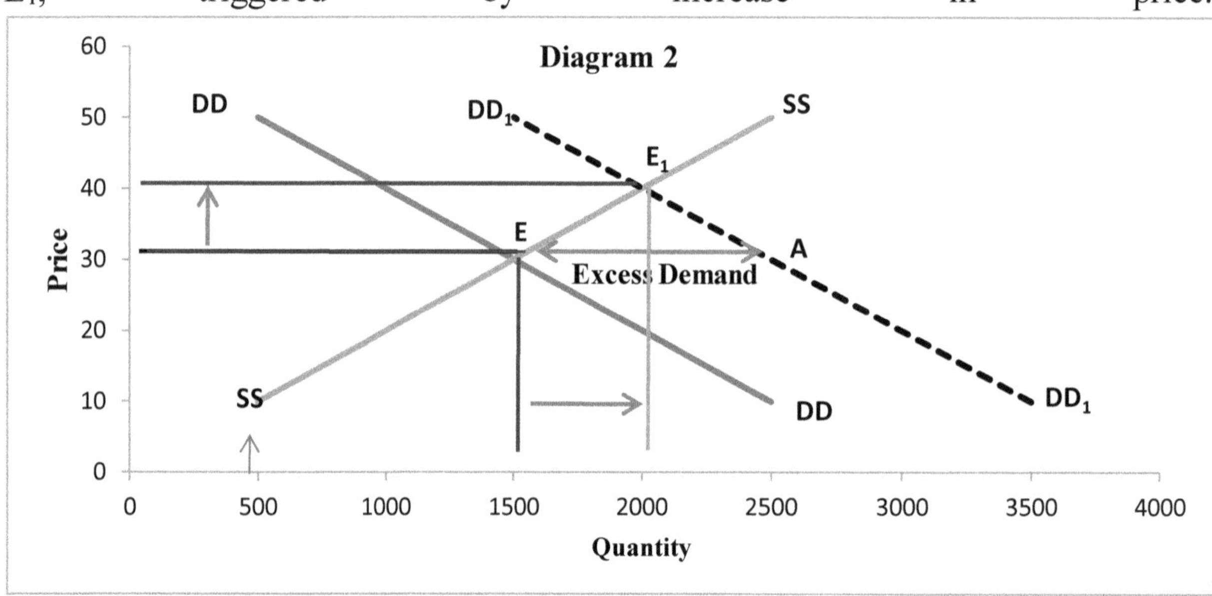

Decrease in Demand: Demand for X- commodity may decrease due to decrease in income, decrease in price of substitute goods, increase in price of complementary goods, expectation of decrease in prices in future, unfavourable change in tastes, unfair distribution of income and decrease in population. This will cause leftward shift in the demand curve of X-commodity from DD to DD_1 to left as shown in diagram 3. As result of shift in demand curve to the left, there will be excess supply (EA as shown in diagram 2) in the market for X-commodity. The excess supply will cause the price of X- commodity to decrease from Rs. 40 to Rs. 30, quantity from 2000 units to 1500 units and shifts market equilibrium from E to E_1. The decrease in price will continue as long as there is presence of excess supply, and will stop rising where excess supply is completely exhausted. Excess supply contracts to zero due to extension in demand from A to E_1 and contraction in supply from E to E_1, triggered by decrease in price.

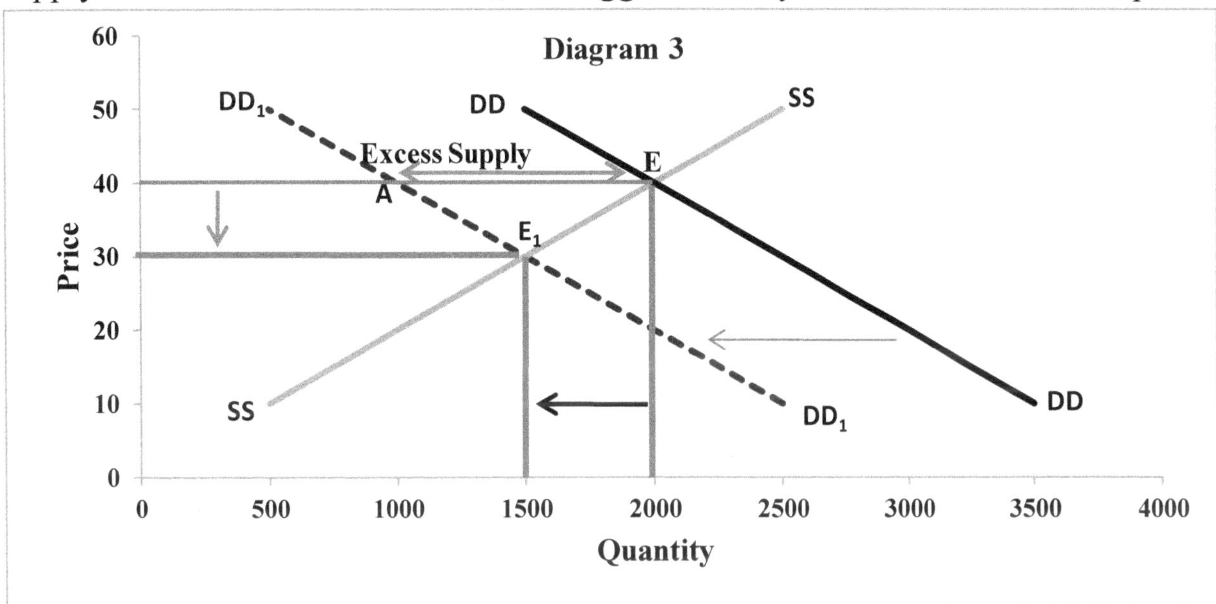

Effect of Change in Supply of X-commodity on Equilibrium Price and Quantity: Change in supply implies increase or decrease in supply of X-commodity. We shall discuss the effects of increase or decrease in supply on equilibrium price and quantity.

Decrease in Supply: Supply of X-commodity may decrease due to decrease in number of sellers, increase in price of inputs, increase in excise duty, indirect taxes, withdrawal of subsidy etc. This will shift the supply curve of X-commodity from SS to SS_0 to the left as shown in diagram 4. Due to the shift in supply curve to the left, there will be excess demand for X-commodity at the given price (Rs. 20). The excess supply (AE or 1000 units) will increase the price from Rs. 20 to Rs. 30 and decrease quantity from 2000 units to 1500 units and shifts equilibrium position from E to E_1.

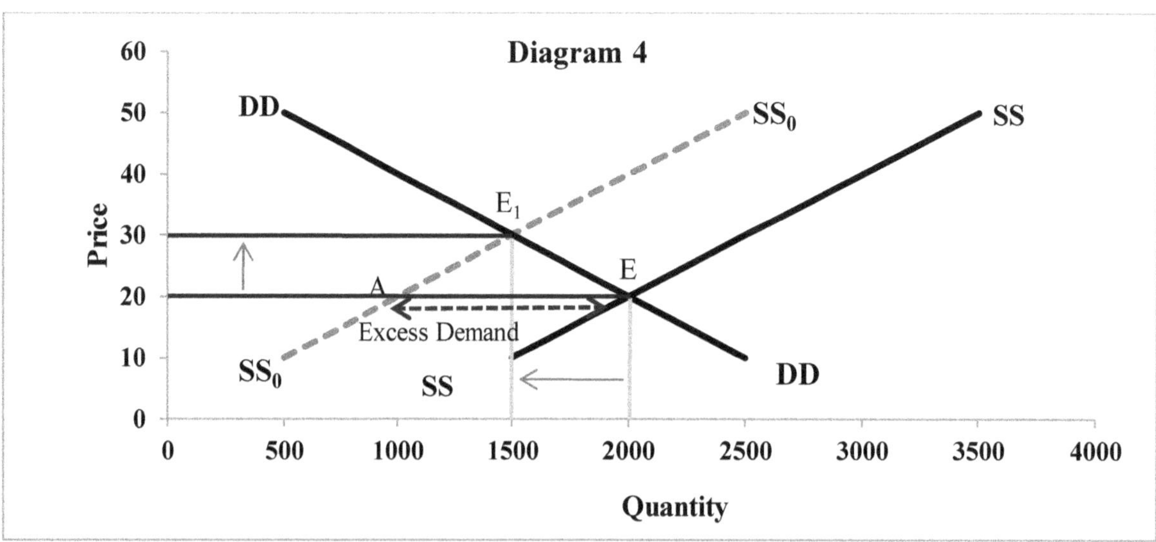

Increase in Supply: Supply of X-commodity may increase due to increase in number of sellers, decrease in price of inputs, decrease in excise duty, indirect taxes, increase in subsidy, improvement in technology etc. This will shift the supply curve of X-commodity from SS to SS_1 to the right as shown in diagram 5.

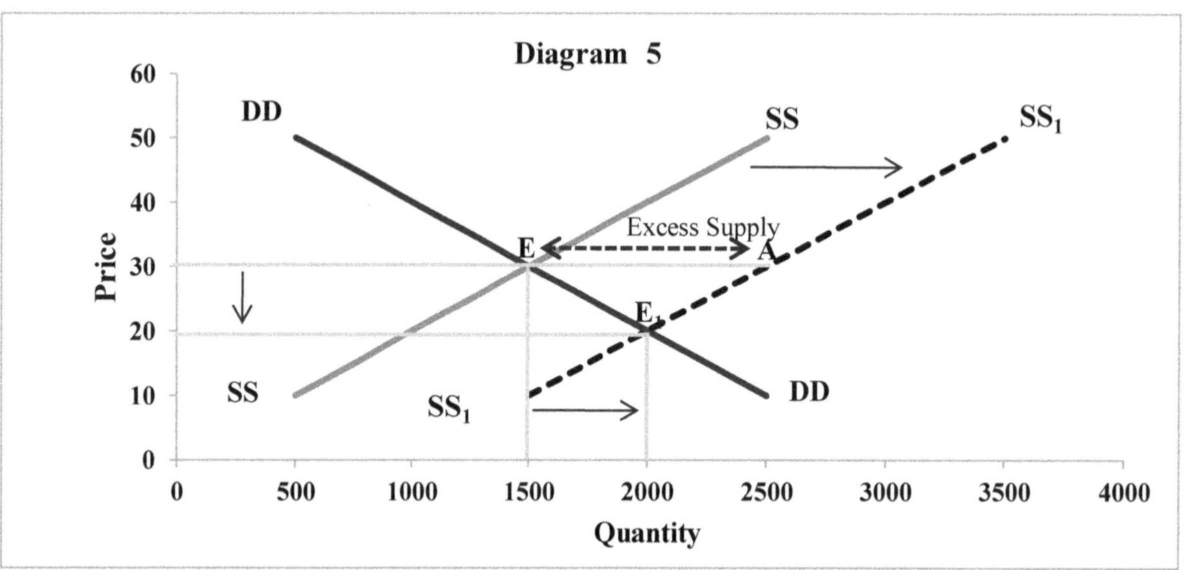

Due to the shift in supply curve to the right, there will be excess supply for X-commodity at the given price (Rs. 30). The excess supply (AE or 1000 units) will decrease the price from Rs. 30 to Rs. 20 and increase quantity from 1500 units to 2000 units and shifts equilibrium position from E to E_1.

Simultaneous Change in Demand and Supply: This implies simultaneous increase and decrease in demand and supply.

Simultaneous Increase in Demand and Supply: There are three possibilities when simultaneous increase in demand and supply will happen. In first case the increase in demand is more than the increase in supply, in second case increase in demand is equal to the increase in supply and final case where increase in demand is less than the increase in supply.

Case I: Increase in Demand > Increase in Supply

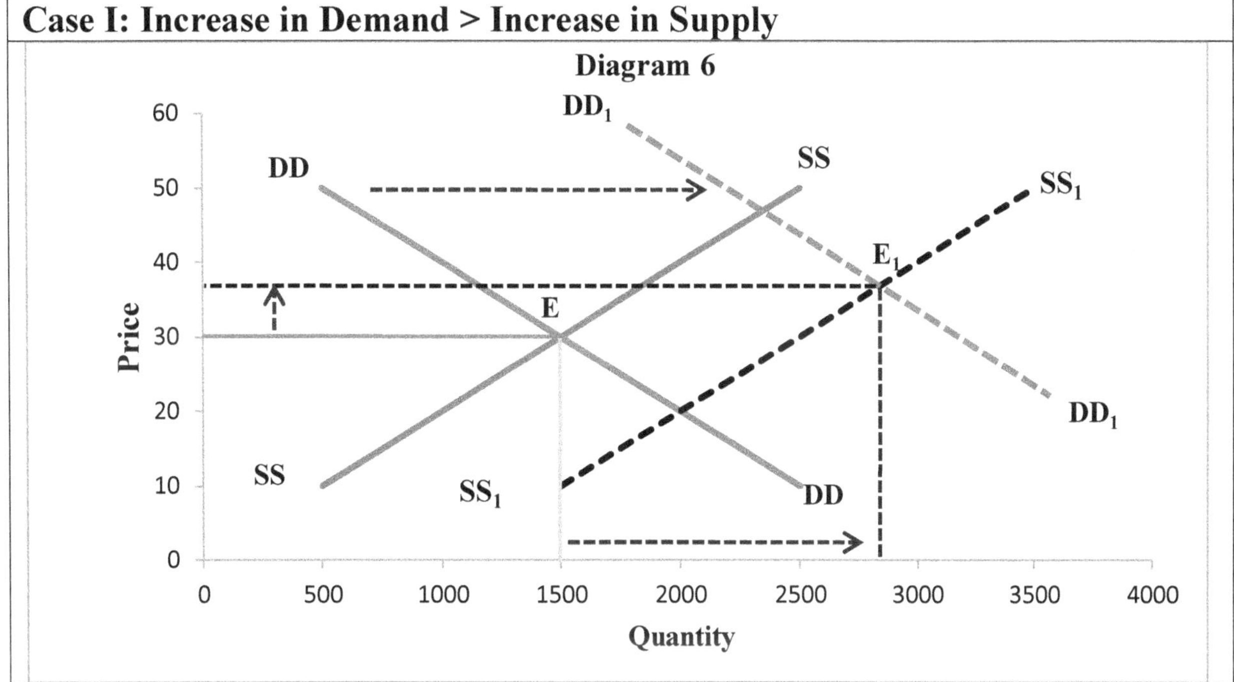

Explanation: When the increase in demand is more than the increase in supply, then equilibrium price will increase along with equilibrium quantity and equilibrium point will shift to the upward in rightward direction (move from E to E₁) where shifted demand and supply curve will intersect as shown in diagram 6.

Case II: Increase in Demand = Increase in Supply

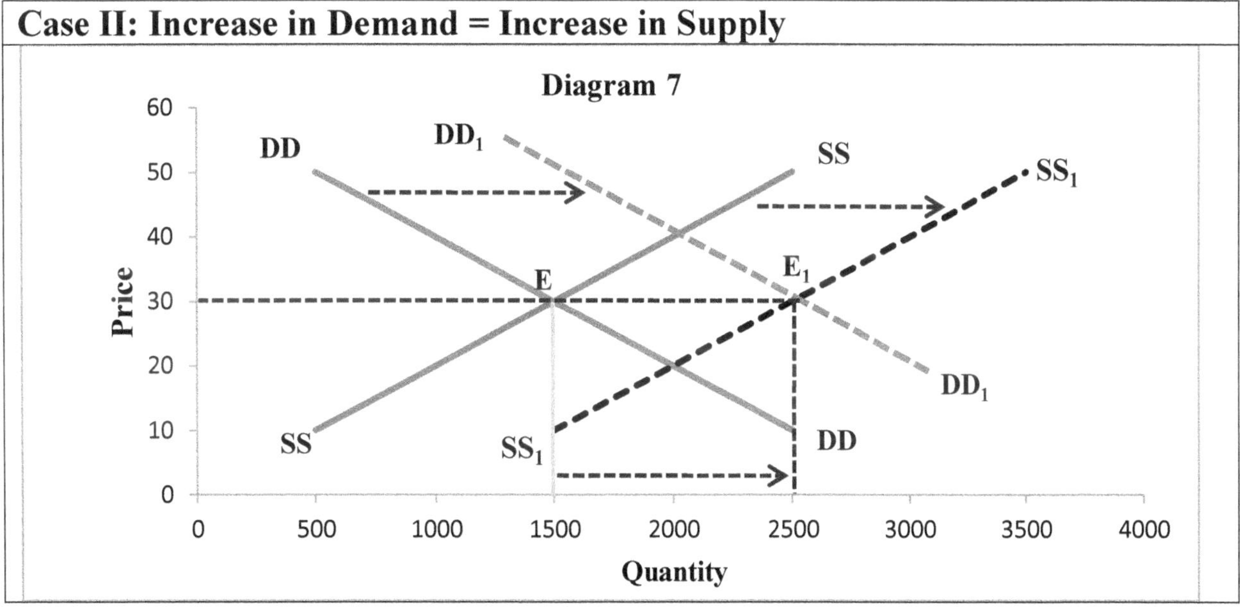

Explanation: When the increase in demand is equal the increase in supply, then equilibrium price will remain unchanged but equilibrium quantity will increase and equilibrium point will shift to the right (move from E to E₁) where shifted demand and supply curve will intersect as shown in diagram.

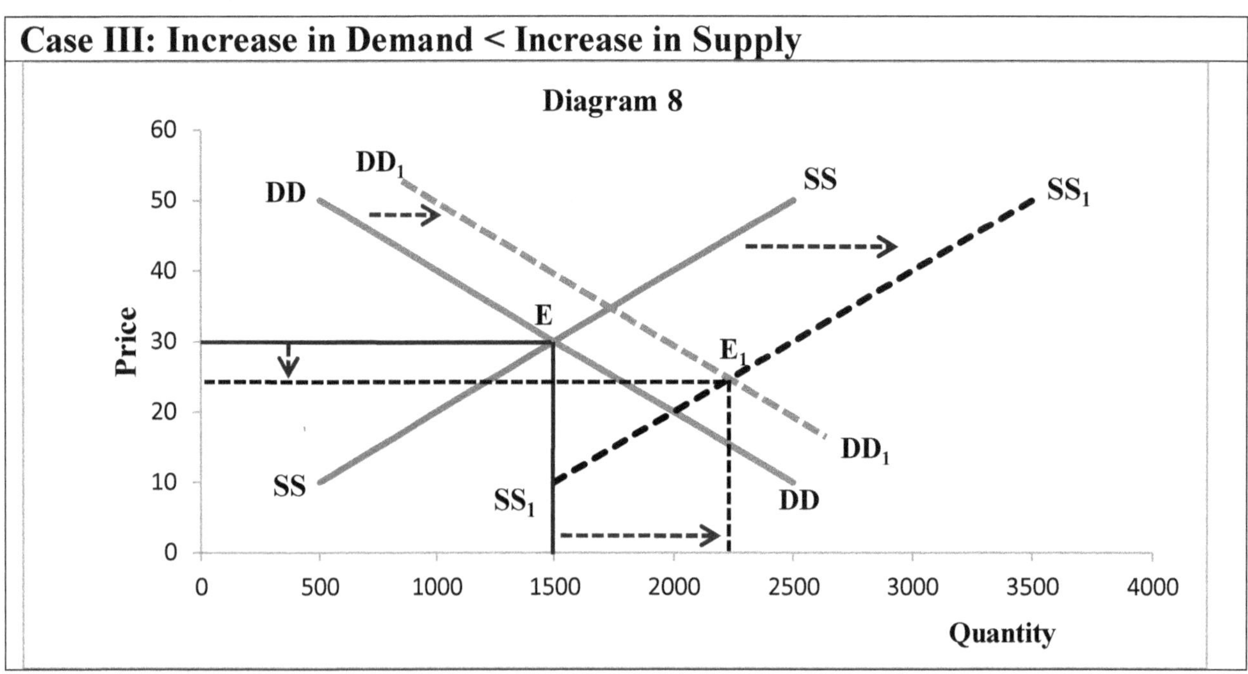

Explanation: When the increase in demand is less than the increase in supply, then equilibrium price will fall but equilibrium quantity will increase and equilibrium point will shift to the down in rightward direction (move from E to E_1) where shifted demand and supply curve will intersect at E_1 as shown in diagram 8.

Simultaneous Decrease in Demand and Supply: There are three possibilities when simultaneous decrease in demand and supply will happen. In first case the decrease in demand is more than the decrease in supply, in second case decrease in demand is equal to the decrease in supply and final case where decrease in demand is less than the decrease in supply.

Case I: Decrease in Demand > Decrease in Supply

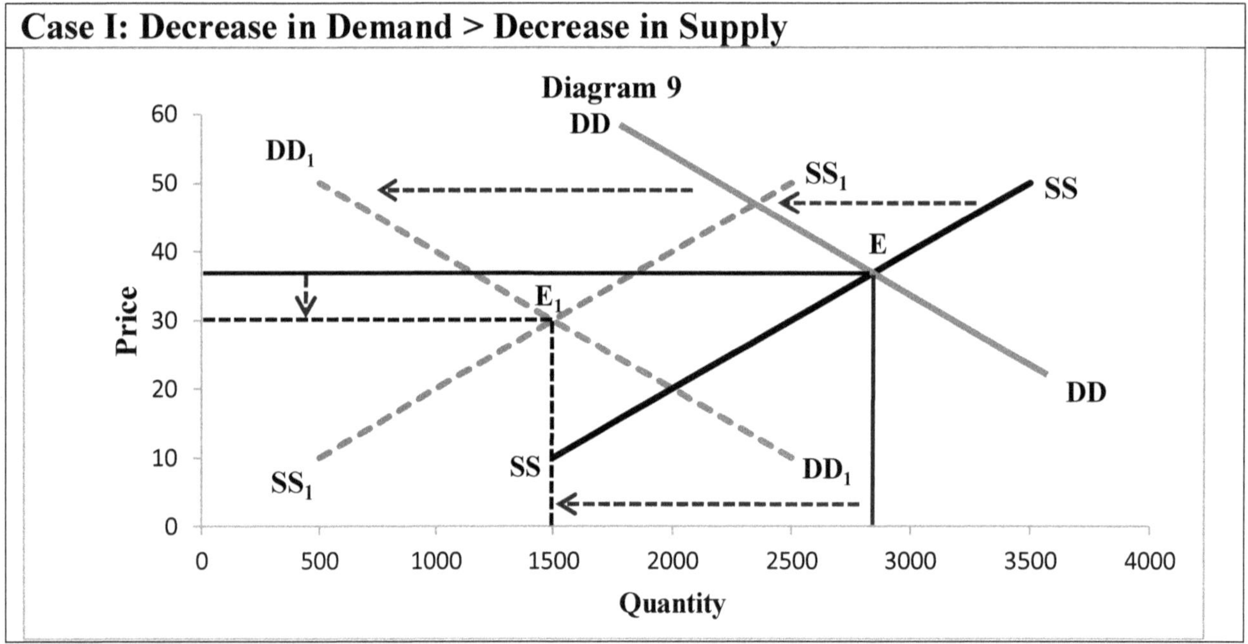

Explanation: When the decrease in demand is more than the decrease in supply, then equilibrium price will fall along with equilibrium quantity and equilibrium point will shift to the downward in leftward direction (move from E to E₁) where shifted demand and supply curve will intersect at E₁ as shown in diagram 9.

Case II: Decrease in Demand = Decrease in Supply

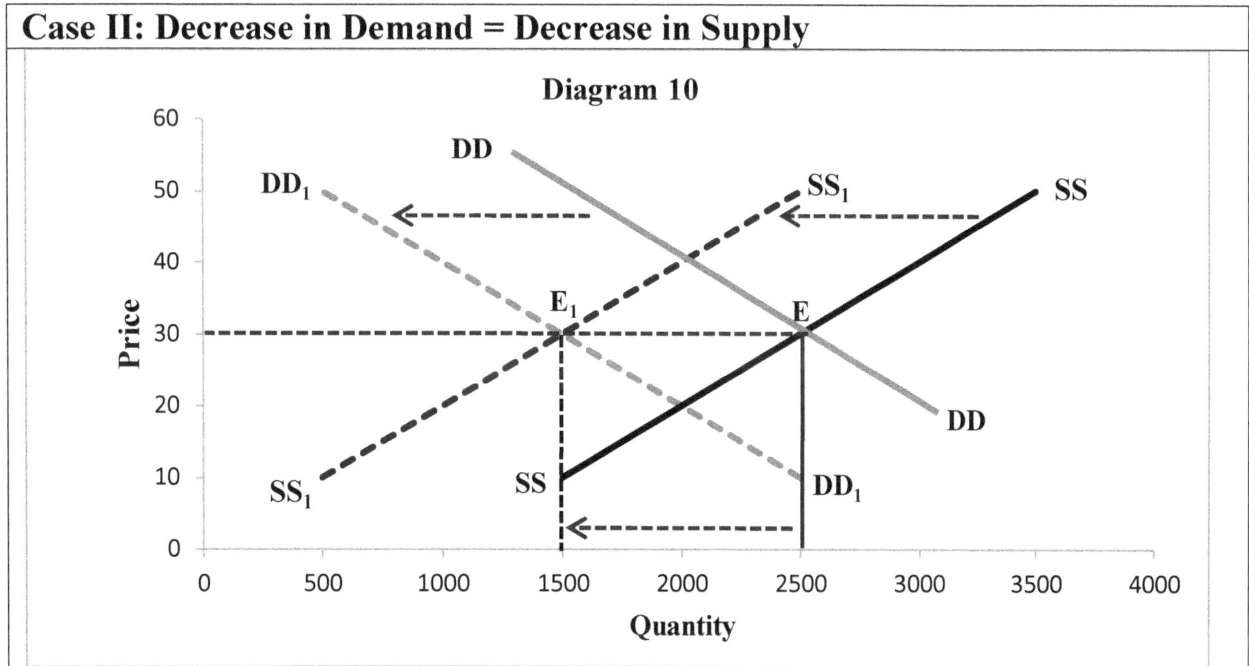

Explanation: When the decrease in demand is equal to the decrease in supply, then equilibrium price will remain unchanged but equilibrium quantity will fall and equilibrium point will shift to the left (move from E to E₁) where shifted demand and supply curve will intersect at E₁ as shown in diagram 10.

Case III: Decrease in Demand < Decrease in Supply

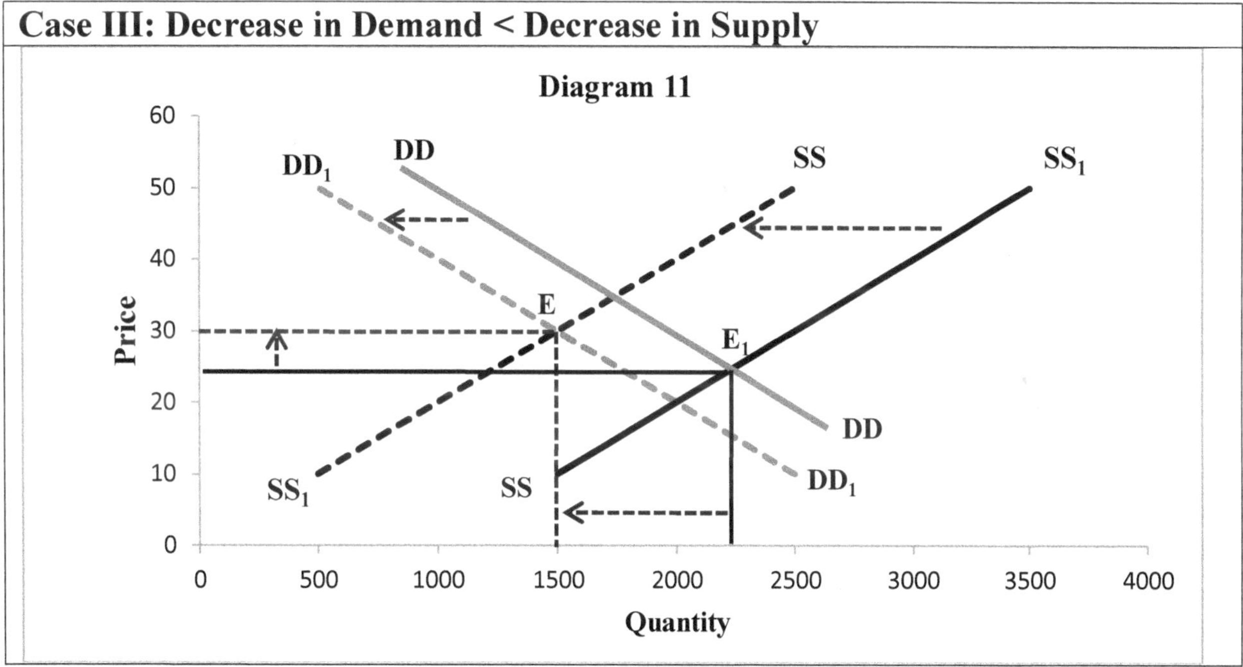

Explanation: When the decrease in demand is less than the decrease in supply, then equilibrium price will rise but equilibrium quantity will fall and equilibrium point will shift to the upward in leftward direction (move from E to E₁) where shifted demand and supply curve will intersect at E₁ as shown in diagram 11.

Special Cases: This will include cases of perfectly elastic demand and supply and perfectly inelastic demand and supply.

When Demand Curve is Perfectly Elastic:	When Demand Curve is Perfectly Inelastic
In this case increase or decrease in supply will have no effect on price but equilibrium quantity will increase with increase in supply and decrease with decrease in supply as shown in diagram 12.	In this case increase or decrease in supply will have no effect on quantity but equilibrium price will increase with decrease in supply and decrease with increase in supply as shown in diagram 13.
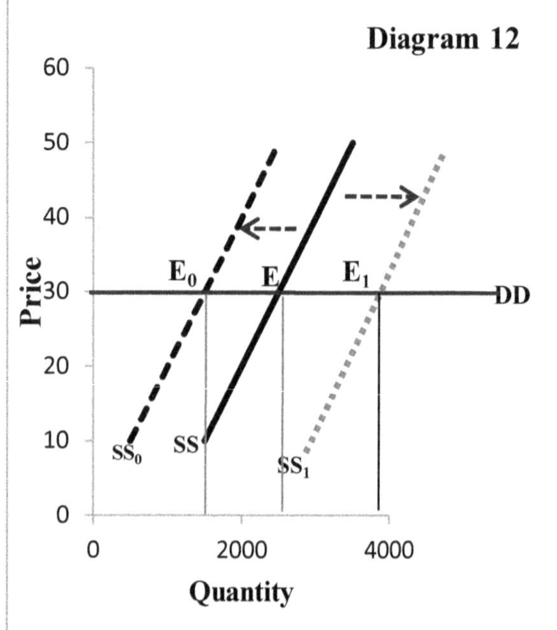	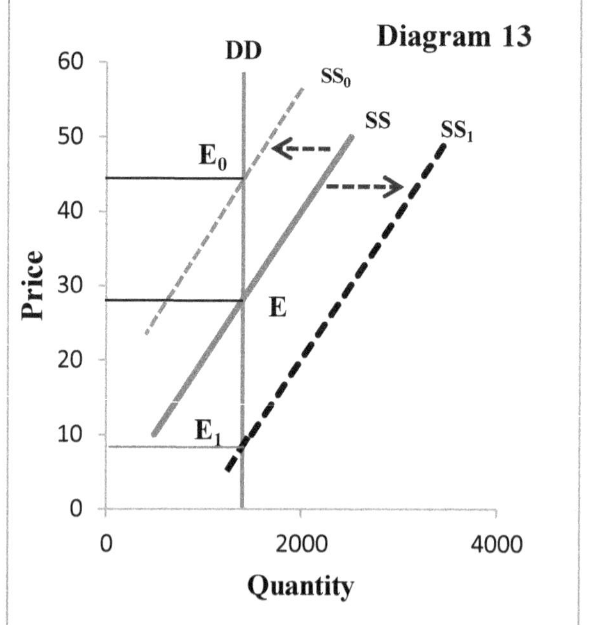
When Supply Curve is Perfectly Elastic	**When Supply Curve is Perfectly Inelastic**
In this case increase or decrease in demand will have no effect on price but equilibrium quantity will increase with increase in demand and decrease with decrease in demand as shown in diagram 14.	In this case increase or decrease in demand will have no effect on quantity but equilibrium price will increase with increase in demand and decrease with decrease in demand as shown in diagram 15.
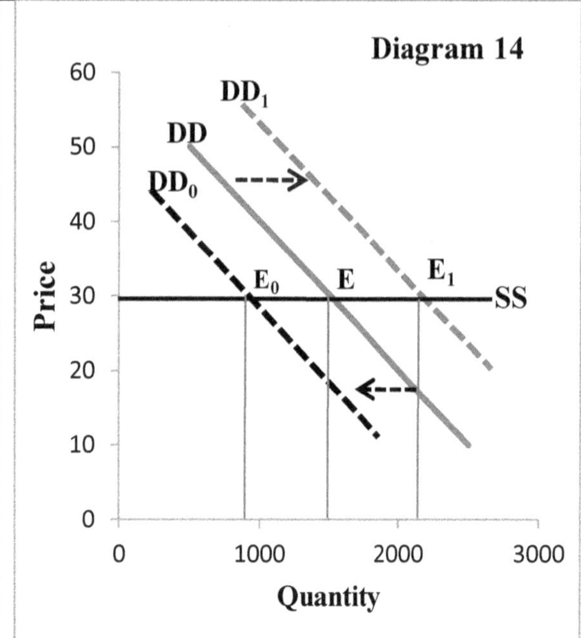	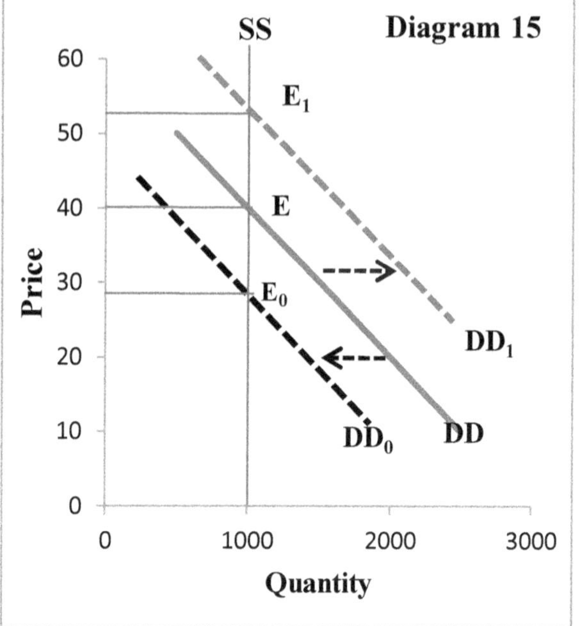

Price Controls

These controls are used to influence the price of commodities through enacting laws, rather by market forces. These include laws setting maximum permissible prices or minimum support prices.

Price Ceiling: A price ceiling is the legal maximum price that a seller is allowed to charge for a product or service from the buyer. This ceiling is generally imposed on essential items like foodstuffs, kerosene oil, cooking gas etc. or to make housing available at an affordable price (rent control). It is always fixed below the market determined price to make essentials affordable for low income families.

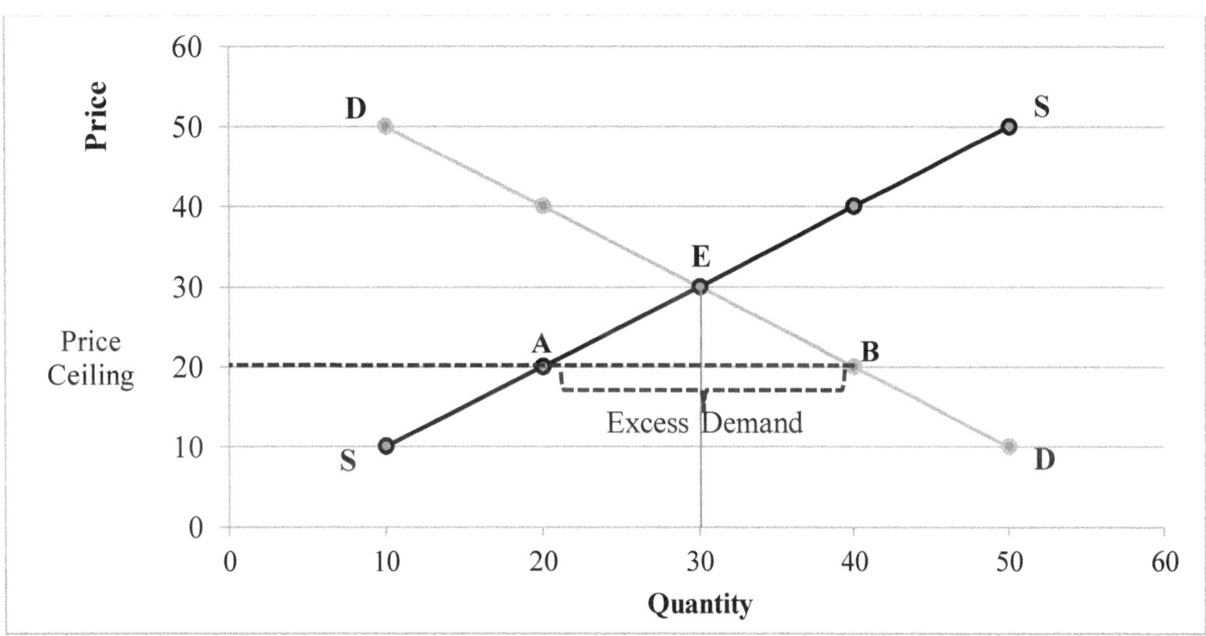

Consequences of Price Ceiling:

There will be shortage of goods in the market. Production will be insufficient to satisfy everyone who wishes to buy the product. Consequently, Long queues will develop at shops to buy the goods. In the absence of any official system of allocating the supply, either only preferred consumers will be entertained by sellers (system of Sellers's preference or allocation by seller's preference), or consumer will get things on the basis of luck. Price ceiling is likely to give rise to black market. Black market is a market in which goods are sold illegally at prices higher than a legally fixed price by the government due to shortage of goods at the price fixed by the government.

Price Floor or Minimum Support Price: It is a legal minimum on the price at which a good can be sold and it is fixed above the market clearing levels or equilibrium price as shown in diagram. The price cannot fall below this level. This price policy may be used to 1. Encourage production of essential articles 2. Provide a fair deal to workers. (Minimum wage policy) 3. Reduce import dependency by encouraging domestic production through price floor and helps to achieve import substitution policy.

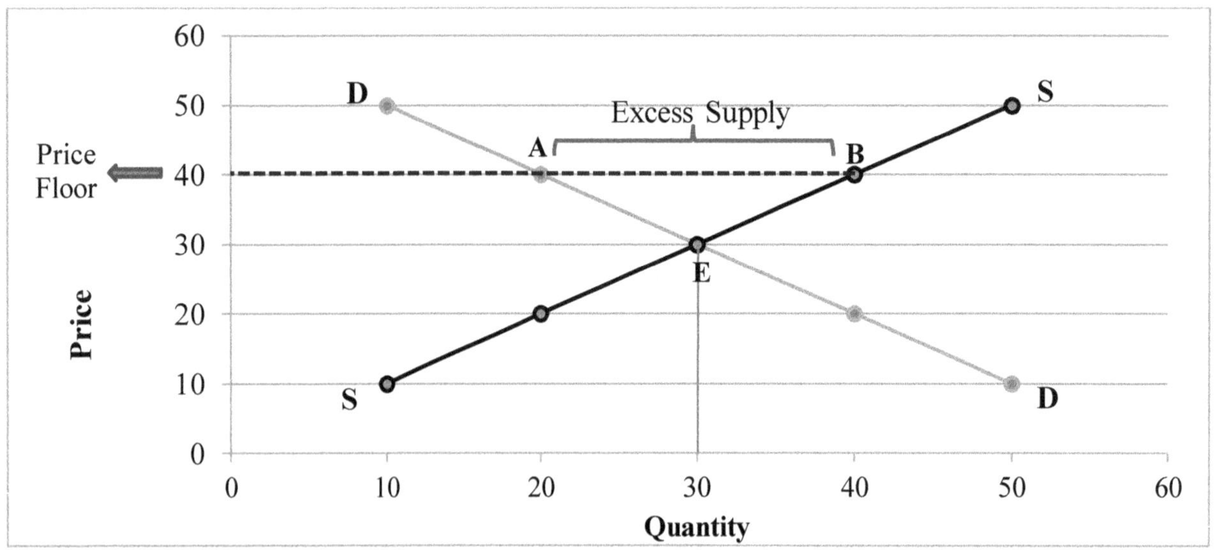

Consequences of Price Floor:

There will be excess supply of goods in the market. Market will be flooded by production of commodity that is protected by price floor. There are chances of transfer of resources towards production of goods protected with price floor and cause misallocation of resources. This may cause shortage of those goods in market that are not covered with price floor and hence cause there price to rise.

Exercise:

1. In the situation of market equilibrium: 1. Market demand = Market supply 2. Market demand > Market supply 3. Market demand < Market supply 4. None of these
2. In a situation of excess supply, market price tends to: 1. Rise 2. Fall 3. Remain constant 4. None of these
3. What will be the effect on equilibrium price if supply is decreased with no change in demand? 1. No change in price 2. Price will fall 3. Price will rise 4. None of these
4. What will happen if both the demand and supply curves shift to right in the same proportion? 1. Only equilibrium price remains unchanged 2. Only equilibrium quantity remains unchanged 3. Equilibrium price remains unchanged but equilibrium quantity decreases 4. Equilibrium price remains unchanged but equilibrium quantity increases

5. Price floor is set 1. Below the equilibrium price 2. Above the equilibrium price 3. Equal to the equilibrium price 4. All of the above

6. The equilibrium market price of the wheat is Rs. 1000 per quintal. Farmers are not happy to sell their produce at this price as it is too low to cover their economic cost. They start protests against government to raise this price to Rs. 1800 per quintal. Keeping in view the elections and to give push to agriculture sector, Govt. decides to set the minimum support price for wheat at Rs. 1700. Farmers withdraw their protests and feel satisfied with Govt's decision. Examine the concept used by government. 1

7. Price ceiling is followed to 1.Protect the interest of Buyer 2. Protect the interest of seller 3. Ensure availability of essential articles to all sections of the society 4. 1 & 3

8. What will be the effect on equilibrium price if there is increase in supply and demand curve is perfectly elastic? 1. Rise 2. Fall 3. Remain constant 4. None of these

9. How will price react to decrease in supply if demand curve is vertical? 1. Fall in price, 2. Increase in price, 3. No change, 4. Information is inadequate

10. Market with seller's preference will prevail as consequence of 1. Price ceiling 2. Price floor 3. Both 1 &2 4. 4. MSP

Answers:

1. 1	2. 2	3. 3	4. 4	5. 2
6. MSP	7. 4	8. 3	9. 2	10.1

Numerical

1. Market demand and supply schedules of mangoes (per day) are given below:

Price (per kg)	9	7	5	3	1
Qd (kg)	4	6	8	10	12
Qs (kg)	14	11	8	5	2

   Find out: 1. Equilibrium price and equilibrium quantity. 2. Excess demand at Rs.3 per kg. 3. Excess supply at Rs.7 per kg. (Ans: 1. 8, 2. 5, 3. 5)

2. Suppose the demand and supply curves of a commodity 'X' in a perfectly competitive market are given by: Qd= 700-p; Qs= 500+3p.Calculate equilibrium price and quantity. (Ans: Equilibrium price Rs. 50, Equilibrium quantity 650 units)

3. The market for audio cassettes has inverse supply and demand curves given by p= 2Qs and p= 42-Qd. Calculate the equilibrium price. (Ans: Rs. 28)

4. Calculate the equilibrium price and quantity for the demand and supply curves of a particular commodity given by: Qd= 10-p and Qs= p. What will happen

when the market price is Rs.7? What will happen when the market price is Rs.3? (Ans: Equilibrium price Rs. 5, Equilibrium quantity 5 units, At P=7, Excess Supply, At P=3, Excess demand)

5. Suppose the demand and supply curves of a commodity are given as: Qd= 200-p Qs= 120+p. Find the equilibrium price and equilibrium quantity. Also show that at price of Rs.30, there is excess demand and at a price of Rs.45, excess supply. (Ans: Equilibrium price Rs. 40, Equilibrium quantity 160 units, At P = 30, Qd = 170, Qs = 150, At P =45, Qd = 155, Qs = 165)

6. Suppose the demand and supply curves of a commodity are given as: Qd= 1000-p Qs= 700+2p. Find the equilibrium price and quantity. Now suppose that the price of an input used to produce salt increased so that new supply curve is Qs= 400+2p. How does the equilibrium price and quantity changes? Suppose that the government has imposed a tax Rs.3 per unit of sale. How does it affect the equilibrium price and quantity? (Ans: Equilibrium price Rs. 100, Equilibrium quantity 900 units, At new supply, Equilibrium price Rs. 200, Equilibrium quantity 800 units, Tax Rs. 3 per unit will change supply function like Qs = 400+2(p-3) and Equilibrium quantity is 898 and Equilibrium price will increase to Rs. 102)

Practice Questions:

1. Explain market equilibrium? How it is determined?
2. What is meant by 'excess supply' of a good in a market? Explain its chain of effects on the market for that good. Use diagram.
3. What is price ceiling? What are its consequences?
4. What is price floor? What are its consequences?
5. When do you say there is excess demand for a commodity in the market?
6. When do we say there is excess supply for a commodity in the market?
7. What will happen if the price prevailing in the market is (a) above the equilibrium price? (b) Below the equilibrium price?
8. Explain how price is determined in a perfectly competitive market with fixed number of firms.
9. How are equilibrium price and quantity affected due to increase or decrease in income?
10. How do the equilibrium price and quantity of a commodity change when price of input used in its production changes?
11. Using supply and demand curves show how an increase in the price of shoes, affects the price of a pair of socks and the number of pairs of socks bought and sold.

12. If the price of a substitute (Y) of Good-X increases, what impact does it have on the equilibrium price and quantity of Good-X?

13. Explain through a diagram the effect of a rightward shift of both the demand and supply curves on equilibrium price and quantity.

14. Suppose the demand and supply curves of salt are given by: $Q_d = 1000 - p$, $Q_s = 700 + 2p$

    1. Find the equilibrium price and quantity
    2. Now suppose that the price of an input used to produce salt has increased so that the new supply curve is: $Q_s = 400 + 2p$
    3. How does the equilibrium price and quantity change? Does the change conform to your expectation?
    4. Suppose the government has imposed GST which raises the cost by Rs.3 per unit of output. How does it affect the equilibrium price and quantity?

15. Market for a good is in equilibrium. There is an "increase "in demand for this good. Explain the chain of effects of this change. Use diagram.

16. Market for a good is in equilibrium. There is change in supply of the good. Explain the chain of effects of this change. Use diagram.

17. Market for a good is in equilibrium. There is simultaneous "increase", both in demand and supply of the good. Explain its effect on market price.

18. Market for a good is in equilibrium. There is simultaneous "decrease" both in demand and supply but there is no change in market price. Explain with the help of a schedule how it is possible.

19. Market for a good is in equilibrium. There is simultaneous "increase" both in demand and supply but there is no change in price. Explain how it is possible. Use a schedule.

20. If equilibrium price of a good is greater than its market price. Explain all the changes that will take place in the market. Use diagram.

21. Farmers may suffer loss even when there is good harvest. Does your supply-demand analysis provide an answer to this paradox?